Public Atti
Policies in

Monika Mischke

Public Attitudes towards Family Policies in Europe

Linking Institutional Context and Public Opinion

Springer VS

Monika Mischke
Siegen, Deutschland

Zugleich Dissertation der Universität Mannheim, 2012

ISBN 978-3-658-03576-1 ISBN 978-3-658-03577-8 (eBook)
DOI 10.1007/978-3-658-03577-8

The Deutsche Nationalbibliothek lists this publication in the Deutsche Nationalbibliografie; detailed bibliographic data are available in the Internet at http://dnb.d-nb.de.

Library of Congress Control Number: 2013947364

Springer VS

Springer VS is a brand of Springer DE.
Springer DE is part of Springer Science+Business Media.
www.springer-vs.de

Acknowledgements

This book is based on my doctoral thesis handed in at the University of Mannheim in September 2012.

First of all, I wish to thank Prof. Dr. Bernhard Ebbinghaus and Prof. Dr. Claus Wendt for supervising this thesis and supporting my research in numerous ways. Both of them provided valuable feedback on the developing manuscript and their doors were always open to discuss questions, ideas, and problems.

I am also grateful to the Mannheim Center for European Social Research (MZES) and the Mannheim Graduate School of Social and Economic Sciences for providing a great research environment with an excellent infrastructure and stimulating seminars and training. I wish to thank all my colleagues and fellow PhD students at the MZES for all of the stimulating discussions and exchanges as well as my coffee-break team for many joyful moments.

My research has also profited from my participation in several summer schools and conferences as well as a research stay at the Swedish Institute for Social Research (SOFI), which was made possible by Tommy Ferrarini and the EQUALSOC Network of Excellence, funded by the EU.

The idea for this thesis was born during our project "Attitudes Toward Welfare State Institutions: New Perspectives for the Comparative Welfare State Analysis," which was funded by the German Research Foundation (DFG) and headed by Claus Wendt. My work greatly benefited from our discussions and the joint research, and I am grateful to my colleagues Michaela Pfeifer and Claus Wendt for the successful and very pleasant cooperation. Furthermore, I would like to thank our student assistants in Mannheim and Siegen for their support, in particular Regina Jutz, Nadine Reibling, Ines Schaurer, and Pia Schütz.

I am especially grateful to Ryan DeLaney, who thoroughly proofread most parts of this thesis, as well as to Miriam Ott, who helped in collecting and editing the family-policy indicators.

Thanks for their support also go to the administrative and IT team at the MZES, namely Sibille Eberle, Josiane Hess, Beate Rossi, Marianne Schneider, Helena Wozniak, Marlene Alle, and Christian Melbeck, and to Susanne Müller at the University of Siegen.

I also wish to thank Christian Albrekt Larsen, Thomas Bahle, Agnes Blome, Tommy Ferrarini, Ulrich Kohler, Einar Overbye, and Stefan Svallfors as well as all members of the EQUALSOC Institutional Change group for their stimulating discussions and helpful comments on my work.

Of the many people who have, in one or the other way, contributed to the completion of this thesis, I would like to extend my appreciation to: Sharon Ashcroft, Jennifer Boothby, Jeff Kavanagh, Gabriele Mischke, and Swantje Schmidt for proofreading parts of this thesis; Claire Corkhill and Wolfgang Mischke for their valuable comments on parts of the manuscript; and Benjamin Branzko for his constant encouragement, emotional support, and delicious cooking.

Last but not least, I am deeply grateful to my family and friends for their continuous support and their unwavering belief in my abilities.

Contents

Abbreviations

CA	Cluster analysis
CI	Confidence interval
CL	Cluster
ESS	European Social Survey
EU	European Union
FPM	Family-policy model
FTE	Full-time equivalents
GDP	Gross domestic product
GRA	Gender-role attitudes
HCA	Hierarchical cluster analysis
ICC	Intra-class correlation coefficient
LFP	Labor-force participation
PT; PTE	Part-time; part-time employment
Ref.	Reference category
OECD	Organisation for Economic Co-operation and Development
OLS	Ordinary least squares
OMC	Open Method of Coordination
PPP	Purchasing power parities
SD	Standard deviation

Country abbreviations

AT	Austria
BE	Belgium
DE	Germany
DK	Denmark
ES	Spain
FI	Finland
FR	France
GR	Greece
IE	Ireland
IT	Italy
LU	Luxembourg
NL	The Netherlands
PT	Portugal
SE	Sweden
UK	United Kingdom

1 Introduction

Welfare-state institutions are based on the idea of social rights and equal opportunities for everyone (Dahrendorf 1988; Sen 1999; Marshall 1950). As part of the institutional and political setting, they enable people to take advantage of opportunities and fulfill their potential. Social-policy institutions reduce economic and psychological insecurity and improve the quality of life of individuals. Consequently, most citizens are financially or socially bound to the welfare state as a pensioner, client of the healthcare system, recipient of unemployment benefits or social assistance, or as a parent using public childcare services.

Moreover, promoting people's well-being and quality of life is a primary goal of the social policy agenda of the European Union (EU), which strongly emphasizes the importance of social inclusion and cohesion for the future of European societies. The idea of social inclusion and cohesion implies that people should have equal opportunities to participate, which includes access to employment, social protection systems, and institutions that promise a generally accepted minimum of basic essentials.

This study focuses on family-policy institutions as one particular example of welfare-state intervention and analyzes public attitudes toward this policy field. The results can show whether the current policy arrangements meet the needs and preferences of the whole population. In comparison with the traditional core fields of the welfare state, such as unemployment protection and healthcare, family-policy measures were introduced later. Most countries introduced universal maternity insurance and child benefits only after the Second World War (Ferrarini 2006; Wennemo 1994). The first countries to expand family services in terms of childcare, residential homes, and home help for the elderly were Denmark and Sweden, followed by Norway in the late 1960s; Finland, Belgium, and France eventually followed in the 1970s (Esping-Andersen 1999). The institutional recognition of fathers' participation in care work began even later. Entitlements for fathers to take advantage of paid parental leave were not introduced until the mid-1970s, and by the year 2000, no more than 10 out of 18 OECD countries had introduced some type of parental-leave transfer directed at fathers (Ferrarini 2006).

Nowadays, family policy is a rapidly changing field of welfare-state intervention and includes different kinds of government benefits that alleviate or address family-related problems. Roughly speaking, family policies are those policies that increase resources of households with dependent children; foster child development; reduce barriers to having children and combining work and family commitments; and promote gender equity in employment opportunities (OECD 2011). This definition indicates the great potential of family-policy measures to impact the main dimensions of social inequality, e.g., inequalities between families and individuals, between men and women, and between families and children from different socio-economic backgrounds. Apart from increasing families' material resources, family-policy measures have far-reaching implications for parents' agency, e.g., in terms of mothers' opportunities to be gainfully employed or fathers' opportunities to provide care (Hobson et al. 2006).[1]

Despite an increased awareness of the necessity of supporting individuals in their ability to reconcile paid work and family life, national family-policy packages differ largely, e.g., with respect to the type of benefits provided or their level of generosity. Moreover, there are differences in the underlying political motives for benefit provision, including the prevention of poverty among families with children, the increase of the fertility rate, female labor-market participation, child well-being, the maintenance of the single wage-earner family, and the decrease of gender inequalities (Wennemo 1994; Kaufmann 2002). Existing differences in family-policy design have been linked to country-specific and long-lasting cultural, religious, legislative, and institutional traditions. Moreover, the power of the (Catholic) Church or women's movements played a key role in the development of distinct family-policy systems. A key feature of the family-policy field is thus the importance of culture, values, and ideals, which are crucial for the understanding of both institutional designs and families' choices and behaviors (Bahle 1995; Gauthier 1996; Pfau-Effinger 1996, 2005b; Kremer 2007; Strohmeier 2002).

Scholars such as Taylor-Gooby (2004) and Bonoli (2005) have argued that the current socioeconomic transformations, including post industrial labor market and family structures, generate so-called "new social risks," such as reconciling work and family life, being a single parent, long-term

---

1 The term agency is inspired by Sen's agency and capability approach (Sen 1993, 1992). As stated by Hobson (2011: 148), this approach asks "not only what individuals do but also what their opportunities to be and do are. For Sen, the core issue is not only what individuals choose, but the choices that they would make if they had the capabilities to lead the kind of lives that they want to lead."

unemployment, being among the working poor, and having insufficient social security coverage. New social risks tend to be concentrated among women, families with small children, the young, and the low skilled – categories that largely overlap – and imply serious welfare losses for these groups. They are labeled "new" because they were merely marginal problems during the "golden age" of post-war welfare states, whereas they are now typical of the post-industrial societies in which we live today. These new social risks pose new challenges to mature welfare states and demand new, innovative social policies aimed at gender equality and an increase in labor-market participation. Among these new, modernizing policies are childcare facilities and the social protection of parenthood and atypical employment (see also Häusermann 2008; Mahon 2002; Esping-Andersen 1999).

The new emphasis on female labor-market participation and work-life balance is related to the processes of social change inherent in advanced industrial economies' transition to post-industrialism (P. Pierson 1998). Pierson pointed out three social processes that lead to increasing pressures on the welfare states of affluent democracies: 1) The slow-down in the growth of productivity (and consequently economic growth) associated with a massive shift from manufacturing to service employment; 2) the maturation and growth to limits (P. Pierson 1998: 541; Flora 1986) of government commitments (especially in the fields of healthcare provision and old-age pensions); and 3) the demographic shift to an older population due to decreasing birth rates and increasing longevity. These processes are accompanied by globalization, which has further accentuated and modified the pressures on welfare states (see also Esping-Andersen 1999; 2002; Taylor-Gooby 2004, 2009). In this "context of permanent austerity" (P. Pierson 1998: 554), welfare states are faced with declining governmental capacity and fiscal strain on the one hand and growing social and demographic needs on the other.

The prevailing responses to these pressing problems are often in line with neo-liberalist ideas and emphasize the mobilization and training of workforces to improve competitiveness, cost-constraint, and cost-efficiency, placing great emphasis on individual responsibility and opportunity (Taylor-Gooby 2009). An overall rise in employment participation is seen as crucial for the viability of the welfare state as well as for the enhancement of social cohesion and inclusion. Moreover, the massive increase in female participation in higher education since the 1960s (Schofer and Meyer 2005) has increased women's opportunities and aspirations to be gainfully employed and pursue careers.

If women and mothers are expected to become increasingly active participants in the labor market, family-friendly policies play a key role in enabling parents to be both earners and caregivers. High-quality, affordable, and flexible childcare arrangements are among the most important preconditions that enable both parents to enter the labor market and combine paid work and family life (Plantenga et al. 2008). Previous studies have shown that women are more frequently employed and more likely to work full-time in countries with high service provision compared with women in countries that provide fewer services or only financial benefits for families (Ferrarini 2006; Kangas and Rostgaard 2007). Moreover, the lack of affordable, high-quality childcare, especially for children under age three, as well as the restricted opening hours of existing facilities, have proven to be the main obstacles in mothers' labor-market participation (OECD 2001; Plantenga and Siegel 2004; European Commission 2005; Bahle 2008a; Saraceno and Leira 2008). In addition, Castles (2003) showed that publicly provided care facilities for children under the age of three, as well as flexible work arrangements, are positively correlated with fertility rates. Early childhood education and care services are additionally important from the perspective of equal opportunity and child well-being, since these institutions can help to reduce the disadvantages of children with special needs or from lower socio-economic backgrounds (OECD 2006).[2]

The common socio-economic and demographic challenges posed to postindustrial societies have resulted in some policy convergence among welfare states and have increased the pressure to support parents in their ability to reconcile gainful employment and family life. Nevertheless, major differences remain in many policy fields, particularly in the field of public support for families (Kautto 2002; Starke et al. 2008; Mahon 2002; Bahle 2003).

Despite an increasing interest in issues of work-family compatibility, there is very limited knowledge about the public's attitude toward family-policy measures in a comparative perspective. Since family-policy issues have not been included in international opinion surveys for a long time, a lack of data is partially responsible for this research gap. Knowledge about the public's attitude toward the welfare state as a whole or toward specific programs, however, is an essential component and indicator of the legitimacy of modern democracies.

According to Svallfors (2006: 18), "'Attitudes' are understood as normative beliefs and opinions about particular social objects. They differ from 'values' in that they are tied to specific existing objects."

In this study, the object of interest is the welfare state and particularly family policy as a specific field of welfare-state intervention. The following

2 For concerns expressed over the use of professional childcare for very young children, please refer to Belsky (2001) and Brooks-Gunn (2002).

chapters investigate normative beliefs and public opinion about the ideal level of government intervention, the evaluation of existing family-policy institutions, and the anticipation of the negative side effects of welfare-state intervention.

Why care about public attitudes toward the welfare state?

Svallfors (2010) argued that there are at least three reasons to care about public opinion toward welfare policies. First, there is a danger of confusing elite opinions with the views of the public as a whole, a problem linked to the question of whether or not existing policy settings are legitimate. Attitudinal research can provide an answer to the question of whether existing social arrangements are accepted and normatively grounded by the people. Huge discrepancies between the public's policy preferences and the actual policy of the government might reduce public support for the political system as a whole (Borre 1998b).

Second, attitudes as well as normative expectations and moral beliefs are rather stable over time and often hard to change (Svallfors 2010). Attitudes can therefore provide stability and function as a counterweight to abrupt policy changes. They can function as a resource as well as a constraint in the process of establishing new policies or reforming existing ones (Brooks and Manza 2007). At the individual level, policy preferences can be expected to impact political behavior in terms of voting behavior as well as in terms of stimulating protest activity in social movements if certain issues are not represented in the legislature (Borre 1998a). In order to understand these dynamics, it is necessary to increase our knowledge about existing attitudes and beliefs.[3]

Third, attitudinal research provides people the means to evaluate public policies by their normative effects on the general public instead of solely looking at the policies' (re-)distributive or economic effects. Whether existing policies tend to foster egoism, narrow-mindedness, and exclusion, or whether they tend to nurture civic-mindedness, tolerance, and concern for others is a fundamental question for a democratic polity (Svallfors 2010: 242). Public attitudes toward welfare policies touch fundamental questions about the goals of society and the means to promote these goals and can serve as indicators of social problems and societal polarization (Borre 1998a).

[3] For a critical opinion about the stability, validity, and impact of public opinion, please refer to Papadakis (1992).

The analysis of public attitudes is thus a fruitful means of achieving a better understanding of the processes of institutional change and stability, respectively, and of the processes of social change and social cohesion. Currently, there is a great deal of policy change in the field of family policy and work- and living arrangements are becoming increasingly heterogeneous. Therefore, it is important to be aware of citizens' perceptions of the ongoing changes as well as their fears, needs, and policy preferences. The investigation of public attitudes can help to narrow the potential gap between society and politics (Borre 1998a). This study applies a cross-country comparative framework, which is especially suited to shed light on the relationship between specific institutional arrangements and attitudinal patterns.

The aim of this study

This study seeks to understand public attitudes toward family policies from both a micro- and macro-level perspective and combines a thorough analysis of existing family-policy measures with an extensive analysis of public attitudes. From a macro-level perspective, this study asks whether attitudinal differences among countries can be explained by country-level characteristics such as the actual family-policy setup and other contextual indicators. At the micro-level, this study is interested in attitudinal differences among individuals or social groups and distinguishes between two mechanisms of attitude formation, namely the calculus approach (i.e., self-interest) and the cultural approach (i.e., norms and values) (see Kangas 1997; Papadakis 1992; van Oorschot 1998, 2002; Jæger 2006a, 2006b; Svallfors 2006).

The calculus approach assumes that individuals support the welfare state because they benefit from the provided benefits or services. Thus, it can be argued that families have a stronger self-interest in family-policy measures compared with individuals.

The cultural approach assumes that group-specific norms about what is proper, just, and acceptable generate different attitudes toward social and political issues. According to this argument, individuals are expected to support specific family-policy measures because they support the underlying political principles and values, e.g., the idea that both mothers and fathers should be able to be gainfully employed and have time to care for their children.

The comparative welfare-state literature assumes that different welfare regimes create systematic variation in the extent to which the public supports welfare-state principles, policies, and programs (e.g., Korpi 1980; Linos and

West 2003; Svallfors 1997; Jæger 2006a; Arts and Gelissen 2001; Bean and Papadakis 1998). Most research in this field assumes that attitudes toward the welfare state are dependent on an individual's position in societal hierarchies (e.g., income or status hierarchies) and on the design of existing social policy arrangements, since these arrangements constitute the context in which citizens' attitudes are shaped (see also Svallfors 1997; Gelissen 2000). Most empirical studies focus consequently on differences in the level of support among the different welfare regime types and among social groups within welfare regimes. This idea has been corroborated by looking at subfields of welfare-state intervention and the impact of specific institutional characteristics on the level and the degree of polarization of public support for these specific fields of welfare-state intervention (Wendt et al. 2010; Wendt et al. 2011; Pfeifer 2009).

The current study complements this research tradition by focusing on family-policy institutions and public opinion toward this field of welfare-state intervention. This study assumes that public attitudes toward particular family-policy measures are systematically related to the actual type and level of government support provided for families. However, not only the policy setup is important but also the broader social context in terms of socio-economic and socio-demographic structures (such as labor-market characteristics, female employment participation, and fertility) needs to be taken into account in order to understand and explain differences in public opinion among countries.

From a micro-level perspective, this study argues that individuals think differently about particular family-policy issues, dependent on both their self-interest (e.g., in terms of being a parent or not) and normative beliefs (e.g., in terms of gender-role attitudes). Moreover, the degree to which both aspects (i.e., self-interest and normative beliefs) influence public opinion is, in turn, expected to vary among countries, dependent on the type and the level of generosity of existing family-policy measures.

Based on these arguments, the key research questions raised in this study are:

1. Which types of family policy exist in the European Union?
2. What do citizens expect from their governments in the field of family policy?
3. How do Europeans perceive existing family-policy institutions?
4. Does the public anticipate the negative consequences of government intervention?
5. To what extent are public attitudes linked to specific family-policy contexts?
6. What are the differences in terms of socio-economic and demographic structures among different family-policy contexts as well as the individual countries?

7. Does the broader social context (in terms of socio-economic and socio-demographic structures) modify public opinion?
8. To what extent do self-interest and cultural values explain differences in public opinion among individuals and are these concepts equally relevant for different dimensions of attitudes?
9. Are the patterns of social polarization universal or instead specific to single countries or certain groups of countries?

Methodologically, this study conducts a secondary data analysis based on social-policy and contextual indicators as well as survey data from the European Social Survey (ESS). In a first step, this study conducts a cluster analysis and develops a family-policy typology based on a variety of family-policy indicators, which mirror different types of government support for families with young children. In a second step, contextual features including economic and socio-demographic structures are described for all countries included in this study. The consideration of both family-policy measures and the broader social context, leads to a slightly adjusted version of the original family-policy typology. Both typologies are used consecutively in a series of pooled regression models, analyzing country-level differences in public opinion toward family-policy measures. In a last step, this study analyzes public attitudes from a micro-level perspective, focusing on socio-demographic and socio-economic differences among individuals.

This approach was chosen because it allows for the investigation of whether particular family-policy institutions generate specific attitudes or whether similar policy profiles can lead to different attitudes, dependent on the broader social context of the respective society. Moreover, the combination of pooled regression models and country-specific models in the second part of the study has the advantage that both general patterns of social polarization as well as country-specific differences among social groups can be analyzed and compared. Table 1.1 provides a synopsis of the research questions, data sources, and statistical methods applied in this study.

Table 1.1: Synopsis of research questions, data sources, and statistical methods

Research question	Data	Statistical method	Chapter
Which types of family policy exist in the European Union?	Family-policy indicators (retrieved from statistical databases, mainly provided by EUROSTAT and the OECD), international policy reviews	Hierarchical cluster analysis	3
What do citizens expect from their governments in the field of family policy? How do Europeans perceive existing family-policy institutions? Does the public anticipate the negative consequences of government intervention?	European Social Survey (ESS), wave 2008	Descriptive statistics, multivariate regression analysis	4, 5, 6
To what extent are public attitudes linked to specific family-policy contexts?	ESS, 2008; Family-policy indicators (see above)	Descriptive statistics, correlation analysis, multi-level regression analysis	4
What are the differences in terms of socio-economic and demographic structures among different family-policy contexts as well as the individual countries?	Contextual indicators (retrieved from statistical databases, mainly provided by EUROSTAT and the OECD)	Descriptive statistics	5
Does the broader social context (in terms of socio-economic and socio-demographic structures) modify public opinion?	ESS, 2008; Family-policy indicators and contextual indicators (see above)	Correlation analysis, multi-level regression analysis	5
To what extent do self-interest and cultural values explain differences in public opinion among individuals and are these concepts equally relevant for different dimensions of attitudes? Are the patterns of social polarization universal or instead specific to single countries or certain groups of countries?	ESS, 2008; Family-policy indicators and contextual indicators (see above)	(Multi-level) regression analysis (pooled, cluster-specific, and country-specific models)	4, 6

Methodological note

Institutional variation is mainly found among countries, thus rendering a cross-national research framework most suited for the analysis of the relationship between the institutional setup and public attitudes.[4] Cross-national research, however, brings about several methodological challenges, some of which are discussed in the following paragraph (see Jowell 1998; Svallfors 2007). The initial challenge is to evaluate the cross-national validity of indicators, be they institutional indicators or micro-level indicators, in order to assess individual-level characteristics. To handle this problem, it is advisable to use only countries of which we have some degree of knowledge and that are similar enough to allow for meaningful comparisons (Jowell 1998). This study restricts the analyses to 15 western, industrialized countries that all belong to the European Union, thereby making the comparison more robust. Additionally, Jowell argues that only data from strictly comparative surveys that apply high methodological standards should be used. Survey questions should be designed in a cross-national framework and be implemented in a uniform manner in all countries. Furthermore, technical standards should be high and apply to all participating countries (e.g., with respect to the sampling method, fieldwork period, and interview technique) (Jowell 1998). In the following chapters, micro-level data stemming from the European Social Survey (ESS) are used. The ESS is a cross-country survey that applies very high methodological and technical standards, thus providing high-quality comparative data (see below for more information on the ESS). The institutional indicators stem from international organizations such as Eurostat and the OECD, ensuring as much comparability as possible.

Another important issue concerns the effect of the wording of the survey questions (see also Gelissen 2000). Kangas (1997) showed that respondents are more committed to social solidarity when questions are formulated in very general terms, but less committed when questions are more specific, e.g., in terms of who should benefit and who should pay (and how much) (see also Papadakis 1992). In the latter case, self-interest comes to the forefront. Additionally, the framing of the question as well as additional information given in the questionnaire impacts on the preferences measured. It is important to keep

[4] This study focuses on attitudinal and institutional differences among different countries. However, it is critical to note that the nation-state may not always be the only or most relevant explanatory unit and that institutional variation is also present within the same nation-state (see Svallfors 1997).

these findings in mind when analyzing and interpreting welfare attitudes in the following chapters.

Data - the European Social Survey

The micro-level data used in this study stem from the European Social Survey (ESS) round 4, conducted in 2008/09 (European Social Survey 2008/09). The ESS included only twelve of the 15 EU member states for which the institutional analysis is conducted. Most parts of this study are therefore restricted to a smaller country sample comprised of Belgium, Denmark, Finland, France, Germany, Greece, Ireland, the Netherlands, Portugal, Spain, Sweden, and the United Kingdom (UK).

The surveyed population consists of persons aged 15 and above who reside in private households in the participating countries, disregarding their nationality, language, or legal status (European Social Survey 2011). The surveyed population was selected by strict random probability sampling, and respondents were interviewed in an hour-long, face-to-face setting. After excluding all cases with missing values on the variables of interest, the total sample size is 20,624 persons. The sample size in the twelve countries varies between 1,384 in Denmark and 2,302 in Germany.

The data are weighted using country-specific design weights. These weights adjust for the slightly different probabilities of selection into the sample, making the sample more representative of a "true" sample of individuals aged 15+ in each country.[5]

The questions analyzed in this study are part of the ESS welfare module that covers attitudes toward welfare provision, the size of claimant groups, views on taxation, attitudes toward service delivery, and likely future dependence on welfare.[6] This ESS-module was first included in the year 2008/09.

5 The design weights are computed as the normed inverse of the inclusion probabilities (for more details, see the ESS documentation Report: European Social Survey 2011).

6 The questionnaire includes no question asking about the likelihood of future dependence on family-policy benefits or services.

Outline of the study

Chapter 2 provides the theoretical backdrop of the study, giving an overview of existing approaches and describing empirical results in the literature. The chapter discusses insights from institutional theory and describes the empirical results from the comparative welfare-state literature. Furthermore, it elaborates on the theoretical mechanisms linking welfare-state institutions and public attitudes. The last section discusses family policy as a special policy field and ends with a description of the hypotheses guiding the empirical analyses in the following chapters.

Chapter 3 examines the diversity of existing family-policy institutions in 15 member states of the European Union and develops a typology of family policies by means of cluster analysis. This part of the study advances our understanding of family-policy variation in Europe by considering up-to-date family-policy indicators from 2008, thus providing a recent picture of the fast changing family-policy landscape in Europe. The countries included are the 15 "old" member states of the European Union, namely Austria, Belgium, Denmark, Finland, France, Germany, Greece, Ireland, Italy, Luxembourg, the Netherlands, Portugal, Spain, Sweden, and the UK. The inclusion of the Southern European countries allows for the investigation of whether these countries form their own, distinct family-policy cluster, as suggested by scholars such as Flaquer (2000) and Bahle (2008a).

Chapter 4 adopts a macro-level perspective and investigates the link between public attitudes toward family-policy issues and the family-policy context. The guiding question is whether and how attitudinal differences among countries are related to the current family-policy setup. Public attitudes toward family policies are captured with the following three attitudinal dimensions: 1) "How much responsibility should governments have in ensuring sufficient childcare services for working parents?" (i.e., responsibility), 2) "What do you think about the provision of affordable child care services for working parents?" (i.e., satisfaction), and 3) "Social benefits and services make people less willing to look after themselves and their family" (i.e., skepticism).

The family-policy setup is represented by the family-policy typology developed in Chapter 3. The first part of Chapter 4 provides a description of differences in public attitudes at the country level, whereas the second part focuses on the relationship between public attitudes and the family-policy setup. This part of the chapter discusses the correlations between single family-policy indicators and the three attitudinal dimensions. Moreover, multivariate regression models are conducted which take into account both individual-level indicators as well as the family-policy clusters. In order to account for the nested structure of the data (i.e., individuals within countries), a multi-level design is applied. With regard to individual-level characteristics, factors representing both the calculus and the cultural approach are included.

Chapter 5 broadens the perspective by taking into account not only the family-policy setup but also the broader social context in order to understand differences in public attitudes. The social context is captured by a set of indicators, such as fertility, female employment participation, gender equality, and child poverty. The first part of this chapter investigates the relationship between the four family-policy clusters and these contextual indicators. The second part then analyzes the relationship between family policies, contextual features, and public attitudes. The aim of this approach is to characterize the wider social context in which family policies operate and simultaneously illuminate differences in the degree of problem pressure. This knowledge can provide important information about the individuals' quality of life, e.g., in terms of work-family compatibility. Finally, this knowledge is used to develop an adjusted version of the family-policy typology, which is then used to explain country-level differences in public attitudes toward family policy.

Chapter 6 adopts a micro-level perspective and focuses on attitudinal differences among social groups both within the adjusted family-policy clusters as well as within the individual countries. Again, the three dimensions of attitudes are analyzed, namely responsibility, satisfaction, and skepticism. This part of the study investigates to what extent self-interest and cultural values explain differences in public opinion among individuals and shows whether these concepts are equally relevant regarding both different dimensions of attitudes as well as different national contexts. This approach thus allows for the investigation of whether patterns of social polarization at the aggregate level can be confirmed for all countries included in the analysis. A high level of attitudinal polarization among social groups is thereby regarded as an indicator for societal conflicts and social inequalities in quality of life.

Chapter 7 summarizes the main empirical results and critically discusses the scientific findings against the background of institutional theory and earlier results from the comparative welfare-state literature. Furthermore, limitations of this study and the applied methodological design are briefly discussed, and implications for future research are pointed out.

2 Theoretical background and literature review

This chapter provides the theoretical backdrop of the study, giving an overview of existing approaches and describing empirical results in the literature. The first section briefly discusses the concept of institutions and describes insights from institutional theory. This section addresses the theoretical relationship between institutions and individuals and the question of how institutions impact on human behavior, preferences, and attitudes.

The second section elaborates on empirical results from the comparative welfare-state literature and discusses the theoretical mechanisms that link welfare-state institutions and attitudes. This part of the chapter describes the hypotheses that have been formulated with regard to attitudinal differences among welfare regimes as well as among social groups and explicates which of these hypotheses have been confirmed empirically. At the end of this section, an analytical framework is provided that depicts the theoretical link between welfare-state institutions and public attitudes.

The last section eventually discusses the distinctiveness of the family-policy field in comparison to other fields of welfare-state intervention. One major feature of this field is the salience of normative beliefs and cultural traditions (e.g., in terms of gender-role attitudes or attitudes toward the best type of childcare) for both the development and the evaluation of family-policy measures. Moreover this section addresses the question of how family-policy institutions structure families' lives and gives an overview of empirical classifications of family-policy systems.

The second part then describes results from earlier studies, which analyzed public attitudes toward family policies and gender-roles, and discusses the question which social cleavages can be expected to matter with respect to attitudes toward family-policy measures. The section ends with a description of the hypotheses guiding the empirical analyses in the following chapters, which analyze the link between existing family-policy institutions, contextual features, and public attitudes toward family polices in a comparative perspective.

2.1 Institutional theory

Institutional theory has been used extensively to illuminate the impact of institutions on political and corporate actors (for an overview, see, Oliver and Mossialos 2005), whereas studies looking at institutions' effects on individuals are rare (Wendt et al. 2011; Mettler and Soss 2004). The basic idea of the institutionalist approach is that actors are embedded in institutional environments that, according to Ebbinghaus (2006: 16), "shape actors' orientations and interests as well as the opportunity structures for the actor constellations." This idea can be applied to both political or corporate actors as well as individuals (see also Ebbinghaus 2011).

A key concept in institutional theory is path dependence, which is used to explain institutional stability as well as institutional change. According to Ebbinghaus (2005: 5), the basic idea of this concept is "that in a sequence of events, the latter decisions are not (entirely) independent from those that occurred in the past." This concept encompasses two distinct approaches: The "trodden trail" approach refers to "micro-level diffusion processes in social networks" (Ebbinghaus 2005: 25) and "stresses the spontaneous evolution of an institution and its subsequent long-term entrenchment" (Ebbinghaus 2005: 5). This model can explain persistence but not institutional change. The second approach - the "road juncture" model - refers to "macro-level institutional arrangements that shape subsequent (political) decision-making" (Ebbinghaus 2005: 25). This model is more flexible and can be used to explain both institutional persistence and change because it "looks at the interdependent sequence of events that structure the alternatives for future institutional changes" (Ebbinghaus 2005: 5). In his study of institutional change in the field of family policy, Bahle (2003) discussed the concept of path dependency and concludes that recent changes in Western European social-service systems indicate a mixture of institutional continuity (in terms of path dependency) as well as institutional innovation.

Institutional theory is divided into three schools of thought: Rational choice institutionalism, sociological institutionalism, and historical institutionalism (for an overview, see, P. A. Hall and Taylor 1996; Oliver and Mossialos 2005). The following paragraph reviews the three approaches briefly, since they constitute useful concepts for the study of welfare-state institutions and their impact on individuals' attitudes. The focus is thereby on two questions: 1) How are institutions defined? And 2) how do institutions impact on individuals? All three traditions focus on the impact institutions have on actors' decisions or behavior and consequently on social and political outcomes.

Rational choice institutionalism arose from the study of American congressional behavior and views politics as a series of collective-action dilemmas (P. A. Hall and Taylor 1996). Rational choice institutionalists apply a typical "calculus approach" in which actors have a fixed and pre-defined set of preferences and behave completely instrumentally and strategically in order to maximize the attainment of these preferences. Political outcomes are seen as the result of strategic interaction through which actors' strategic behavior is affected by expectations about how others are likely to behave. Institutions are then able to solve collective-action dilemmas by structuring alternative options as well as providing information and enforcement mechanisms, thus reducing uncertainty about the behavior of others. The origination of institutions is hence assigned to the involved actors themselves, who create institutions in order to realize gains from cooperation.

Sociological institutionalism has developed in the subfield of organizational theory and explains institutional forms and procedures in cultural terms (P. A. Hall and Taylor 1996). Sociological institutionalists follow a variant of the "cultural approach" and apply a broad definition of institutions, which tends to include culture itself as a form of institution. As Hall and Taylor (1996: 947) pointed out, institutions are not only the formal rules, procedures, or norms, "but the symbol system, cognitive scripts, and moral templates that provide the 'frames of meaning' guiding human action" (see also Rothstein 1996).

The relationship between institutions and individual action is seen as highly interactive and mutually constitutive. Following this approach, institutions influence behavior by providing the cognitive scripts and models that are necessary to interpret the world as well as the behavior of others. According to Hall and Taylor (1996: 948), institutions "influence behavior not simply by specifying what one should do but also by specifying what one can imagine oneself doing in a given context." Hence, they affect individuals' most basic preferences, self-images, and identities. This approach does not deny rationality or purposeful action but claims that what an individual views as rational is itself socially constituted. The emergence of new institutional forms or practices, finally, is explained by a "logic of appropriateness" in contrast to a "logic of instrumentality" (Campbell, cf. P. A. Hall and Taylor 1996: 949), i.e., organizations (or individuals) aim primarily at enhancing social legitimacy within their broader cultural environment.

Finally, according to Hall and Taylor (1996: 938), **historical institutionalism** defines institutions "as the formal or informal procedures, routines, norms and conventions embedded in the organizational structure of the polity or political economy. They can range from the rules of a constitutional order or the standard operating procedures of a bureaucracy to the conventions governing trade unions behavior or bank-firm relations." Research following this tradition is especially interested in power and asymmetrical power relations and assumes that institutions distribute power unevenly across social groups, e.g., with regard to access to the decision-making process. Applying the path-dependency concept, institutions are seen as relatively persistent over time. When explaining institutions' impact on human action, historical institutionalists apply both approaches - the calculus and the cultural approach.

According to the calculus approach, human behavior is based on strategic calculation and seeks utility maximization given a set of individual goals and preferences. This argumentation is in keeping with rational choice institutionalism. Institutions structure individual action through the provision of more-or-less certainty regarding the behavior of other actors at the present and in the future (e.g., through the provision of information, enforcement mechanisms, or penalties for defection). As Hall and Taylor (1996: 940) stated it, "institutions persist over time because they embody something like a Nash equilibrium," which means that individuals are better off when following the institutionally suggested pattern of behavior.

The cultural approach, in contrast, is more in line with sociological institutionalism and stresses the impact of established routines and the individual's interpretation of the situation on human action resulting in bounded rationality. Following this approach, institutions structure individuals' interpretations and actions by providing moral or cognitive templates. Hence, institutions not only provide strategically useful information but also "affect the very identities, self-images and preferences of the actors" (P. A. Hall and Taylor 1996: 939). Institutions and the conventions associated with them are persistent over time because they are taken-for-granted and simply not called into question.

Each of these three schools of thought has its own strengths and weaknesses and could benefit from a greater exchange with the others (P. A. Hall and Taylor 1996). Rational choice institutionalism has developed a precise model of the relationship between institutions and behavior. However, this model rests on rather simplistic assumptions about human action, focusing on rationality, instrumentality, and strategic calculation. It therefore misses important dimensions of human behavior, such as social norms and values. Sociological institutionalism is better equipped to account for these dimensions, for it specifies ways in which institutions can affect the underlying preferences or very identities of actors. However, one of the major weaknesses of this approach is the broad definition of institutions, which makes the empirical application of the concept difficult (see also Rothstein 1996). Historical institutionalism, finally, is best suited for integrating the advantages of the other two types of institutionalism. Since it applies both calculus and cultural approaches, it provides the most all-encompassing theory when analyzing the relationship between institutions and individuals (see also Wendt et al. 2011). The main weakness of this approach is that it has not clearly specified the causal mechanisms through which institutions affect social actors.

In order to define the concept of institutions for this study, Hall and Taylor's definition of institutions as "the formal or informal procedures, routines, norms and conventions embedded in the organizational structure of the polity or political economy" (P. A. Hall and Taylor 1996: 938), serves as a useful starting point. Focusing on welfare-state institutions, however, a narrower definition of institutions is needed that includes only formal political institutions. This study therefore applies the definition provided by Svallfors (2006). His definition restricts the concept of an institution to "politically decided objects and their implementation. By this definition, institutions are thus systems of formal rules and procedures, manifested in phenomena such as social security systems, election systems, and family law" (Svallfors 2006: 23). When broken down to the subfield of family-policy institutions, which are the focus of this study, this definition includes institutions such as parental leave, childcare services, and family allowances. Regarding this specific field of welfare-state intervention, the calculus approach suggests that those groups that are most likely to benefit from family-policy benefits and services should be most in favor of these policies. This argument applies, e.g., to parents with small children and especially to low-income families. The cultural argument, in contrast, emphasizes normative beliefs, which play a crucial role in the family-policy field (see Section 2.6). Normative beliefs about the social roles of men and women (and particularly of mothers) and about the provision of social care are key aspects in the understanding of public opinion toward family policy.

2.2 The link between institutions and welfare attitudes

Variation among welfare regimes

A key hypothesis in the comparative welfare-state literature is that the different welfare regimes create systematic variation in the extent to which the public supports welfare-state principles, policies, and programs (e.g., Korpi 1980; Linos and West 2003; Svallfors 1997; Jæger 2006a; Arts and Gelissen 2001; Bean and

Papadakis 1998). The most influential classification of welfare states is Esping-Andersen's "The Three Worlds of Welfare Capitalism" (1990). Based on the concepts of social stratification and "de-commodification," Esping-Andersen distinguishes three distinct welfare regimes, namely the liberal (e.g., the US), the conservative (e.g., Germany), and the social-democratic welfare state (e.g., Sweden). According to Esping-Andersen (1990: 21/22), "De-commodification occurs when a service is rendered as a matter of right, and when a person can maintain a livelihood without reliance on the market." The level of de-commodification describes the degree to which "citizens can freely, and without potential loss of job, income, or general welfare, opt out of work when they themselves consider it necessary" (Esping-Andersen 1990: 23). Briefly summarized, the social-democratic regime is characterized by a high level of de-commodification and universal welfare policies, whereas the liberal regime coincides with low de-commodification and strong individualistic self-reliance. The conservative regime is characterized by corporatism and a modest level of de-commodification. Although Esping-Andersen's classification has not remained uncontested (e.g., Scruggs and Allen 2006), the bulk of empirical studies interested in the relationship between welfare states and public opinion use this classification as the point of departure.[1]

The distinct welfare regimes don't only comprise a specific set of social policy arrangements and assign a different level of responsibility to the state, the market, and the family for the provision of welfare; they also create collective patterns of institutionalized solidarity and social justice beliefs. As Esping-Andersen (1990: 58) stated it, "each case will produce its own unique fabric of social solidarity." These moral and normative beliefs have developed over time, are embedded in the culture, and have been institutionalized in welfare-state institutions, which in turn impact on public discourse and individual orientations (e.g., P. Hall 1986; Rothstein 1998; Mau 2004). According to Mau (2003, 2004), different norms of reciprocity and fairness result in different "moral economies" of the welfare state, which are understood as sets of institutionalized normative assumptions about who should get what, for what reasons, and under what conditions. These normative assumptions function as generalized frames of reference for the public's judgment of what the appropriate scope of public welfare is and which social groups deserve public aid (see also Jæger 2006a; Edlund 1999; Svallfors 2003). Following these arguments, redistributive policies

[1] For critics and extensions made by other scholars, please refer to Leibfried (1992), Castles and Mitchell (1993), Ferrera (1996), Bonoli (1997), Arts and Gelissen (2002), and Scruggs and Allen (2006).

should gain public support as long as they are consistent with socially valid reciprocity norms (Mau 2003). This means that people support a certain welfare arrangement not only out of self-interest but also because the arrangement in question is morally plausible and perceived as fair. Reciprocity thereby does not imply the "equality of burdens or obligations" or a "balancing out of material costs and benefits" (Mau 2003: 188). According to Mau's conceptualization, "reciprocity means that people expect some kind of recompensation for their efforts, but these recompensations can be either in the form of having a stake in a collective endeavour, a protection promise, welfare entitlement returns or in the form of norm-conforming behaviour on the part of the beneficiaries. [...] From the recipient's perspective, reciprocity is a pattern of exchange that entails certain obligations or actions as repayments for benefits received" (Mau 2003: 188). What exactly the public considers fair and equitable, both in terms of burdens and benefit level, varies across different fields of welfare-state intervention and among distinct welfare regimes and is partly contingent upon public discourses, the press, and political actors (Mau 2003).

In addition to providing social services and income maintenance, welfare states function as an agent of social stratification (Esping-Andersen 1990; see also Gelissen 2000). The different policy arrangements can increase or lessen societal cleavage structures and conflict lines and generate very different patterns of coalition in the electorate. Authors such as Esping-Andersen (1990), Svallfors (2006, 2007), and Korpi and Palme (1998) emphasize the role of the middle classes in the development and persistence of welfare-state arrangements. The middle class is either believed to form a "welfare-coalition" with the working class or an "anti-welfare-coalition" with the upper class (Albrekt Larsen 2008: 147). Scholars argue that encompassing or universal welfare states foster a broad coalition among the electorate in favor of government intervention, whereas welfare states relying primarily on targeted and means-tested policies enhance hostile attitudes toward the welfare state (Korpi 1980; Korpi and Palme 1998; Edlund 1999; Rothstein 2001).

Most research in this field assumes that attitudes toward the welfare state are dependent on an individual's position in societal hierarchies (e.g., income or status hierarchies) and on the design of existing social policy arrangements since these arrangements constitute the context in which citizens' attitudes are shaped (see also Svallfors 1997; Gelissen 2000). Most empirical studies focus consequently on differences in the level of support among the different welfare regime types and among social groups within welfare regimes.

Scholars have hypothesized that support for redistribution should be highest in the universal and highly redistributive social democratic regime type, lowest in the liberal regime type, and in-between in the conservative welfare regime type (see Svallfors 1997; Gelissen 2000; Arts and Gelissen 2001; Andreß and Heien 2001). Empirically, the findings are not completely clear cut. All studies find substantial differences among countries with regard to attitudes toward redistribution (e.g., Edlund 1999; Svallfors 1997; Arts and Gelissen 2001; Linos and West 2003), solidarity beliefs (e.g., Arts and Gelissen 2001), and government responsibility for other aspects of welfare provision (e.g., Gelissen 2000; Svallfors 2003, 2004; Blekesaune and Quadagno 2003; Lipsmeyer and Nordstrom 2003; Bean and Papadakis 1998). However, these patterns correspond only roughly to the welfare regime typology (see also Jæger 2006a; Svallfors 2010).

Studies focusing on support for specific welfare programs have confirmed the expected pattern. Universal and encompassing programs, such as healthcare and old-age pensions, receive higher public support compared with targeted and means-tested programs, such as housing and social assistance (e.g., Bean and Papadakis 1998; Rothstein 2001; Coughlin 1980, 1979). The latter type of program is also more likely to produce suspicion regarding abuse or cheating. Blekesaune and Quadagno (2003) showed that support for programs helping the unemployed varies with different levels of unemployment. If unemployment is high, support for programs helping the unemployed is comparatively high as well (see also Wendt et al. 2011).

Regarding the strength of conflict lines among social groups within the different welfare regime types, it has been hypothesized that class cleavages should dominate in the liberal regime, whereas the conservative regime type is expected to create conflicts between labor-market insiders and outsiders (i.e., between those who have a good labor-market position and those who are unemployed or have a weak labor-market position). The social democratic regime, in turn, is hypothesized to create strong gender and sectoral conflicts between the public sector, which is mainly populated by women, and the private sector, which is predominantly occupied by men (Esping-Andersen 1990). Empirical results, however, are inconsistent with some studies confirming the expected cleavage patterns among different welfare regimes (e.g., Andreß and Heien 2001; Linos and West 2003), whereas others find that most conflict lines are present in all welfare regimes (e.g., Svallfors 1997, 2010; Edlund 1999; Bean and Papadakis 1998; Svallfors 2003).

An important methodological extension of this field is the work done by Jæger (2006a, 2009), who argues that individual countries should not be treated as perfect empirical representations of their respective theoretical welfare regimes. Therefore, instead of using welfare regimes, Jæger includes regime-type indicators measured at the country-level to assess a country's empirical resemblance to the welfare regimes. These indicators mirror what states actually do in terms of welfare provision and cover the three dimensions of welfare provision, namely the state, the market, and the family. Jæger (2006a) used indicators such as the total scope of public social spending and the composition of cash benefits versus social services (state dimension), unemployment benefit generosity (market dimension), and the scope of benefits and services to families (family dimension). This approach allows for the approximation of a country's degree of membership in the different regime types and introduces more cross-national variation (Jæger 2006a). Jæger concluded that empirical support for the regime hypothesis is mixed. In a later study, he (2009) analyzed not only the level of public support for redistribution but also the variance of support in 15 countries. With respect to the level of support, he found the strongest support in the conservative regime, followed by the social democratic regime, whereas the level of support is lowest in the liberal regime. The rank order with respect to the variance in public support differs slightly: The variance is strongest in the social democratic regime, followed by the conservative regime, and is lowest in the liberal regime. Jæger argues that the results are coherent with the idea that the actual level of redistribution and ideological and political controversy regarding redistribution affects attitudinal polarization at the individual level (Albrekt Larsen 2006; Svallfors 2004; Pfeifer 2009).

The findings described above show that there is variation both in the level of public opinion among welfare regimes as well as in the patterns of social polarization among individuals within these regimes. The current study amends existing research by investigating both the level and variability of public opinion toward family policy in distinct family-policy regimes as well as in individual countries. This stepwise approach sheds light on the interrelatedness of the family-policy setup and public attitudes. Moreover, it is argued that other contextual features are important for the understanding of the link between the policy setup and public opinion. The approach of welfare arrangements (Pfau-Effinger 2005a) theoretically captures the interrelatedness of different aspects of a society that potentially impact on public opinion. This approach is described in the following section.

The approach of welfare arrangements

Complementing the comparative welfare-state literature, Pfau-Effinger (2005a) reflected on the relationship between culture and welfare-state policies in a comparative perspective and introduced the approach of welfare arrangements. According to this approach, welfare-state policies of a given society are embedded in the broader societal context that includes the following interrelated elements: The cultural system, the welfare system, social structures, and political and individual actors (see Figure 2.1).

At the macro-level, the cultural system includes the welfare culture, which forms the basis of the welfare arrangement and captures the relevant ideas surrounding the welfare state in a given society. The welfare culture comprises "the stock of knowledge, values and ideals to which the relevant social actors, the institutions of the welfare state and concrete policy measures refer" (Pfau-Effinger 2005a: 4). The welfare system comprehends the institutional system of a given society, including the institutions of the welfare state as well as other central institutions, such as the family and the labor market. The social structures cover existing social inequalities, power relations, and the division of labor (Pfau-Effinger 2005a: 4).

At the meso- and micro-level, political- and individual actors are taken into account. Political actors (in terms of both collective and individual actors) are assumed to be involved in conflicts, negotiation processes, and discourses on values and ideals, whereas individual actors play an important role in terms of their social practices and behavior. A key feature of the welfare-arrangement approach is the interrelatedness of all elements. The relationship of culture and welfare-state policies is thus conceptualized as "a complex, multi-level relationship which is embedded into the specific context of a particular society and which can develop in contradictory ways" (Pfau-Effinger 2005a: 16).

Figure 2.1: The welfare arrangement

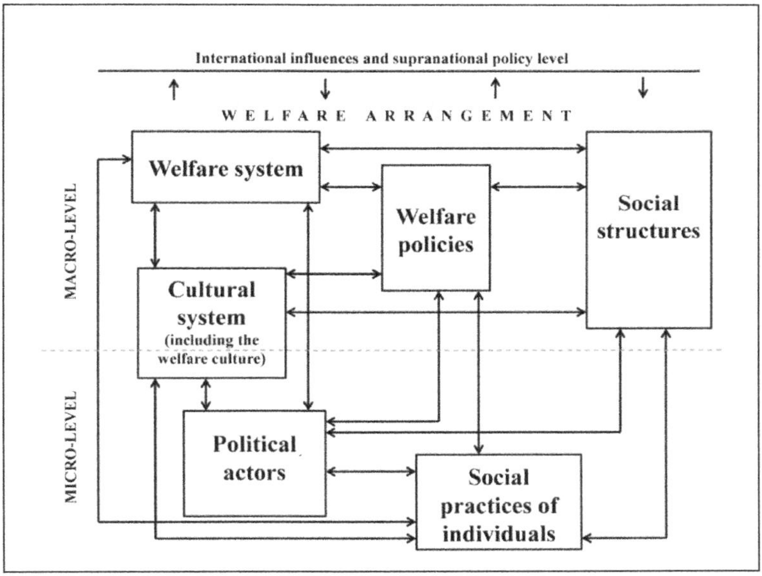

Source: Adopted from Pfau-Effinger (2005a: 5).

Furthermore, Pfau-Effinger (2005a) argues that there is not one coherent welfare arrangement that applies to all policy fields in a given welfare state. Instead policy-field specific welfare arrangements may coexist and in part overlap within each welfare state. Each type of arrangement has its own welfare culture, i.e., cultural values and models on which it is based. Pfau-Effinger distinguishes the arrangement concerning social security and the societal arrangement of family and gender relations. Family policies, which are embedded in the latter, can consequently be founded on different cultural models of the family, such as the dual-earner- or the male breadwinner family model. This argument highlights the importance to take into account not only the design of the whole welfare state but instead the design of particular social-policy fields (Wendt et al. 2011).

The concept of welfare culture is a key element in Pfau-Effinger's approach (Pfau-Effinger 2005a). It comprises cultural ideas about different aspects of society, such as employment, the state-market relationship, social services, the welfare mix, the family, notions of solidarity, social integration and social exclusion, and cultural assumptions about justice and redistribution. The welfare culture thus includes ideas about what is "normal" in terms of employment biographies or forms of employment, values concerning the labor market integration of certain groups of the population (e.g., migrants or mothers of young children), cultural ideas about the degree to which the state should intervene in the market (e.g., neo-liberal ideas versus traditional social democratic values), and ideas about social welfare and social services and how they should be provided (e.g., the extent to which the state, the family, and the market are regarded as the key areas for the provision of services and welfare).

In order to explain the relationship between culture and welfare-state policies, Pfau-Effinger (2005a) distinguishes three levels of welfare culture. The first level concerns the welfare-state policies that are embedded in certain cultural values and models and are justified and legitimized by these values. The second level refers to the attitudes in the population toward the welfare state. Various social groups refer to the cultural values and models related to the welfare-state policies. Predominant and challenging ideas as well as marginalized ideas can thereby be distinguished. Finally, social actors (i.e., collective and individual actors) use potentially contradictory and conflicting cultural values and models as the basis for policy discourses and debates aiming at reforming or changing existing policies.

The welfare-arrangement approach thus suggests that public attitudes toward welfare-state policies constitute part of the welfare culture and that all elements of the welfare arrangement (i.e., the cultural system, the welfare system, welfare-state policies, social structures, political actors, and social practices of individuals) are likely to interact with these attitudes (and vice versa).

A well-established welfare arrangement implies that the cultural and normative basis of the welfare arrangement is anchored in societal institutions as well as in the behavior of social actors (Pfau-Effinger 2005a). In this situation, policy context and public attitudes actually reinforce one another and the status quo of welfare-state intervention is broadly accepted and in accordance with public preferences. However, general processes of social and cultural change can result in a decline of the degree of the cultural and social integration of the welfare arrangement. As a result of these processes, the welfare arrangement itself can become the object of conflict and negotiation processes. New and challenging ideas, which may be imported from the international context (e.g., the European Union), then start to compete with older ideas within the cultural system (e.g., in terms of innovative cultural models or new institutional arrangements). A change in policies is most likely to occur if social and political actors can establish a link with the cultural orientations of the general population and thus attract the support of potential voters. However, social or cultural change does not inevitably result in policy adjustments, or as Pfau-Effinger stated, "Change in welfare-state policies does not necessarily follow cultural change, but can develop at a different rate" (Pfau-Effinger 2005a: 14).

The welfare arrangement approach clearly demonstrates the interrelatedness of public attitudes, the current policy setup, and other cultural and societal characteristics. A main advantage of this approach is furthermore the consideration of social or cultural change (including influences from the international context, such as the European Union) which can lead to a decline of cultural and social integration of the welfare arrangement.

As pointed out previously, many Western welfare states face similar demographic and socio-economic challenges in terms of new welfare needs, low fertility rates, and ageing societies. At the micro-level, women increasingly want to participate in the labor market and pursue a career, and family forms as well as work-family arrangements have become increasingly diverse. Consequently, the traditional male-breadwinner family model can no longer be considered the norm, and work-life balance has become a key issue both for policy makers and individuals. The ongoing processes of social and cultural change might increase public preferences for welfare-state interventions supporting the dual-earner model of the family. The lack of these policies, in turn, might result in a decline of cultural and social integration of the welfare arrangement and generate a gap between the welfare needs and preferences of the population and the actual policy setup. This study analyzes public opinion toward family policy and can shed light on the question of whether existing welfare arrangements meet the needs and preferences of the public. The welfare arrangement approach serves as a starting point for the selection of contextual features that mirror important aspects of a society, such as existing social inequalities, labor-market characteristics, and the degree of problem pressure. This study argues that these aspects are crucial for understanding country-level differences in public opinion.

2.3 Differences among social groups

This study is not only interested in country-level differences in public opinion but also in attitudinal differences among social cleavages (i.e., borders between social categories, such as different social classes, ethnic groups, gender, or generations (Svallfors 2007: 9)). The basic idea is that an individual's attitudes are related to his or her position in the social structure (see also d'Anjou et al. 1995). Based on institutional theory (e.g., P. A. Hall and Taylor 1996), two mechanisms are distinguished that can result in different attitudes among social groups (Kangas 1997; Papadakis 1992; van Oorschot 1998, 2002; Jæger 2006a, 2006b; Svallfors 2006). The first mechanism is self-interest, or the calculus approach, which argues that attitudes may differ because different social groups are more or less well equipped with crucial resources, such as money or qualifications, and are more or less exposed to risks, such as unemployment or poverty, resulting in different individual interests. Following this line of reasoning, people or social groups support the welfare state because they benefit from the provided benefits or services.

The second mechanism is the cultural approach, which includes norms and individual political and ideological orientations. Here, the idea is that different social groups are placed differently in networks of interaction and communication, resulting in group-specific norms about what is proper, just, and acceptable. These norms then result in different orientations toward social and political issues. According to this argument, individuals are expected to support the welfare state because they support its underlying political principles and values. The relationship between social cleavages and orientations is again affected by the institutional frameworks people are embedded in as well as by the political articulation prevalent in different polities (see Svallfors 2007).

The self-interest perspective suggests that both recipients of welfare transfers and people who are at risk of becoming dependent on the welfare state are generally more likely to be supportive of the welfare state. Consequently, the unemployed, pensioners, students, people with low incomes, and other members of the so-called "transfer classes" (Alber 1984; Lepsius 1990) are expected to be more in favor of public welfare provision. Empirical studies have mainly confirmed that low-income groups are more in favor of welfare-state intervention compared with high-income groups (e.g., Arts and Gelissen 2001; Jæger 2006b, 2009; Andreß and Heien 2001). Studies have also found that the unemployed and those not in the labor market are indeed more in favor of welfare-state intervention compared with those in regular employment (e.g., Svallfors 2004, 1997; Andreß and Heien 2001; Linos and West 2003; Jæger 2006a; Svallfors 2006; Gelissen 2000, 2002; Jæger 2009; Blekesaune and Quadagno 2003; Arts and Gelissen 2001). Results are less clear-cut with regard to pensioners' attitudes (e.g., Bean and Papadakis 1998; Andreß and Heien 2001; Jæger 2006b; Gelissen 2000).

Scholars have also argued that self-interest results in different support levels across different social classes (Esping-Andersen 1990; Bean and Papadakis 1998; d'Anjou et al. 1995; Svallfors 1997, 2006; Robinson and Bell 1978). Individuals' class membership, which is normally derived from individuals' occupational position, is a crucial measure for one's social position in society.

Both important resources, such as money, qualifications, and social status, as well as social risks, such as unemployment, poverty, or sickness, are systematically tied to the position within the social stratification system (Svallfors 1997). It follows that social classes must have diverging interests in either preserving or reducing the scope of welfare-state intervention. From a cultural perspective, members of social classes are differently placed in networks of interaction and communication, resulting in class- specific norms about what is proper, just, and acceptable (Svallfors 1997). Consequently, we might expect not only class-specific interests but also class-specific values and normative beliefs following from individuals' location in the social structure. Most studies in the field have confirmed the hypothesized class differences in support for welfare-state intervention (e.g., Gelissen 2000, 2002; Svallfors 2006; Linos and West 2003; Svallfors 1995, 1997, 2004). These effects have primarily been attributed to the self-interest argument.

With regard to gender differences, scholars found that women are more supportive of welfare-state intervention than men (e.g., Svallfors 1997, 2004; Linos and West 2003; Jæger 2009, 2006a; Blekesaune and Quadagno 2003). One argument for these differences is the gender-specific risks of welfare-state dependency. Due partly both to gender norms and to other disadvantages in the labor market, women show lower rates of continuous labor market participation. Moreover, they are often responsible for the provision of unpaid (child)care and therefore more likely to depend on welfare benefits (e.g., Svallfors 1997; Gelissen 2000). A second argument emphasizes the different socialization experiences of men and women. Women are more likely to embrace a "rationality of caring" in which concern, consideration, and devotion for others are more prominent, whereas men prefer a "rationality of individualism" in which the merit principle prevails (Svallfors 1997; d'Anjou et al. 1995; Andreß and Heien 2001). The hypothesized gender differences in support of welfare-state intervention have been empirically confirmed, not only with regard to welfare-state intervention (e.g., Svallfors 1997, 2004; Linos and West 2003; Jæger 2009, 2006a; Blekesaune and Quadagno 2003) but also with regard to the preferred level of solidarity (e.g., Arts and Gelissen 2001).

The effect of education is discussed more ambivalently. On the one hand, people with a higher level of education have better labor market opportunities and are therefore less likely to become dependent on welfare benefits. In line with the self-interest perspective, this might result in lower levels of support for government intervention among the more highly educated (Andreß and Heien 2001; Gelissen 2000). On the other hand, it is argued that a higher educational level goes hand-in-hand with enlightenment due to a longer socialization to democratic values and therefore generates greater commitment to social equality and social rights (Robinson and Bell 1978; d'Anjou et al. 1995; Andreß and Heien 2001). These arguments are in line with the cultural perspective and suggest that more highly educated persons should be more supportive of welfare-state intervention. Empirical results are rather clear cut with respect to the effect of education, the bulk of studies suggesting a negative impact of education and thus supporting the self-interest hypothesis (e.g., Jæger 2006b; Andreß and Heien 2001; Linos and West 2003; Jæger 2009; Arts and Gelissen 2001). However, Gelissen finds a positive effect of education on welfare-state support, albeit only in interaction with other socio-political orientations (Gelissen 2000).

The effect of age is also discussed ambivalently. In line with the self-interest perspective, Gelissen (2000) argues that both the younger and older cohorts face a higher likelihood of being dependent on welfare-state benefits compared with the middle-aged and are therefore more supportive of welfare-state intervention. Younger workers, on the one hand, run a greater risk of unemployment due to lack of seniority and are more vulnerable to market fluctuations due to lack of savings and other resources. Retirees, on the other hand, are out of the labor market, and most are already dependent on welfare benefits via pensions. Other older workers may anticipate soon leaving the labor market and therefore being dependent on welfare benefits in the near future (Gelissen 2000; see also Blekesaune and Quadagno 2003). It has also been argued that the age effect might be especially strong with regard to age-specific benefits and that the old might be more supportive of old-age and sickness benefits since they are the main beneficiaries of these programs (Blekesaune and Quadagno 2003).

In line with the cultural approach and with reference to Inglehart (1977), Andreß and Heien (2001) suggested that younger and middle aged people should be expected to be more supportive of welfare-state intervention than older cohorts. Younger age groups and the middle-aged are more likely to have internalized post-materialistic values, such as solidarity and social justice, and should therefore also more strongly support government intervention compared with older birth cohorts. The results of age are empirically ambiguous (e.g., Andreß and Heien 2001; Bean and Papadakis 1998; Arts and Gelissen 2001; Gelissen 2000), and neither hypothesis has been confirmed univocally. The idea that the age effect is program-specific has also not been confirmed unambiguously (Blekesaune and Quadagno 2003), and several studies have not included age at all (e.g., Linos and West 2003; Svallfors 1997).

Furthermore, some researchers have argued that public-sector employees (as the producers of welfare) are more in favor of the welfare state than are private-sector employees (e.g., Svallfors 1995, 1997; Hoel and Knutsen 1989). On the one hand, public-sector employees have an interest in save-guarding their employment conditions, e.g., in terms of wages or job security. This argument clearly emphasizes self-interest. On the other hand and more in line with the cultural approach, public-sector employment can be seen as a specific socialization experience through which employees show solidarity with other public-sector employees and their clients and patients. Based on arguments provided by Müller (2000, 1998), who analyzed voting behavior in Germany, the cultural argument should apply especially to professionals in social and cultural services (e.g., in the fields of healthcare, education, and social care), where employees develop specific value orientations due to their daily work experiences. Despite having received clear support within the Scandinavian group of countries (e.g., Svallfors 2004, 1997; Hoel and Knutsen 1989) and Canada (Jæger 2006b), this hypothesis has not been confirmed empirically in an international framework (Svallfors 1997).

Finally, it has been suggested and empirically shown that parents who receive family benefits or use public childcare institutions have a strong self-interest to support the welfare state (Jæger 2006b; Pettersen 2001). These results, however, cannot be generalized because they are based on single-country studies.

The political-values hypothesis suggests that individuals' internalized political values and beliefs are decisive in determining the level of their support of welfare-state intervention. The underlying idea is that support for welfare-state intervention is embedded within a coherent system of political and ideological orientations (Feldman and Zaller 1992; Blekesaune and Quadagno 2003; d'Anjou et al. 1995). A more conservative or rightist political orientation, e.g., in terms of market justice or economic individualism, is consequently related to a weaker support of welfare-state involvement. From this ideological position, the welfare state appears to be uneconomic, unproductive, inefficient, ineffective, and to deny freedom (C. Pierson 1997: 48; cf. Gelissen 2000: 289). In contrast, a more leftist political position, as well as a post-materialist value orientation that includes values such as social justice, equality, and solidarity with the weak in society (Inglehart 1977), is related to a positive evaluation of welfare-state intervention. From this perspective, the welfare state is seen as fostering equality and social integration (see also Gelissen 2000). Empirical studies have shown that pro-welfare attitudes are correlated with other ideological beliefs, such as the subjective position on the left-right continuum (Bean and Papadakis 1998; Gelissen 2000; Arts and Gelissen 2001; Jæger 2006b), beliefs about social justice and social mobility (Linos and West 2003), egalitarian ideology (Andreß and Heien 2001; Blekesaune and Quadagno 2003), and post-materialist values (Gelissen 2000).

D'Anjou et al. contend that the "ideology thesis" is in fact a refinement of the "self-interest thesis" because ideology is strongly affected by the individual's structural position in terms of income, class, gender, and race (d'Anjou et al. 1995). This is in line with some of the arguments given above, suggesting that attitudinal differences among specific social groups can be attributed to either self-interest or specific normative beliefs. This holds, e.g., with regard to differences among social classes and between men and women, different age-groups, and public- versus private-sector employees. Scholars such as Mau (2003) or Svallfors (2006) use the term "moral economy" to emphasize that the normative ideas of reciprocity, obligation, and responsibility should complement a pure self-interest perspective on preferences and attitudes toward the welfare state.

Albrekt Larsen (2006) distinguished a third mechanism, namely the formation of class interests and coalitions, or the power-resources approach. This approach regards particular welfare-state arrangements to a great extent as outcomes of distributive conflicts between class-related groups and political parties (Korpi 2003: 590). The formation of class interests can thus be seen as a preceding process in the course of institution building and institutional change in social policy (Korpi 2003, 1989; Esping-Andersen 1990; Bean and Papadakis 1998). Once institutions are in place, they impact on the long-term development of interests, preferences, and coalition formation among citizens (Korpi and Palme 1998).

This study views the current family-policy setup as a given and investigates the relationship between existing family-policy institutions and public attitudes. The processes of institution building or institutional change are thus not taken into account here.[2] A key issue guiding the following analyses concerns the emergence of social cleavages in public opinion. The subsequent chapters thereby focus on two mechanisms of attitude formation, namely the cultural and the calculus approach. It is asked, e.g., if women are more in favor of a strong role of the state than men, or whether individuals are more skeptical toward the unintended side effects of government intervention than are families. Section 2.9 elaborates on these questions and discusses which social cleavages are to be expected regarding public opinion toward family policy.

---

2 See Ferrarini (2006: Chpt. 3) for a thorough analysis of the political determinants of family-policy development, such as class-political factors and women's role in political decision making.

2.4 Deservingness perceptions and feedback processes

The deservingness literature deals with the question of which criteria individuals use to judge whether a person or a group deserves help, e.g., welfare-state benefits and started with Coughlin's pioneering studies (Coughlin 1979, 1980). In a comparative framework, Coughlin analyzed public support for different welfare-state programs and concluded that there is "a universal dimension of support" - that is, the ranking of the deserving groups follows the same pattern in all countries (see also Papadakis 1992). People are most in favor of programs for the old, followed consecutively by programs for the sick and disabled and by programs for needy families with children. The least deserving groups, in contrast, are the unemployed and people on social assistance and finally, immigrants (van Oorschot 2006). Van Oorschot (2006; 2000) discussed the following five criteria on which the public builds its judgment of deservingness: Control, need, identity, attitude, and reciprocity. The extent to which a group or a person fulfills these criteria is then decisive for the public's judgment of this group's or person's deservingness. This implies that the degree of perceived deservingness is higher 1) the less a group or a person is seen as being in control of neediness (control); 2) the greater the level of need (need); 3) the more people have a feeling of shared identity or belonging (identity); 4) the more grateful, docile, and compliant recipients are (attitude); and 5) the higher previous or future paybacks are (reciprocity).

In his book "The Institutional Logic of Welfare Attitudes," Albrekt Larsen (2006: 22) criticized that the theoretical links between welfare-state regimes and attitudes toward public policy "[...] suggest a too mechanic formation of attitudes towards welfare policy [...]." He argued that attitudes toward public policy are partly a result of public debate and suggested a "*political man* theory, where the individual's attitudes towards public policy are open to discussions of the common good, justice, necessity, suitability in relation to the experienced reality" (Albrekt Larsen 2006: 22). He claimed that the regime effect on public attitudes toward welfare policies is mainly caused by the regime effects on public perceptions of reality. Theoretically, Albrekt Larsen therefore combined welfare regime theory and the literature on deservingness perceptions. He showed that the public's perception of the poor and unemployed as well as attitudes toward welfare policies supporting these groups are more favorable in times of high unemployment. These results corroborate the idea that public discourses, the press, and political actors have an impact on what people perceive as being fair and appropriate in the field of welfare provision (Mau 2003, 2004; see also Papadakis 1992).

This study focuses on attitudes toward family policies. The group of beneficiaries is thus parents and their children. How needy families are strongly depends on the economic situation of the household in question, at least with regard to financial resources, yet it is always clear that children are not in control of their neediness. Furthermore, two deservingness criteria can be regarded as being fulfilled by families in general, namely the criterion of identity (i.e., they belong to us,) and the criterion of reciprocity.[3] Through labor-market participation, most parents have contributed or still contribute to the system of social security via taxation and contributions and children can be expected to contribute to this system in the future and to help secure the future of society as such. Taken together, these arguments suggest a rather high level of deservingness and hence strong public support for family-policy measures. Furthermore, both the perception of working parents and issues of work-family reconciliation, which are partly shaped by public discourses and the media, can be assumed to impact on the formation of attitudes toward family policies.

In line with these arguments, Kumlin (2002: 31) emphasized the importance of experiences with welfare-state benefits and services and argued that people build their opinions on "personally experienced welfare-state information." Hence, experiences with welfare-state services (e.g., in terms of availability, affordability, and quality) can be assumed to shape citizens' opinions about these services. Whether people make positive or negative experiences is, in turn, strongly related to the institutional design of existing policies.

A related strand of research analyzes the potential feedback effects welfare attitudes have on policy development. The "new politics of the welfare state" thesis by Pierson (1996; 2001: Chpt. 13) states that in times of austerity, the clients of the welfare state (e.g., pensioners, health-care consumers, the disabled, and welfare-state employees) successfully resist government attempts to cut back on benefits. Pierson sees a "blame-avoidance logic" at work in which politicians do not pursue unpopular retrenchment policies since they fear electoral backlash (for a critical voice, see Korpi 2003). In line with Pierson's argument, Brooks and Manza (2007) asked "why welfare states persist" and concluded that feedback processes exist between attitudes and institutions and that welfare attitudes play a key role in welfare policy development. The authors showed that mass preferences "exert a significant constraint on retrenchment pressures" (Brooks and Manza 2007: 99). These results complement research on attitude

---

3 An exception might be the group of migrant families. However, the topic of migration and the social rights of migrants, e.g., in terms welfare state entitlements go beyond the scope of this study. For a discussion of these issues, see Alesina and Glaeser (2004) and Mau and Burkhardt (2009).

formation and suggest that feedback processes between attitudes and institutions work in both directions (Svallfors 2010; see also Mettler and Soss 2004).

These arguments emphasize the necessity to investigate public opinion toward welfare-state policies because they play a crucial role in elections and thus in the process of policy making. In contrast to many other fields of welfare-state intervention, however, public expenditures for family-policy measures and social services are expanding (e.g., Fagnani and Math 2008; Castles 2009; Bahle 2008b). Häusermann (2008), who analyzed family-policy reforms in Switzerland and Germany, showed that new conflict lines that cross-cut existing social divisions emerge in the political arena. New value-cleavages emerge between libertarian values (i.e., being in favor of participation, individualization, and gender equality) and authoritarian values (i.e., traditional family values and communitarian structures). A key issue in the processes of family-policy reform and coalition building is whether family policies should reward and promote female labor-market participation or rather women's caring and educational tasks (Häusermann 2008: 8, 18).

The author's findings suggest that the position both of policy makers and political parties on these normative issues might increasingly become an important factor during election campaigns. A "blame-avoidance logic" might then be at work not regarding unpopular retrenchment (P. Pierson 1996) but regarding unpopular normative or ideological positions with respect to gender roles and family values.

Policy field specific studies

The latest stream of research in the comparative welfare-state literature analyzes welfare attitudes against the backdrop of specific welfare-state programs such as healthcare systems (Wendt et al. 2011; Wendt et al. 2010), minimum-income protection systems (Pfeifer 2009; Wendt et al. 2011), and family policies (Wendt et al. 2011). Instead of analyzing the overall welfare state, these studies analyze subfields of welfare-state intervention. Since this approach investigates program-specific policy designs and citizens' evaluations of these specific programs, researchers are able to establish a more specific link between welfare policies and public attitudes. As Wendt et al. (2011: 18) asserted, the main argument in favor of this approach is that "people generally do not have a picture of the whole welfare state in mind but would like to know whether they will have a sufficient income when old, healthcare services when ill, family benefits when raising children, and, if unemployed or poor, whether unemployment benefits and social assistance will be available." This argumentation underlines the fact that differences in attitudes toward government intervention are not only explainable by self-interest and (political) values and norms but also by individuals' personal experiences with particular welfare-state institutions. So far, results confirm that specific policy features have an impact on public attitudes and that the level of support for specific policies as well as the level of societal polarization among social groups varies with respect to the policy field in question as well as with respect to the field-specific institutional setup.

Particular policy designs are assumed to impact on public opinion by mediating citizen's personal experiences with welfare-state intervention and by shaping public awareness of societal problems, the salience of group differences within a political community, deservingness perceptions, and the perception of the appropriate solution and level of government intervention (Mettler and Soss 2004). In these processes, institutions have a mediating effect on orientations but do not causally determine them. As Svallfors (2007: 10) put it, the relationship between institutions and attitudes "is instead a probabilistic one as well as one of mutual dependency and development. Certain institutions tend to make some orientations more likely than others; given a certain set of orientations, some institutions are more easily implemented or changed than others."

2.5 A conceptual framework

Flora, Alber, and Kohl (1977) defined the welfare state as a specific aspect of state interventionism characterized by the following two criteria: 1) The state takes the responsibility for the (re-) distribution of specific material (or cultural) commodities and resources and 2) these interventions are based on legal entitlements of specific groups of the population or the population as a whole. The interventions thereby pursue the goals of socio-economic security and/or socio-economic equality (Flora et al. 1977: 705). A key function of welfare-state policies is hence the distribution and redistribution of resources, which has an impact on living conditions, social stratification patterns, and belief systems (e.g., Esping-Andersen 1990; Jæger 2009).

Studying attitudes toward welfare-state policies, Roller (1992: 38-47) conceptually distinguished three objects of evaluation. She argued that attitudes can bear reference to *goals*, *means*, and the *consequences* of policies.

Concerning *goals*, Roller distinguishes two dimensions, namely the *extensity* (or range) and *intensity* (or degree) of government intervention. *Extensity* refers to whether the government should take over responsibility for achieving a specific goal, such as providing benefits for the unemployed, poor, ill, or disabled. *Intensity* refers to the intensity of government activity within a policy goal or area given that the government is held responsible for achieving this goal. Intensity captures, e.g., whether the state should spend more or less on certain welfare benefits and services.

The concept of *means* (or outputs) refers to the evaluation of specific institutions or programs of welfare-state intervention. According to Roller's conceptualization, *institutions* cover people's evaluation of long-term social policy (e.g., how fair the actual pension system is), whereas *programs* refer to the evaluation of short-term social policy programs (e.g., what an appropriate measure would be to secure the financing of future pensions).

With respect to the *consequences* (or outcomes) of state intervention, finally, Roller contrasted people's evaluation of *intended consequences* with the evaluation of *unintended consequences*. *Intended consequences* cover the extent to which the intended policy goals have been achieved (e.g., the goals of socio-economic security or socio-economic equality), whereas *unintended consequences* cover the positive and negative side effects that have not been intended, such as the abuse of social-policy benefits.

In accordance with other scholars (e.g., Kangas 1997; Papadakis 1992; van Oorschot 1998; Jæger 2006a; Svallfors 2006), Roller distinguished two determinants of individual policy preferences, namely self-interest (i.e., the calculus argument) and norms and values (i.e., the cultural argument) (Edeltraud Roller 1992). She argued that self-interest is the prevailing determinant of attitudes when these attitudes bear reference to policies that aim at increasing socio-economic security, whereas normative beliefs are more salient in the case of policies that try to further socio-economic equality.

This study analyzes the relationship between family-policy institutions and public attitudes. In the process of attitude formation, the specific institutional setup of existing family policies as well as the broader social context is assumed to affect the salience of self-interest versus political values and norms. Both mechanisms – the cultural (i.e., values and norms) and the calculus (i.e., self interest) approach – are taken into account when investigating attitudes toward family policies in the following chapters (for a similar approach, see Wendt et al. 2011). The analyses take into account three objects of evaluation (or dimensions of attitudes). Concerning the evaluation of goals, the aspect of the extensity of welfare-state intervention is taken into account by asking whether the state should be responsible for the provision of childcare services. Concerning the evaluation of means, this study focuses on childcare services as one particular institution and asks how satisfied the public is with existing childcare services.

With regard to the evaluation of consequences, finally, the aspect of unintended consequences is taken into account by asking whether the public agrees that public benefits and services make people less willing to care for themselves and their families. Based on Roller's conceptualization as well as modifications made by Wendt et al. (2011), the following figure (2.2) depicts the analytical framework applied.

Figure 2.2: Public perception of government intervention. A conceptual framework

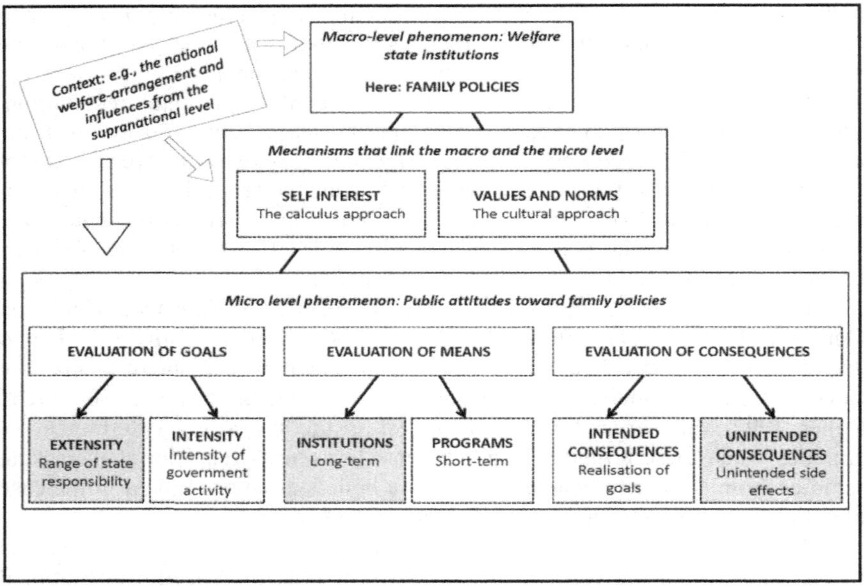

Source: Adapted from Roller (1992: 47), Wendt et al. (2011: 22) and Albrekt Larsen (2006: 14).
Note: The grey-shaded fields represent the attitudinal dimensions analyzed in this study.

The point of departure in this framework is the actual policy setup, whereas the preceding processes of institution building or policy reform go beyond the scope of this study and are not discussed here (e.g., Korpi 2003, 1989; Esping-Andersen 1990; Bahle 1995, 2003; Ferrarini 2006). Accordingly, this framework uses the actual institutional setup of family policies as it is given. Existing institutions are then assumed to impact on the development of interests, preferences, and coalition formation among citizens (Korpi and Palme 1998) as well as on citizen's evaluation of policy goals, means, and consequences.

The mechanisms distinguished by Mettler and Soss (2004) are helpful in explaining how the institutional setup can impact on attitude formation and the salience of self-interest versus norms and values. Based on the concept of policy feedback, the authors distinguished five mechanisms that can explain feedback effects between public policies and public opinion. First, policies define membership in the political community in terms of who is included and to what degree. Any policy that applies eligibility criteria for granting benefits or rights implies that certain individuals are fully included and others are not included at all or to the same degree. According to Mettler and Soss (2004: 61), public policies thus define the content and meaning of citizenship and influence "the ways individuals understand their rights and responsibilities as members of a political community." Second, policies can influence patterns of group identity either by increasing the level of cohesion or alternatively by fostering group divisions by actively constructing and positioning social groups and defining their boundaries and political meaning. Policies can affect citizens' ideas about which groups are deserving or undeserving, thereby influencing the ways a target group is viewed in the society at large. Third, policies can affect citizens' capacities for civic and political engagement, e.g., by shaping citizen's personal experiences with the government, stimulating political learning, and affecting patterns of political belief. Fourth, public policies frame policy agendas, societal problems, and evaluations of government actions. Social policies define the meaning and origins of societal problems by identifying target groups for government action and by defining policy solutions. Social policies then shape citizens' perceptions as to whether an issue is a public or a private problem and eventually whether this problem should be solved by society as a whole or by the individual, him- or herself. Public policies thus affect the salience of issues as well as the public's evaluations of governments and their actions. Finally, public policies may structure and stimulate political participation by influencing individual or group mobilization. Policy designs can thereby actively encourage or discourage demand-making. For instance, programs that have a low visibility can foster under-utilization, especially by those groups who tend to lack information about their own eligibility.

These considerations again underline the importance of taking into account the policy design of specific policy fields and public attitudes toward these fields instead of the whole welfare state. The five mechanisms distinguished by Mettler and Soss (2004) can be assumed to play a role in every subfield of welfare-state intervention; however, the specific outcomes in terms of public opinion and the emphasis of either self-interest or norms and values can be expected to differ not only among different welfare states but also across different policy fields within welfare states.

Looking at the field of family policy, gender relations and the division of paid and unpaid work between parents are structured by the design of the respective institutions. The design therefore has important implications for the agency, actions, orientations, and living conditions of individuals (Korpi 2000; Ferrarini 2006). The actual type and level of government intervention in the sphere of the family can affect public opinion concerning the question of whether the government is generally regarded as being responsible for providing support for families and whether it is a private or public responsibility to solve parents' conflicts between work and family life. Moreover, the public's perception of family-policy institutions is potentially affected by institutional variations in eligibility criteria (e.g., means-tested versus universal benefits or variation with respect to the number and age of children), benefit levels (e.g., the level of income replacement of financial compensation), the type of remuneration (flat-rate versus income related), and fees (e.g., the costs of public childcare). Based on arguments provided by the approach of welfare arrangements (Pfau-Effinger 2005a), it is argued that not only the actual family-policy setup impacts on the public's perception of existing family-policy institutions. Instead, public attitudes are assumed to be embedded into the specific context of a particular society that includes different aspects, such as culture, social structures, and other institutions. Different aspects, such as labor market characteristics and opportunities or normative beliefs about gender roles, could have a modifying effect on public opinion. Furthermore, influences from the international-level, such as the European Union, play a role in the formation of attitudes. Citizens are aware of the social benefits and services provided in other EU countries and might adjust their preferences and expectations accordingly. Moreover, the EU social policy agenda itself impacts on policy reforms in the member states (e.g., Ferrarini 2006; Plantenga et al. 2008; Rostgaard 2002).

2.6 Family policy as a special policy field

Post-war welfare regimes across the OECD hardly absorbed the family-related burden; on the contrary, these regimes built their social-policy arrangements under the assumption that the male-breadwinner family model was the norm and that mothers would be housewives and care for children and other dependent family members (Esping-Andersen 1999). Nowadays, this model has been superseded by the dual-earner family model (Mahon 2002; Lewis 2001), which is increasingly viewed as the standard in Western Europe and places emphasis on both parents as earners and caregivers (Mahon 2002; Abrahamson 2007; Saraceno and Leira 2008). Questions concerning the compatibility of parenthood and paid employment have become increasingly relevant for individuals and policy makers in Europe, and the boundaries between private and public responsibilities are now being re-examined (Saraceno and Leira 2008; Bahle 2003).

The growing attention paid to family-policy interventions becomes significantly evident at the supranational level of the European Union. In 1996, the European Council passed a directive that obliges all member states to introduce legislation on parental leave that would enable parents to care full-time for their children over a period of at least three months, thus guaranteeing a certain minimum standard in all member states (Plantenga and Siegel 2004; Rostgaard 2002). Recognizing that the lack of affordable, high-quality childcare is among the main obstacles in mothers' labor-market participation (Plantenga and Siegel 2004; Bahle 2008a; Saraceno and Leira 2008; OECD 2001; European Commission 2005; Rostgaard 2002), the European Council also set ambitious targets for the provision of childcare services. In 2002, the member states agreed upon coverage rates of 33% for children under age three and 90% for children from age three to compulsory school age. This coverage was to take effect by the year 2010 (Plantenga and Siegel 2004; Saraceno and Leira 2008). Resulting from the open method of coordination (OMC), these target percentages are not obligatory, and no sanctions exist for non-compliance (Plantenga et al. 2008).

During recent decades, there has been a tendency in most member states to introduce or reform existing policies to provide more support for the dual-earner family model and thus support parents in their ability both provide childcare and be gainfully employed. The countries began with varying levels of dual-earner support and implemented reforms with different foci and priorities. Hence, despite similarly pressing challenges in most European countries and a rhetorical consensus concerning the type of family policies needed, great variation in the way and extent to which families are actually supported within particular welfare states persists.

Since maternity and parental leave regulations have often been considered to constrain employers' liberty, the United Kingdom and Ireland have, e.g., long opposed the European regulation projects concerning these entitlements (Meulders and O'Dorchai 2007). Both countries continue to provide only a short period of parental leave that is not compensated financially. Instead, both countries provide a long period of maternity leave, which is partly compensated financially, and which was easier for employers to accept (Lewis et al. 2008b).

The two countries are usually classified as liberal welfare states (e.g., Esping-Andersen 1990), and have a tradition of "non-involvement by the state in the private sphere of the family" (Lewis et al. 2008b: 271). Social care is thus regarded as mainly a private responsibility, except in the case of poor families and "at risk" children (Lewis et al. 2008b: 270; Del Boca et al. 2005).

In contrast, the national childcare strategy of the British Labour government (which rose to power in 1997) represented a major shift in policy because the state took responsibility for the development of childcare for all children (Rake 2001). By 2004, free part-time nursery care was being offered to all children over the age of three years. However, until the year 2008, there was no legal obligation on the local authorities to provide these care services (Lewis et al. 2008b: 270).

Another example of a considerable policy shift is Germany's reform of parental leave, which came into effect in 2007. Through this reform, the means-tested flat-rate benefit was replaced by an unconditional wage replacement of 67% (up to a ceiling of 1,800 Euros per month). Benefit duration was cut to 14 months, including 2 non-transferable months for the partner who assumes less leave, usually the father (Wersig 2007; Henninger et al. 2008).

In comparative perspective, the development of family policies has been partly influenced by women's movements emphasizing diverging gender ideologies (Korpi 2000; Ferrarini 2006). The "difference" line of argumentation thereby stresses gender differences and argues that women's rights and position in society should be based on women's unpaid caring work. Consequently, care-related benefits have been promoted. The "equality" line of argumentation, in contrast, stresses gender equality and women's equal rights, and promotes policies which enable women to participate in the labor market on equal terms with men (Korpi 2000: 140; Ferrarini 2006: 34; Sainsburry 1999). Not surprisingly, the dominant gender ideology had a strong impact on the historical development of country-specific family-policy arrangements. Ferrarini (2006: 143) argued that these policy arrangements have far-reaching "implications for agency, actions, orientations and living conditions of individuals in terms of childbearing, female labor force participations, poverty among households with young children as well as gender role attitudes."

Differences in policy design go hand-in-hand with both diverging preferences regarding the organization of work and care and varying attitudes toward the best type of childcare and mothers' labor-market participation (Mahon 2002; Lewis et al. 2008a; Kremer 2007). This relationship points to an important peculiarity of the family-policy field, namely the salience of moral norms and values that affects the development, change, and stability of family-policy institutions, as well as the choices, actions, and attitudes of individuals. Cultural approaches explain existing differences in the extent and kind of public support for families, as well as families' diverging work-and-care arrangements with long-lasting cultural traditions, values, and ideals (e.g., Pfau-Effinger 1998).

Kremer (2007) showed that families, and particularly mothers, base their behavior on country-specific, culturally shaped care ideals. According to Kremer (2007: 171), ideals of care "can be loosely translated as 'what is considered to be good-enough caring'." The divergent ideals of care, in turn, impact women's labor-market participation differently. The ideal of professional care is most inclusive for all women and is the best "guilt-reduction strategy" for working mothers. This ideal, however, may not be suitable for all European welfare states due to parents' diverging and country-specific ideals of care. According to Anttonen et al. (2003), this prominence of moral norms and values can be explained by the degree of "plasticity" inherent in social care. Plasticity describes the fact that the production and consumption of social care are highly substitutable between the sector of the household, the market, and the state. If the state does not provide care services, the domestic economy steps into the breach and absorbs the inadequacies of the social care policies (Anttonen et al. 2003). Such a substitution by the domestic sector is not possible in other fields of social welfare provision, such as healthcare services or education (see also Jensen 2008).

These arguments certainly do not deny the possibility of social change. As Pfau-Effinger (1998) argued, alternative and competing cultural systems facilitating social and cultural change may exist. The way social actors deal with contradictions and alternatives in value systems can influence these value system and institutions. Parents' practices can thus be atypical in their inconsistency with regard to either or both the dominant care ideal and institutional structure. In times of women's increasing labor-market aspirations and participation, many families want to (or have to) combine work and family life. Additionally, policy makers have an interest in raising fertility and female employment rates in order to sustain the viability of the welfare state and enhance economic prosperity (see also Daly and Klammer 2006; Lewis et al. 2008b).

The current socio-demographic and socio-economic changes are accompanied by (normative) discussions about who should provide social care for dependent family members and under which conditions this care should be provided (e.g., in terms of financial compensation or the qualification of care providers). Despite the long-lasting cultural traditions and care ideals, Anttonen et al. (2003: 195) contended that "there is a certain inevitability to state-regulated, universal social care services based upon individual citizenship entitlements." However, the prominence of moral norms and values in the family-policy field has to be kept in mind when studying differences in the development, change, and stability of family-policy institutions or differences in the choices, actions, and attitudes of individuals.

There are several examples that illustrate this salience of moral norms and values in the emergence of different family-policy systems. The Nordic countries, e.g., were the first countries that have introduced comprehensive family-policy benefits and services, which explicitly supported the dual-earner / dual carer model of the family. Family policies were introduced to promote gender equality, in terms of both mothers employment participation and fathers participation in childcare (Haataja and Nyberg 2006; Hiilamo 2006; Hilamo and Kangas 2009).

In France, family-policy measures have been introduced primarily in order to increase fertility and policies continue to favor large families (Fagnani and Math 2008; Fagnani 2007). In the 1980s, France created the nursery school system (école maternelle), which has increased the acceptance of public childcare services among the population. Childcare services were seen as being important for children's intellectual and emotional awakening and general well-being (Fagnani 2007: 42). A policy orientation toward work-family compatibility then progressively evolved.

In West Germany, in contrast, "the family was long considered the best environment for raising a preschool age child," and family policies promoted the male-breadwinner model of the family, holding up the principle of subsidiarity (Fagnani 2007: 43).[4]

When searching for the implications that different family-policy institutions have for the division of paid and unpaid work between men and women as well as the gender dimension of social inequality within societies, it is essential to take into account agency-inequality (Korpi 2000; Orloff 1993; Hobson et al. 2006; Hobson 2011). As Korpi stated (2000: 128), the agency concept reflects "potential or latent aspects of inequality, indicated by the range of alternative achievements and accomplishments between which an actor has the capability to choose" (see also Archer 1996; Sen 1992; Hobson et al. 2006). Korpi argues that the labor market is the central arena for socio-economic stratification processes in modern societies. Individuals who are excluded from these processes are usually disadvantaged in terms of material resources as well as social rights,

4 The idea of subsidiarity implies "that social services should be provided for at the lowest possible level in the community, public authorities playing a role only in the event that churches and families are unable to do so" (Fagnani 2007: 43).

which are often conditioned upon economic activity. Furthermore, labor-market participation affects a person's self-perception and identity, which again influences a person's capabilities and freedom in many different areas of life. A more equal distribution of paid work between men and women is also likely to affect the distribution of intra-family bargaining power, which might be crucial for achieving changes in the distribution of care work within the family (Korpi 2000). Traditionally, many women have been excluded from the labor market with far-reaching consequences for gender inequalities in society. Assuming an increasing economic necessity and individual preference to combine labor-market participation and family life, family-policy institutions can either intensify or mitigate gendered agency inequalities depending on whether they support the traditional male-breadwinner model of the family or the dual-earner model. As Ferrarini pointed out, family policies can affect agency not only for existing parents and children but also for potential parents who anticipate possible consequences that come along with their childbearing decision, e.g., in terms of labor-market participation and economic well-being (Ferrarini 2006).

The following section discusses existing attempts to classify family-policy institutions. These attempts refer more-or-less explicitly to the agency concept by taking policy implications for the division of paid and unpaid work into account.

2.7 Classifications of family-policy institutions

Several attempts have been made to provide a more general classification of welfare states and it has been pointed out previously, that Esping-Andersen's "The Three Worlds of Welfare Capitalism" is the most prominent. His typology, however, has not remained undisputed (see Scruggs and Allen 2006), and several scholars have proposed alternative classifications (e.g., Castles and Mitchell 1993; Ferrera 1996; Bonoli 1997; Leibfried 1992; Arts and Gelissen 2002; Scruggs and Allen 2006). Feminist scholars have called for an integration of a gender perspective into the analysis of welfare states. In particular, they have criticized the concept of de-commodification[5] because it does not account for the different lifestyles of men and women and the fact that women provide the bulk of unpaid domestic labor and social care work (e.g., Daly 1994; Sainsbury 1996; Orloff 1993). Orloff (1993: 318-319) argued that two additional dimensions

---

[5] I.e., "when a service is rendered as a matter of right, and when a person can maintain a livelihood without reliance on the market" (Esping-Andersen 1990: 21/22).

should be taken into account when assessing the quality of social rights, namely "access to paid work" and "the capacity to form and maintain an autonomous household." The first dimension covers the degree to which women's labor-market participation (or "the right to be commodified") is promoted or discouraged by the state. The second dimension refers to women's economic dependency and covers the degree to which women can "survive and support their children without having to marry to gain access to breadwinners' income."

The work of Lewis and Ostner (1994) has provided a major step toward the inclusion of a gender perspective in the analysis of welfare states. The authors suggested an alternative categorization of welfare regimes based on the gender division of work, and they used the strength of the male-breadwinner / family-wage model as a proxy measure, distinguishing among "strong" (Great Britain and Germany), "moderate" (France), and "weak" (Denmark) male-breadwinner states. Sainsbury (1994) provided an alternative approach, identifying the "male-breadwinner" and the "individual" model as the two poles of a continuum. In the prototypical breadwinner model, there is a strict division of labor between husband and wife; in the individual model, each spouse is individually responsible for his or her own maintenance, and husband and wife share the tasks of financial support and childcare.

Gornick and colleagues (1997) made a more specific attempt to classify family policies by focusing on policies that support mothers' employment. The authors differentiated among support for mothers' employment with children in three different age groups: Those from birth to the age of three, three to school age, and school-aged children. The authors analyzed 16 indicators that mirror public policies in the area of family policy and that potentially affect a mother's decision to enter or remain in paid work in a variety of countries (the United Kingdom, Australia, the United States, the Netherlands, Germany, Norway, Canada, Denmark, Finland, France, Sweden, Italy, Belgium, and Luxembourg). Three kinds of policies are considered: Benefits for new parents, childcare services, and public-school policies. With respect to policies aimed at children under age six, the findings suggest that there are three country groups. The countries with the most supportive policies are France and the three Nordic countries (Finland, Denmark, and Sweden), followed by Belgium and Italy. The group ranking in the middle consists of five countries, namely Luxembourg, Germany, Canada, the Netherlands, and Norway. The least-supportive countries for this age group are the three English-speaking countries: Australia, the United Kingdom, and the United States.

Korpi (2000) provided an additional approach in his family-policy typology, explicitly taking into account the relevance of policy institutions in shaping gender relations and agency. He arranged family-policy institutions along two dimensions, depending on whether they support the traditional family (general family support) or a dual-earner family (dual-earner support). General family support, on the one hand, maintains a family type with a traditional division of paid work and care work between men and women and within society. In this family type, the father is the main earner and the mother is mainly responsible for childcare. Dual-earner support, on the other hand, is oriented toward mothers' participation in both labor-market careers and in care work at home. Dual-earner support may also provide incentives for fathers to engage in childcare. On the basis of these two dimensions, Korpi distinguished the following three ideal-typical models of family-policy strategies, depicted in Figure 2.3 a "general family support model" (with high general family support), a "dual-earner support model" (with high dual-earner support), and finally a "market-oriented family-policy model" (with less-developed family policies along both dimensions). In the latter model, market forces shape gender relations and individuals have to find private solutions for the work-family conflict.

Figure 2.3: Dimensions and ideal-typical family-policy models according to Korpi (2000) and Ferrarini (2006)

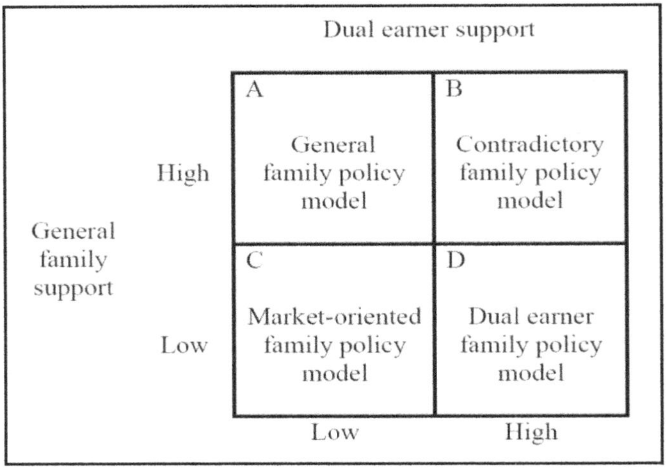

Source: Ferrarini (2006: 13).

Based on this typology, Ferrarini (2006) studied family-policy developments from 1950 to 2000. He took maternity insurance, dual-parental insurance, and paternity insurance into consideration in order to capture dual-earner support. The general family-support dimension was captured using childcare leave, child benefits, marriage subsidies, and maternity grants. Ferrarini methodologically calculated the net generosity of support per dimension in percent of the national average-production-worker's wages. His results support the distinction among the three policy models. Austria, Belgium, France, Germany, Ireland, Italy, and the Netherlands are grouped into the "general family policy model," while Denmark, Finland, Norway, and Sweden belong to the "dual-earner family policy model." The third cluster, the "market-oriented family-policy model," includes Australia, Canada, Japan, the United Kingdom, and the United States, which have less-developed family policies along both dimensions. In addition, Ferrarini described a fourth cluster that could potentially exist, namely the "contradictory family policy model." This model reflects a situation of institutional pluralism with high support for both the traditional family and the dual-earner family (i.e., the top right cell (B) in Figure 2.3). However, this model was not identified in the original typology (Korpi 2000) or in Ferrarini's study.

Most studies so far have included other non-European countries, such as the United States and Australia, but excluded the Southern European countries, such as Greece, Portugal, and Spain (e.g., Gornick et al. 1997; Korpi 2000; Ferrarini 2006). An exception is the work done by Bahle (2008a), who included all 25 EU member states in his study entitled "Family policy patterns in the enlarged EU." Based on data from the year 2004, Bahle developed a "cultural map" in which he categorized the countries based on the following two dimensions: 1) "State interference into the family-work relationship" (including maternity and parenting benefits as well as childcare services) and 2) "state-provided family income" (i.e., family allowances) (Bahle 2008a: 116-117). He distinguished the following five groups: The first group, representing "the universality model," consists of Denmark, Sweden, Finland, Estonia, and Latvia. The second group comprises France and Belgium and combines characteristics of the first and the third group. The third group, named the "subsidiarity group," is the largest and most heterogeneous group and includes Germany, Luxembourg, Austria, Hungary, the Czech Republic, Poland, Lithuania, and Slovenia. The fourth group, representing the "autonomy model," comprises the Netherlands, the United Kingdom, and Ireland. Finally, the fifth group is characterized by familism and comprises the Southern European countries of Italy, Portugal, Spain, Greece, Cyprus, and Malta.

Based on family-policy classifications or single family-policy indicators, several comparative studies have confirmed the positive impact of policies supporting the dual-earner model of the family. Measures promoting the dual-earner model are positively associated with female labor-market participation (Ferrarini 2006; Kangas and Rostgaard 2007), fertility (Ferrarini 2006; Sleebos 2003), and egalitarian gender-role attitudes (Sjöberg 2004; Ferrarini 2006), as well as lower rates of child poverty and increased child well-being (Bradshaw and Finch 2002; Kamerman et al. 2003).

This study investigates the link between family policies and public opinion toward these policies. The focus is thereby on public opinion toward the ideal level of government intervention, the evaluation of existing family-policy institutions, and the anticipation of the negative side effects of welfare-state intervention. This study argues that it is crucial to be aware of citizens' perceptions of the ongoing changes in the field of family policy. The investigation of the public's needs and policy preferences can reveal whether existing policy arrangements are accepted and normatively grounded by the people (Svallfors 2010) as well as point out which policy reforms might be successful or rather difficult to implement.

In a first step, this study investigates the current family-policy setup in 15 member states of the European Union. Chapter 3 selects several family-policy indicators, which capture the ideal-typical dimensions of general family support and dual-earner support. This distinction allows for capturing pluralistic policy orientations as well as policy implications for agency and gender inequality. The chosen indicators are then used in a cluster analysis in order to develop a family-policy typology and thereby contribute to the understanding of family-policy types in Europe. The analyses amend existing research by including the Southern European countries, which allows for the investigation of whether these countries form their own, distinct family-policy cluster, as suggested by Flaquer (2000) and Bahle (2008a).[6] Furthermore, the cluster analysis considers a great variety of up-to-date family-policy indicators, thus providing a recent picture of the changing family-policy landscape in Europe.

2.8 Attitudes toward family policies – state of the art

There are currently only a limited number of comparative studies that analyze attitudes toward public family policies. Since family-policy issues have not been included in international opinion surveys for a long time, a lack of data is

---

6 For a discussion of the distinctiveness of the Southern European countries, see also Ferrara (1996) and Karamessini (2008), who discussed the distinctiveness of this group of countries with respect to several fields of welfare-state intervention.

partially responsible for this research gap. An exception is the International Public Policy Acceptance Study (IPPAS), which covers 14 East and Central European countries. Based on this dataset, Stopnik and Sambt (2007) analyzed preferences for a hypothetical improvement of parental leave and a rise in child allowances, as well as the potential impact of these measures on citizens' family-planning decisions. Results show that people are in favor of improved parental leave benefits as well as higher child allowances. Furthermore, the potential impact of these policy measures on one's own family-planning decisions is estimated to be high. The authors have not analyzed attitudinal differences among different social groups (see also Valentova 2007).

Based on the "work family and well being module" of the 2004/05 wave of the European Social Survey (ESS), Lewis and colleagues (Lewis et al. 2008a) analyzed how parents in 13 Western European countries reconcile employment and childcare. The authors concluded that working hours are a crucial element of families' reconciliation practices. In terms of policy preferences, they found that mothers are rather content with the amount of available childcare services. In contrast, demand for more formal childcare is strong in Portugal, France, and Spain. Unfortunately, differences among societal groups have not been analyzed in detail. However, the authors reported that demand for more childcare is slightly stronger among mothers with the lowest and the highest level of education, which might be due to group-specific employment preferences and practices. Mothers with low educational qualifications might need to work more due to economic pressures, while those with high qualifications might want to work more (Lewis et al. 2008a: 34).

Lewin-Epstein et al. compared public attitudes toward family policy in Germany and Israel (Lewin-Epstein et al. 2000). Using data from the International Social Survey Programme (ISSP), they analyzed the level of respondents' agreement with the following two statements: 1) "Working women should receive paid maternity leave when they have a baby," and 2) "Families should receive financial benefits for child care when both parents work." The authors conducted pooled regression models using an additive index of the two items as dependent variable. The models revealed that women, more highly educated persons, young persons, and married persons are more supportive than men, lesser educated persons, old persons, and unmarried persons, respectively. Social class also matters: The higher the class position, the lower the support for state assistance to families. Finally, whether or not a young child (up to 12 years) lives in the household has no effect on family-policy support, whereas a positive attitude toward children (i.e., "Watching children grow up is life's greatest joy") increases support. Regarding the key variables of age, religiousness, and social class, the authors provided country-specific results indicating that differences among social groups are context specific. In West Germany, young persons, lower-class members, and non-religious persons are most supportive of family-policy benefits, whereas in Israel, age does not matter and lower-class members and religious individuals are most supportive.

A single-country study conducted by Pettersen (2001) confirms most of the previously described social cleavage patterns. Based on data from Norway, Pettersen showed that support for different types of family policies declines with increasing income, whereas a higher education correlates with increased support for public spending on schools and education. Pettersen demonstrated that families are more supportive of family policies than individuals are. The type of policies supported most, however, differs according to the age of the children living in the respondents' households. Families with children in all age-groups are in favor of increased child allowances, whereas support for daycare centers is higher among families with children below school age. Families with children who have reached school age are more in favor of higher spending for schools and education.

Although the described results cannot be generalized due to the small set of countries included or the limited analyses of group differences within individual countries, the cited studies provide valuable evidence about which social cleavages might play a role in attitudinal differences toward family policies. Section 2.9 elaborates on these issues.

Attitudes toward gender roles

The aspect of moral norms and values inherent in questions concerning the work-family conflict has been covered by a broad range of comparative studies that analyze gender-role attitudes and attitudes toward female labor-market participation. This strand of research captures people's normative beliefs concerning the roles of men and women in society, the gendered division of paid- and unpaid work, and the positive and negative consequences of female (or mothers') labor-market participation. The attitudinal differences have, in turn, been related to societal outcomes such as female labor-market participation and families' work- and care arrangements. Researchers use responses to the following survey items to capture egalitarian versus traditional gender-role attitudes:

- A working mother can establish just as warm and secure a relationship with her children as a mother who does not work.
- A preschool child is likely to suffer if his or her mother works.
- All in all, family life suffers when the woman has a full-time job.
- A job is all right – but what most women really want is a home and children.
- A man's job is to earn money; a woman's job is to look after the home and the family.
- Being a housewife is just as fulfilling as working for pay.

Most studies analyze gender-role attitudes focusing on differences among social groups, among countries, on changes over time, or on a combination of the three (e.g., Crompton et al. 2005; Bolzendahl and Myers 2004; Sjöberg 2004; Motiejunaite and Kravchenko 2008; Sundström 1999; Knudsen and Wærness 2001a). The results of these studies show that over time, gender-role attitudes have become more egalitarian, and polarization across social groups has become smaller, indicating increasing public agreement for these issues (e.g., Bolzendahl and Myers 2004; Crompton et al. 2005). Women, more highly educated persons, and those persons whose mothers were employed during their childhood have more egalitarian attitudes. Religiousness and age, in contrast, increase support for traditional attitudes. Despite a general trend toward more egalitarian gender-role attitudes, considerable differences among countries persist. Knudsen und Wærness (2001b) compared gender-role attitudes between Sweden, Norway, and Great Britain. Their study revealed the most egalitarian attitudes in Sweden and the most traditional attitudes in Norway. The authors explained the relatively high level of egalitarian attitudes in Great Britain with the country's history of early industrialization and urban married women's employment. Both developments may have potentially created a favorable climate for mothers' labor-market participation despite the fact that government policy has largely ignored the needs of working parents and that a range of policies actually discourage married women's employment.

Sundström (1999) analyzed differences in gender-role attitudes in Germany, Italy, and Sweden. She showed that differences among the age groups are greater in Italy and Germany and that attitudes have become quite similar among the three countries when focusing on the younger age groups. For the German case, results indicate an "increasing gap between people's attitudes to working mothers and the ambivalence in German social and family policies" (Sundström 1999: 203). These policies encourage a traditional division of paid and unpaid work between men and women. The findings indicate contradictions between the value system of the population and existing institutions, a situation that can facilitate social and institutional change (Pfau-Effinger 1998).

In a 13-country study, Sjöberg (2004) analyzed the role of dual-earner versus general family support in structuring attitudes toward gender-roles in terms of female labor-market participation. Based on a multi-level analysis, he showed that respondents in countries in which family policies support a dual-earner family model have significantly more positive attitudes toward female labor-force participation (see also Ferrarini 2006).

Kangas and Rostgaard (2007) analyzed the correlation between preferences (regarding the organization of family- and working life) and institutional structures (in terms of parental leave and childcare services) on mothers' employment participation. The authors found that more home-centered women work less hours, a finding that is in line with preference theory (Hakim 2002). However, Kangas and Rostgaard also showed that institutional factors, such as the availability of childcare services and paid parental leave, positively impact female labor-market participation, corroborating the importance of family policies in structuring individuals' preferences, behavior, and labor-market decisions (see also Ferrarini 2006).

In his book "The moral economy of class," Svallfors (2006) analyzed class difference in gender ideology in Sweden, Britain, Germany, and the United States. Confirming earlier findings, Svallfors (2006: chpt. 6) showed that women and young persons tend to have more equality-oriented attitudes than men and older persons. Furthermore, he concluded that there are considerable class differences in attitudes toward men's and women's paid work and household work. Irrespective of age and gender, the working class displays more conservative attitudes than the service class does in all four countries. Svallfors argued that these class differences can hardly be explained by class-related self-interest; rather, a class-specific ideology (or a "class-based moral economy") would better explain these differences (Svallfors 2006: 120).

Alongside the general trend toward egalitarian gender-role attitudes and women's increasing ambitions and opportunities to pursue a career, women also hold on to private-sphere life goals, such as getting married, becoming a mother, and caring for young children (Sjöberg 2010; Novack and Novack 1996; see also Bielby and Bielby 1984). This means that women are increasingly confronted with two potentially conflicting orientations, namely the pursuit of a career and becoming a mother. Sjöberg (2010) investigated individuals' conflicting orientations by looking at ambivalent gender-role attitudes. He argued that attitudinal ambivalence indicates a disjunction between people's aspirations and the structural possibility of realizing those aspirations. Sjöberg used data from 26 countries and showed that attitudinal ambivalence tends to be higher when the lag between the growth in women's educational attainment and the development of societal institutions that enable women to reconcile gainful employment and care work is greater. Ambivalent attitudes are especially widespread in the two Southern European countries included (Spain and Portugal). In both countries, the growth of female educational attainment has outpaced the growth in female labor-market participation, indicating a mismatch between women's aspirations to pursue a career and the structural possibility of realizing those aspirations.

2.9 Public attitudes toward family policies: Hypotheses

The present study combines the analysis of family-policy institutions as well as the broader social context with an investigation of public attitudes. The aim of this endeavor is to provide valuable information concerning the potential gap between politics and society. The exploration of public attitudes thereby highlights potential social problems and societal polarization that have implications for social inclusion and cohesion as well as the stability and legitimacy of modern democracies.

This section consolidates the theoretical arguments and empirical research results that have been discussed so far, and develops hypotheses concerning attitudinal differences toward family policies both among countries and among social groups within these countries.

Based on the distinction proposed by Roller (1992), this study takes into account three objects of evaluation (or dimensions of attitudes), namely the evaluation of goals, means, and the consequences of welfare-state intervention (see Table 2.1 for a synopsis of these dimensions). Concerning the evaluation of goals, the focus is on the dimension of extensity. This dimension is captured by asking respondents how much responsibility governments should have to ensure sufficient child care services for working parents. In the remainder of this study, this dimension is referred to either as extensity or responsibility.

The second dimension, the evaluation of means, covers attitudes toward existing childcare services by asking respondents what they think about the provision of affordable child care services for working parents. This dimension is referred to as satisfaction.

The third dimension, the evaluation of unintended consequences, finally, indicates to what extent people anticipate the negative side effects of welfare-state intervention. This dimension is related to two major concerns about welfare-state programs: 1) The possibility of (financial) cheating (Edlund 1999;

Jensen and Svendsen 2009); and 2) the concern that welfare programs undermine social capital and civil society, which are, in turn, crucial for the quality of democracy (Putnam 1993; for a critical discussion, see Kumlin and Rothstein 2005). Critics have argued that welfare benefits and services would "crowd out" norms of reciprocity and citizens simply "refer their more unfortunate sisters and brothers to the broad system of social and welfare programs" (Kumlin and Rothstein 2005: 340). Here, the degree of skepticism toward the welfare state is captured by asking to what extent respondents agree (or disagree) that social benefits and services make people less willing to look after themselves and their families. This dimension is referred to as skepticism.

Table 2.1: The three dimensions of attitudes

Dimension according to Roller (1992)	Abbreviation	Survey question (ESS 2008)
The evaluation of goals or extensity	Responsibility	How much responsibility do you think governments should have to ensure sufficient childcare services for working parents?
The evaluation of means or institutions	Satisfaction	What do you think about the provision of affordable childcare services for working parents?
The evaluation of unintended consequences or negative side effects	Skepticism	To what extent do you agree or disagree that social benefits and services in [country] make people less willing to look after themselves and their family?

Studies analyzing public support for different fields of welfare-state intervention have shown that programs supporting needy families with children enjoy a medium level of support. In contrast, programs supporting the old or the sick are most popular, whereas programs supporting the unemployed or poor are least popular (Coughlin 1979, 1980; van Oorschot 2006). Unlike the field of healthcare, in which all people have a great interest in good access to services throughout their whole lives, family-policy measures target a specific period of the life cycle and are only relevant for few groups, i.e., families with young children (Wendt et al. 2011). Simultaneously, the group of potential beneficiaries of family policies is large and more heterogeneous compared with the group of beneficiaries of more targeted fields of welfare-state intervention, such as unemployment benefits and social assistance schemes. The latter are typically financed by the whole population, whereas beneficiaries represent a minority of the population and the risk of abuse by clients can be considered comparably high (Wendt et al. 2011). Regarding family policies, in contrast, the risk of abuse can be considered low, and a majority of the population – if not currently benefitting – will either benefit from family-policy measures in the future or already benefitted in the past. Taking these arguments into consideration, the general level of public support for family-policy measures is expected to be rather high, and polarization among social groups moderate.

Which social cleavages can be expected to matter with regard to attitudes toward family policies? This section discusses in very general terms which group differences are expected to emerge based on the self-interest and the cultural approaches. Due to an assumed lack of quality and availability of existing childcare services in most countries, this study argues that those groups that are expected be more in favor of government responsibility for the provision of childcare services, should also be less satisfied with existing childcare services as well as less skeptical regarding the negative side effects of welfare-state benefits and services.

With reference to the self-interest argument, **families** should be more in favor of family policies than are individuals because families are directly affected by these policies. Parents with young children should be most supportive of a strong role of the state. Furthermore, families are expected to be less satisfied with existing childcare services as well as less skeptical toward the negative side effects of social benefits and services.

Women are expected to be more in favor of public support for families than men. Women are furthermore expected to be less satisfied with the status quo of existing childcare services as well as less skeptical toward unintended side effects. From a self-interest perspective, these gender differences are related to the fact that women provide the bulk of unpaid care work, take the bulk of leave, do the main work organizing childcare arrangements, and are more likely to depend on welfare benefits (see above as well as Svallfors (1997); Gelissen (2000)). From the cultural perspective, women have different socialization experiences than men and are more likely to embrace a "rationality of caring" instead of a "rationality of individualism" (see above as well as Svallfors (1997); d'Anjou et al. (1995); Andreß and Heien (2001)).

With respect to **birth cohorts**, it is argued that younger generations are more supportive of a strong role of the state as well as less satisfied and less skeptical compared with older generations. Younger people either have children or anticipate that they might become parents in the future. A higher probability to be affected by family policies and the work-family conflict personally then results in a stronger self-interest in government support for families.

In line with the cultural approach, younger age groups and the middle-aged are more likely to have internalized post-materialistic values, such as solidarity and social justice, and should therefore more strongly support government intervention compared with older birth cohorts (Inglehart 1977; Andreß and Heien 2001). This idea is in line with research on gender-role attitudes which has shown that younger persons hold more liberal gender-role attitudes compared with older persons (e.g., Crompton et al. 2005; Bolzendahl and Myers 2004; Knudsen and Wærness 2001b; Sundström 1999). However, it could also be argued that older generations might support government interventions for families because they show solidarity with their children and grandchildren (Goerres and Tepe 2010).

With regard to **education**, more highly educated individuals are assumed to be more supportive of government intervention for families as well as less satisfied and less skeptical. The self-interest argument applies to highly educated women, for this group can be expected to have a stronger labor-market attachment and thus be in need of parental leave arrangements and public childcare services in order to combine paid employment and family life. In line with the cultural approach, it has been argued that higher education goes hand-in-hand with enlightenment due to a longer socialization to democratic values and therefore generates greater commitment to social equality and social rights (Robinson and Bell 1978; d'Anjou et al. 1995; Andreß and Heien 2001). Previous studies have confirmed that more highly educated individuals have more egalitarian gender-role attitudes (e.g., Bolzendahl and Myers 2004; Crompton et al. 2005). The calculus as well as the cultural approach would thus suggest higher support for family policies among the more highly educated groups of both men and women.

High-income groups are expected to be less supportive of family policies because they are less dependent on public solutions, especially in terms of financial compensation. Lower-income groups, in contrast, are particularly in need of public childcare services due to their lack of financial means to purchase private solutions (see also Wendt et al. 2011). Moreover, the labor-market participation of both parents is often an economic necessity among low-income groups, which might increase their support for public policies, such as public childcare services (Lewis et al. 2008a). Lower-income groups are thus expected to be more in favor of a strong role of the state in the provision of childcare services as well as less satisfied with the status quo and less skeptical toward unintended side effects.

Respondents' **employment status** is often used to control for current dependency on welfare benefits, and it has been argued that the transfer classes (such as the unemployed or pensioners) are more in favor of public welfare provision compared with those in regular employment (Alber 1984; Lepsius 1990). As described above, previous studies have shown that the unemployed stand out with a strong preference for redistribution (e.g., Svallfors 2004, 1997; Andreß and Heien 2001; Linos and West 2003; Jæger 2006a; Svallfors 2006; Gelissen 2000, 2002; Jæger 2009; Blekesaune and Quadagno 2003; Arts and Gelissen 2001). Regarding family-policy benefits and services, the arguments are less clear cut. On the one hand, transfer classes might have a strong preference for state involvement and thus also for family-policy measures. On the other hand, those working are more in need of public support for families in terms of childcare services or employment protection, especially if both partners are gainfully employed. Regarding childless respondents, it is argued that those currently working are more aware of what it means to combine gainful employment and family life, even though they might not face this challenge personally. It is therefore hypothesized that those currently working are more in favor of family-policy benefits and services, less satisfied with the status quo, and less skeptical compared with persons who are not involved in the labor market.

Both the self-interest approach as well as the cultural approach to attitude formation suggests that **public-sector employees** are more in favor of welfare-state interventions compared with private-sector employees (e.g., Svallfors 1995, 1997; Hoel and Knutsen 1989). Emphasizing self-interest, public-sector employees have an interest in safe-guarding their employment conditions (e.g., in terms of wages or job security); from a cultural perspective, this group shares a specific socialization experience involving solidarity with other public-sector employees and their own clients or patients. Arguments provided by Müller (1998, 2000) suggest that the latter especially applies to professionals in the social service sector, e.g., in the fields of healthcare, education, or social care. Public-sector employees are therefore expected to be more in favor of family polices, less satisfied with existing childcare services, and less critical concerning the unintended consequences of welfare-state intervention. Empirically, however, the relationship between public-sector employment and support for the welfare state has mainly been confirmed in the Scandinavian countries and was not significant elsewhere (e.g., Svallfors 2004, 1997; Hoel and Knutsen 1989). The current study investigates whether public-sector employment matters at all in the field of family policies and if so, whether the effects are more pronounced in the Scandinavian countries.

Normative beliefs, such as **gender-role attitudes**, attitudes toward motherhood, and attitudes toward the socialization of childcare, are crucial factors for understanding individuals' preferences and practices as outlined above. This study includes gender-role attitudes as well as religiousness in order to capture these normative and cultural aspects. Individuals with more egalitarian gender-role attitudes are thereby expected to be more in favor of public support for the dual-earner model of the family, less satisfied with existing childcare services, and less critical concerning the unintended consequences of welfare-state intervention. Earlier research has shown that women, younger persons, more-highly educated persons, and members of the service class hold more egalitarian gender-role attitudes, whereas religiousness increases support for traditional gender-role attitudes (Crompton et al. 2005; Bolzendahl and Myers 2004; Knudsen and Wærness 2001b; e.g., Sundström 1999; for class differences: Svallfors 2006: chpt. 6). For women and the more-highly educated persons, cultural arguments are thus coherent with expectations based on the self-interest approach.

Regarding **religiousness**, it has been shown that the Church and Church-state relations have been important factors in the development of different family policies (Bahle 1995; Kremer 2007; Pfau-Effinger 2005b; Strohmeier 2002; Bahle 2003, 2008a; Korpi 2000). Confessional parties, mostly related to Catholicism, have thereby played a key role in the formation of public family policies in many countries. They have supported social norms, values, and policies promoting the maintenance of the traditional family (with women as mothers and housewives), which is seen as the moral basis for a good society (Korpi 2000). It could be argued that the (ideological) impact of these groups is mirrored in the actual design of existing family-policy institutions and that this design is rather consistent with the (ideological) preferences of more-religious persons.

In line with these thoughts, Lewin-Epstein et al. (2000) stated that more-religious persons might regard public family policies as an infringement on the private sphere of the family. Furthermore, religiousness is associated with support for traditional gender-role attitudes (Bolzendahl and Myers 2004; Crompton et al. 2005), which in turn impact the actual division of paid and unpaid work between spouses. Routine household maintenance and childcare responsibilities are thereby regarded as the tasks of women (and especially mothers) (DeMaris et al. 2011; Voicu et al. 2009). Consequently, more-religious persons are expected to be less in favor of family policies supporting the dual-earner model of the family. More-religious persons are furthermore expected to be more satisfied with existing childcare services and more skeptical toward unintended side effects.

Moreover, respondents' **place of living** is included in the empirical analyses as a control variable. Previous research has shown variation within countries in the levels of childcare service provision across municipalities and regions (Melhuish and Moss 1991; OECD 2001) as well as between rural and urban areas (OECD 2001: 57). Due to data limitations, differences across specific regions cannot be analyzed in this study, but it is possible to examine the question of whether attitudinal differences emerge between rural and urban areas.

For Germany, this study additionally distinguishes between **East and West Germany**.[7] After reunification in October 1990, the eastern part of the country adopted the West German constitution (known as the Basic Law) and existing West German institutions (Rosenfeld et al. 2004). With regard to family policies, however, differences remain, e.g., in terms of childcare facilities. Childcare coverage rates for all age groups are higher in the East, where care is provided mainly on a full-time basis (European Commission 2005; OECD 2006). Furthermore, attitudinal differences between East and West Germans persist, East Germans being more in favor of a strong role of the state (Edeltraut Roller 2002; Lewin-Epstein et al. 2000; Mau 2003). Additionally, both public childcare and mothers' labor-market participation are much more accepted in the eastern part of the country (Rosenfeld et al. 2004; Pfau-Effinger 2006). Considering existing differences in past experiences and living conditions (e.g., state socialism versus market economy, availability of childcare services, mothers' labor-market participation) as well as in attitudes (e.g., normative beliefs as well as welfare-state attitudes), East German respondents are expected to be more supportive of a strong role of the state, more satisfied with existing services, and less critical regarding negative side effects compared with their West German counterparts.

It could be argued that social class matters as well and should be included in the analyses. Based on the self-interest argument, lower social classes and especially the working class should be more in favor of government intervention. From a cultural perspective, in contrast, it has been argued that lower social classes have more traditional value orientations. For instance, it has been shown that they are more conservative regarding gender-role attitudes compared with the service class (Svallfors 2006: Chpt. 6). Lower social classes might also

---

7 After the Second World War, Germany was divided into two countries. Between 1949 and 1989, the "German Democratic Republic" (East Germany) had a state socialist system with a centrally planned economy with socialist employment and family policies, whereas the "Federal Republic of Germany" (West Germany) had a multi-party parliament, a market economy, and a conservative-corporatist welfare state (Rosenfeld et al. 2004: 103).

potentially oppose mothers' labor-market participation and consequently also those policies that promote the dual-earner model of the family. Furthermore, it has been argued that class cleavages might be less pronounced regarding attitudes toward policies covering new social needs, such as the reconciliation of work and family life (Taylor-Gooby 2004: 11; Häusermann 2008). Instead, new conflict lines might emerge that cross-cut existing social divisions. In the multivariate models, social class is not included due to the problem of multicollinearity. Instead, the income situation, the level of education as well as gender-role attitudes and religiousness are included separately. These factors are also relevant from the class perspective.

To sum up, the following attitudinal disparities among social groups are expected: Families (especially those with young children), women, more highly educated persons, and lower-income groups should have a stronger self-interest in government intervention in the field of family policies, be less satisfied with existing childcare services, and less skeptical regarding the negative side effects of welfare-state intervention. Furthermore, public-sector employees and those currently working (in contrast to pensioners, the unemployed, students, and homemakers) are expected to be more supportive as well as less satisfied and less skeptical. Regarding the cultural approach, those who possess more egalitarian gender-role attitudes as well as less-religious persons are expected to be more supportive of government intervention, less satisfied with the status quo, and less skeptical toward negative side effects.

The analytical distinction between the calculus and the cultural approach is most convincing with regard to questions concerning the dimension of extensity of government intervention (Edeltraud Roller 1992). This dimension is captured by the question of whether the government should take responsibility for the provision of childcare services. The other two dependent variables capture attitudes toward means (i.e., satisfaction) and unintended consequences (i.e., skepticism). Here, the applicability of the calculus versus the cultural approach is less clear. As pointed out above, this study assumes a lack of quality and availability of existing childcare services in most countries. Consequently, it is hypothesized that those groups who are supportive of a strong role of the state for the provision of childcare services are also more critical regarding the current quality of these services. Regarding the evaluation of unintended consequences, those favoring a strong role of the state are expected to be less critical and anticipate fewer negative side effects of welfare-state policies. Table 2.2 summarizes the hypotheses.

Table 2.2: Hypotheses regarding attitudinal differences among social groups

	Dimensions of attitudes		
Social groups	Responsibility	Satisfaction	Skepticism
Self-Interest			
Women vs. men	+	-	-
Families vs. individuals	+	-	-
Young birth cohorts versus older cohorts	+	-	-
High vs. low education level	+	-	-
Low vs. high income	+	-	-
Public vs. private sector	+	-	-
Working vs. not in the labor market	+	-	-
Normative beliefs			
Egalitarian gender-role attitudes	+	-	-
Religiousness	-	+	+
Control variables			
Place of living (city / town / countryside)			
East vs. West Germany (relevant only in DE)	+	+	-

Note: + indicates a positive effect, – a negative effect comparing the first group with the respective reference group. Reading example: Compared with individuals, families are expected to be more in favor of government responsibility (+), less satisfied with existing services (-), and less critical regarding negative side effects (-).

The calculus and the cultural approach and perceptions of reality

The distinction between self-interest and value orientations as modes of attitudes is first and foremost a theoretical one. Empirically, however, this distinction is less clear-cut (compare Edeltraud Roller 1998). In this study, self-interest is captured with socio-demographic variables such as gender, income, and education, whereas value orientations are covered using gender-role attitudes and religiousness. However, D'Anjou et al. (1995) argue that ideology and value orientations are strongly affected by individuals' structural position. Empirically verified attitudinal differences between particular social groups can therefore not be unambiguously ascribed to either self-interest or specific normative beliefs.

Albrekt Larsen (2006) argues that the "perception of reality" (Albrekt Larsen 2006: 22) has an impact on attitude formation. How people experience reality can thus impact on attitudes toward certain groups and eventually on attitudes toward policies intended to ease the problems certain groups face.

In line with these thoughts, Kumlin (2002) argues that the public's perception of the welfare state is shaped partly by the information provided by elite actors and the mass media. Beyond the impact of public debate, he emphasizes the importance of experiences with welfare-state benefits and services and argues that people build their opinion on "personally experienced welfare-state information" (Kumlin 2002: 31). Consequently, those who have actually had their own experiences with welfare-state policies – e.g., parents who have used public childcare services – might differ in their attitudes compared with those who have not had this experience. Positive experiences can thereby be assumed to increase satisfaction, whereas negative experiences have the opposite effect. Whether people have positive or negative experiences is, in turn, strongly related to the institutional design of existing institutions. So whether parents have good experiences with public childcare services depends on the characteristics of existing services, e.g., in terms of quantity, quality, affordability, and accessibility. Unfortunately, the ESS questionnaire includes no questions concerning the actual or past use of family-policy benefits or childcare services, so these aspects cannot be covered empirically. The use of childcare services is captured indirectly via the presence of children in the household.

Existing institutions appear to have an impact on attitude formation and must be taken into account when trying to explain attitudinal differences among countries or social groups. This observation requires a modification of the hypotheses formulated above, for it implies that the analyses might not identify the same cleavages in all countries but will identify country-specific patterns of social polarization. This is in line with earlier research results (e.g., Lewin-Epstein et al. 2000; Svallfors 2006) as well as theoretical arguments that emphasize the interdependency of welfare-state regimes and social cleavages (Esping-Andersen 1990; Korpi and Palme 1998; Svallfors 2006, 2007).

The importance of norms and values, finally, has to be taken into account not only at the individual level but also at the macro level because of the existence of country-specific care ideals and family-policy traditions (e.g., Pfau-Effinger 1998; Kremer 2007). Country-level characteristics (e.g., in terms of existing policies and gender arrangements) are expected to impact on attitudes toward family-policy measures with regard to both the level of public support and the degree of societal polarization. In accordance with the comparative welfare-state literature (e.g., Korpi 1980; Korpi and Palme 1998; Svallfors 2006;

Esping-Andersen 1990), different family-policy regimes may create systematic variation in the extent to which the public supports specific policy measures. Moreover, the distinct family-policy arrangements may affect societal cleavage structures and conflict lines, resulting in varying levels of attitudinal polarization among social groups within the distinct family-policy contexts.

The more recently a new and innovative policy has been introduced and the more the policy in question contradicts existing policies (or policy traditions), the stronger societal polarization is expected to be. In contrast, rather homogenous patterns are expected in countries that have a long tradition of dual-earner policies and practices. Alternatively, dual-earner policies or practices might activate normative counter movements among women who are not gainfully employed. In a study conducted in ten Western European countries, Banaszak and Plutzer (1993) found that women who live in areas with high female labor-market participation tend to express the most conservative values concerning feminist attitudes. Such a conservative reaction in some parts of the population could explain societal polarization despite a tradition of dual-earner policies and practices.

The current challenges in terms of new social risks, changing family structures, low fertility rates, and financing problems within the established branches of social security (e.g., healthcare and pension systems) (e.g., Taylor-Gooby 2004; Bonoli 2005) might increase public awareness of the struggles faced by working parents and impact on the "perception of reality" (Albrekt Larsen 2006: 22). Public debate, problem awareness, changing gender-role attitudes, and increasing female employment participation might then result in broad public support for policies facilitating female labor-market participation and work-family reconciliation, independent of the current policy setup. The question of whether and how family-policy regimes impact on the level and structure of public attitudes toward government intervention that promotes the dual-earner model of the family therefore remains mainly an empirical question and is analyzed in the upcoming chapters.

3 Family policies in Europe – a cluster analysis

This chapter examines the diversity of existing family-policy institutions in 15 member states of the European Union and develops a typology of family policies by means of cluster analysis.[1] The countries included are Austria, Belgium, Denmark, Finland, France, Germany, Greece, Ireland, Italy, Luxembourg, the Netherlands, Portugal, Spain, Sweden, and the United Kingdom.

As pointed out before (see Chapter 2), most existing studies include other non-European countries, such as the United States and Australia, but exclude the Southern European countries, such as Greece, Portugal, and Spain (e.g., Gornick et al. 1997; Korpi 2000; Ferrarini 2006: an exception is the work done by Bahle (2008)). The current study contributes to existing research in this field and advances our understanding of family-policy variation in Europe in at least three ways. First, the focus on the 15 "old" member states of the European Union reduces complexity to some extent and keeps some influences constant, e.g., the influences from the supranational level, particularly the European Union. The results thus give an impression of the variability among countries belonging to the same economic and political union. Second, the inclusion of the Southern European countries allows for the investigation of whether these countries form their own, distinct family-policy cluster, as suggested by Flaquer (2000) and Bahle (2008a) as well as by Ferrera (1996) and Karamessini (2008), who discussed the distinctiveness of the "Southern Model" with regard to various fields of welfare-state intervention. Third, by considering up-to-date family-policy indicators from 2008, this study provides a recent picture of the fast-changing family-policy landscape in Europe.

Following the approach suggested by Korpi, the choice of indicators used to classify the 15 countries is restricted to the structure of family-policy institutions and does not include policy outcomes (e.g., female labor-market participation). This restriction allows for understanding institutions as "intervening variables," which mediate between causal factors and policy outcomes (Korpi 2000: 141).

1 The family-policy indicators used in this chapter were collected during the research project "Attitudes Toward Welfare State Institutions: New Perspectives for the Comparative Welfare State Analysis," which was funded by the German Research Foundation (DFG) between 2006 and 2009. I already analyzed and published these indicators in the first part of the chapter "Family policy - one for all?" (Wendt et al. 2011).

Along these lines of argumentation, the following chapters (4 to 6) apply the obtained typology as a conceptual framework for the interpretation of variations in public attitudes toward family-policy issues in the EU member states.

This chapter proceeds with some considerations of the typology concept and a brief description of the family-policy typology suggested by Korpi (2000) and Ferrarini (2006). The following sections discuss the indicators used in this study (Section 3.1) as well as data and methods (Section 3.2). Section 3.3 then presents the obtained family-policy typology resulting from the cluster analysis. The last section (3.4) concludes and discusses the potential relationship between the family-policy typology and public attitudes.

According to Ebbinghaus (2006: 52-53), two types of typologies have to be distinguished. With reference to Max Weber, the first kind of typology – the so called "ideal-type" – refers to theoretical models of reality, not reality as such. Typologies of this kind can serve as conceptual instruments for a comparison with and measurement of reality (see also Arts and Gelissen 2002). The family-policy typology developed by Korpi, which is used here as point of departure, is an example of such an ideal-typical typology. The second type of typology – the "real-type" – refers to classifications of empirically observed patterns. This kind of typology is used to reduce empirical complexity and to describe typical patterns found in reality (see also Obinger and Wagschal 1998; Shalev 2007). The typology developed in this chapter is a real-type typology that provides a classification of existing patterns of family-policy institutions in 15 EU member states.

Family policy is a rapidly changing field of welfare-state intervention and includes different kinds of government benefits that relieve or solve family-related problems. The focus in this study is on policies that are meant to contribute to the health and well-being of families with young children before their start in compulsory schooling. What this study does not capture are policy measures supporting the care for the elderly or other dependent family members. However, even this focus does involve a broad range of different policy measures, including direct cash transfers, taxation, in-kind benefits, direct services, and healthcare- and working-time policies (Gornick et al. 1997; Gornick and Heron 2006). Therefore, the selected indicators used here to classify and describe existing family-policy institutions in Europe inevitably represent only a limited variety of the diversity in this policy field. The selection of indicators is based on the ideal-typical family-policy typology provided by Korpi (2000) and Ferrarini (2006) (see also Chapter 2).

Based on the policy implications for gendered agency inequality in terms of labor-market participation, Korpi (2000) distinguished welfare states along the two ideal-typical policy dimension of general family support and dual-earner support. The first dimension, general family support describes a situation in which the state supports the traditional family model assuming a gendered division of paid and unpaid work both within families as well as in society more generally. The second dimension, dual-earner support, in contrast, implies that the state supports a dual-earner family model and encourages women's labor-market participation and a more equal distribution of social care work within the family as well as in society. Based on these two dimensions, Ferrarini (2006) distinguishes four ideal-typical family-policy models. The first model is the "general family-policy model," which provides a high level of general family support and a low level of dual-earner support. The second model is the "dual-earner family-policy model," in which dual-earner support is high but general family support is low. The third ideal-typical model is the "market-oriented family-policy model," which implies that neither general nor dual-earner support is very well developed. In this model, market forces are assumed to shape gender relations and individuals have to find private solutions in order to reconcile work and family responsibilities. The fourth theoretical model, finally, is the "contradictory family-policy model." This model is characterized by a high level of both general family and dual-earner support.

The main advantages of this typology are at least two-fold. First, the two dimensions explicitly focus on policy implications for agency inequalities in terms of female labor-market participation as well as fathers' involvement in social care work and thus underline the role public policies play in structuring both gender relations and the opportunity structures for individual actors. Second, the inclusion of different types of family support (i.e., general versus dual-earner support) allows for capturing contradictory or pluralistic policy orientations (Ferrarini 2006). Since countries are never completely clear cut regarding the type of family model they support, capturing this plurality is crucial, especially if the typology is meant to provide a framework for the interpretation or explanation of international variation in social outcomes or public attitudes that are potentially contradictory or pluralistic.

A disadvantage, in contrast, is the fact that existing institutions usually do not unequivocally conform to ideal types. An empirical analysis of actually existing institutions therefore inevitably results in a more heterogeneous picture. Moreover, one must keep in mind that typologies are useful means for reducing the complexity of reality, but this simultaneously implies a danger of neglecting important details of institutional variation. As Korpi (2000: 144) stated, "At best, typologies can give us a bird's-eye view of the general contours of the landscape, thus facilitating orientation without giving guidance in details."

3.1 Indicators for the construction of family-policy types

Based on the distinction between general family support and dual-earner support, this study selects up-to-date policy indicators from the year 2008 that capture leave entitlements (i.e., maternity, paternity, and parental leave), childcare services, child allowances, and tax incentives. These indicators are then used in a cluster analysis in order to detect country groups with similar policy profiles. The subsequent paragraphs describe the chosen indicators, data sources, and coding decisions in more detail and specify which indicators represent the general family support dimension and the dual-earner support dimension. Table 3.1 provides a brief summary of the indicators and the last part of this section presents the country-specific values for all indicators.

Leave entitlements. Three types of leave are included: Maternity-, paternity-, and parental leave. Maternity leave is a break from employment related to maternal and infant health and welfare. It is available only to women and usually limited to the period just before and after confinement. Paternity leave is only available to the father and refers to an entitlement to take a short period of leave immediately following the birth of a child. Parental leave and childcare leave are two forms of leave provided for childcare purposes. Parental leave starts after maternity leave, whereas childcare leave can usually be taken immediately after parental leave, thereby creating one continuous period of leave. Both forms are considered together here, although conditions, such as benefits paid, need not be the same. Earnings-related leave benefits have particular potential to increase female labor-market participation and attachment and to encourage a more equal distribution of paid and unpaid work if fathers are also entitled to such benefits (Ferrarini 2006; O'Brian et al. 2007; Kangas and Rostgaard 2007).[2] Moreover, generous earnings-related parental leave benefits reduce the poverty risk contingent upon childbirth and can ease the childbearing decisions for potential parents (Ferrarini 2006). In contrast, a major concern associated with low paid, flat-rate parental leave benefits is that "mothers with lower levels of education, who have worked in less skilled occupations, are most likely to take these low-paid leaves, which may further marginalize them from the labor market" (OECD 2001: 33).

2 For a brief overview of divergent opinions about the effect of leave on women's labor-market attachment, see Kangas and Rostgaard (2007).

Table 3.1: Indicators for the comparative analysis of family policies

Indicator	Measurement	Description
Leave entitle-ments	Effective maternity-, paternity-, and parental leave	The effective leave variables mirror the length of leave (in weeks) as well as level and type of remuneration (flat-rate, income-related, or unpaid). Both parental leave, which is remunerated in relation to the former income, and maternity leave strengthen mothers' labor-market attachment and therefore represent the dimension of dual-earner support. Paternity leave stimulates fathers' involvement in care work and therefore also represents the dual-earner support dimension. Parental leave that is remunerated either flat-rate or not at all represents the general family support dimension.
Childcare services	Childcare usage (children under age three, in hours/week) Childcare usage (children aged three to compulsory school age, in hours/week)	The indicators are a proxy for the availability of childcare services. The higher the availability of services, the more they facilitate mothers' labor-market re-entry and participation. Services for the youngest age-group (under three) represent the dual-earner support dimension, while services for older children represent the general family support dimension.
Cash benefits	Child allowances (in PPPs per 1,000 children (0-4))	Cash benefits for families with dependent children are captured via child allowances and increase financial resources of the household. These benefits are rather neutral with regard to female labor-market participation and represent the dimension of general family support.
Tax incentives	Difference in net transfers to the government (single-earner couples versus equal dual-earner couples, in %)	Higher percentages indicate stronger incentives for an equal sharing of paid work between husband and wife, and thus also for the dual-earner model of the family.

Source: Wendt et al. (2011: 71).

Consequently, maternity- and paternity leave represent dual-earner support, since maternity leave supports female labor-market attachment and paternity leave encourages fathers' participation in care work and thus a more equal sharing of paid and unpaid work between men and women. With regard to parental leave, income-related benefits indicate dual-earner support. Flat-rate benefits, as well as time rights without any financial compensation, in contrast, indicate general family support, since these types of parental leave do not stimulate women's labor-market participation and attachment. Longer and better-remunerated periods of leave indicate a higher level of support. More generous financial-compensation rates provide larger economic resources to the household and therefore increase the attractiveness and actual use of the entitlement.

Prior to the cluster analysis, effective leave indicators for maternity-, paternity-, and parental leave were calculated, taking into account information on the length, type, and level of remuneration (see Table 3.2). Information on length and payment was mainly taken from the country notes published in the "International Review of Leave Policies and Related Research" by Moss and Korintus (2008). This approach takes into account that a comparison of the sheer length of leave entitlements would say little about the actual impact given the huge differences in payment levels. It can be assumed that a higher level of payment increases the rates of leave take-up (Plantenga et al. 2008; for a similar approach, see Plantenga and Siegel 2004). The effective leave indicators were calculated as the multiple of the length of leave (in weeks) and generosity of wage replacement (as a percentage of wages) divided by 100. In the case of paternity leave, information on length was measured in days instead of weeks. All flat-rate benefits were recalculated as percentages of wages using the national median wage as a reference. The obtained values can be interpreted as the number of weeks (or days in the case of paternity leave) for which leave is provided and remunerated with 100% of former earnings.

Table 3.2: Effective leave indicators

Country	Length of maternity leave (weeks)	Maternity leave pay (% of wage)	Effective maternity leave[a]	Length of paternity leave (days)	Paternity leave pay (% of wage)	Effective paternity leave[a]
Austria	16.00	100.00	16.00	0	0.00	0.00
Belgium	15.00	76.87	11.53	10	87.40	8.74
Denmark	18.00	100.00	18.00	14	100.00	14.00
Finland	17.50	80.67	14.12	18	70.00	12.60
France	16.00	100.00	16.00	11	100.00	11.00
Germany	14.00	100.00	14.00	0	0.00	0.00
Greece	17.00	100.00	17.00	2	100.00	2.00
Ireland	42.00	43.33	18.20	0	0.00	0.00
Italy	20.00	80.00	16.00	0	0.00	0.00
Luxembourg	16.00	100.00	16.00	2	100.00	2.00
Netherlands	16.00	100.00	16.00	2	100.00	2.00
Portugal	17.14	100.00	17.14	5	100.00	5.00
Spain	16.00	100.00	16.00	15	100.00	15.00
Sweden	10.00	80.00	8.00	10	80.00	8.00
United Kingdom	52.00	15.61	8.12	10	8.23	0.82

Table continued on next page.

Table 3.3: Effective leave indicators (continued)

Country	Length of parental leave (flat-rate) (weeks)	Parental-leave pay (flat-rate) (% of wage)	Effective parental leave (flat-rate)[a]	Length of income-related parental leave (in weeks)	Parental-leave pay (income related) (% of wage)	Effective parental leave (income related)[a]
Austria	65.00	50.50	32.82	0.00	0.00	0.00
Belgium	13.00	46.63	6.06	0.00	0.00	0.00
Denmark	0.00	0.00	0.00	32.00	100.00	32.00
Finland	120.67	22.21	26.80	26.33	70.95	18.68
France	156.00	36.62	57.13	0.00	0.00	0.00
Germany	0.00	0.00	0.00	52.00	67.00	34.84
Greece	0.00	0.00	0.00	0.00	0.00	0.00
Ireland	0.00	0.00	0.00	0.00	0.00	0.00
Italy	0.00	0.00	0.00	26.00	30.00	7.80
Luxembourg	26.00	69.02	17.95	0.00	0.00	0.00
Netherlands	0.00	0.00	0.00	0.00	0.00	0.00
Portugal	0.00	0.00	0.00	0.00	0.00	0.00
Spain	0.00	0.00	0.00	0.00	0.00	0.00
Sweden	4.50	36.07	1.62	47.50	80.00	38.00
United Kingdom	0.00	0.00	0.00	0.00	0.00	0.00

Note: [a] Effective-leave variables were calculated as follows: (length of leave (in weeks) * level of payment (in % of wages)) / 100. The numbers can be interpreted as the number of weeks that are remunerated with 100% of wages. Flat-rate benefits were recalculated as percentages of wages using the national median wage as a reference. The length of paternity leave is presented in days instead of weeks. Effective paternity leave was consequently calculated as follows: (Length of leave (in days) * level of payment (in % of wages)) / 100. The numbers can be interpreted as the number of days paternity leave is provided and remunerated with 100% of former earnings.
Source: Wendt et al. (2011: 76). Data Sources: Moss and Korintus (2008); for Luxembourg: Euraxess Luxembourg (2010) and Sellier and Mouris (2010).

Childcare services. High quality, affordable, and flexible childcare arrangements are among the most important preconditions that enable both parents to enter the labor market and combine paid work and family life (Plantenga et al. 2008). Childcare places for children from birth to three years of age are thereby a key factor for facilitating mothers' return to the labor market after childbirth. However, facilities for this age group are especially scarce and demand clearly exceeds supply. This study therefore interprets a high availability of childcare services – especially for the youngest age group – as support for the dual-earner family model.

Studies have shown that women are more frequently employed and more likely to work full-time in countries with high service provision compared with women in countries with less or only financial support for families (Ferrarini 2006; Kangas and Rostgaard 2007). In addition, Castles (2003) showed that both public childcare facilities for children under the age of three as well as flexible work arrangements are positively correlated with fertility rates. Early childhood education and care services are additionally important from the perspective of equal opportunity and child well-being, as these institutions can help to reduce the disadvantages of children with special needs or from a lower socio-economic group (OECD 2006).[3]

Despite the unquestioned importance of childcare services for facilitating both parents' labor-market participation, reliable and internationally harmonized data on available services are scarce (Plantenga et al. 2008; Eurostat 2004). A common approach to overcome the lack of data is to use survey data that provide information on the actual use of childcare services as indicated by the parents, themselves. In this study, data from the EU-SILC provided by Eurostat (2010a) are used. The disadvantage if this indicator is that it includes different types of formal childcare arrangements that do not strictly distinguish between services provided by the (local) government and those provided by other organizations or private persons (e.g., registered childminders). Here, data on the actual hours per week children spend in formal childcare services function as a proxy for the availability of childcare facilities. Using the hours children are cared for institutionally has the advantage of indicating to what extent existing services are sufficient in facilitating mothers' employment. Two age-groups of children are distinguished. The weekly hours used by children under age three represent the dimension of dual-earner support; those used by children aged three to

[3] For concerns expressed over too early usage of professional childcare, please refer to Belsky (2001) and Brooks-Gunn et al. (2002).

compulsory school age represent the general family support dimension (for a similar approach, see Ferrarini 2006).

Cash benefits. This study uses child allowances to capture cash benefits. Child allowances are periodical flat-rate payments made to a member of a household with dependent children. These payments help with the costs of raising children and increase families' net income. However, they are futile with respect to their effects on parents' labor-force participation and likely to reproduce existing labor-market inequalities between men and women. Child allowances therefore represent the general family support dimension (Korpi 2000; Ferrarini 2006). This type of family support is captured by public expenditure data obtained from Eurostat (2010b). Child allowances were calculated in purchasing power parities (PPPs) per 1,000 children (between 0 and 4 years of age) in order to correct for differences in the age-specific composition of the population in the analyzed countries.

Tax incentives. The tax system is traditionally regarded as a powerful means for vertical redistribution of incomes. Additionally, tax policies may have differentiated effects on the labor supply of men and women and have often decreased female participation in the labor force (Montanari 2000; Smith et al. 2003). If wives' earnings imply a heavy marginal tax on husbands' income, the opportunity cost of wives' employment becomes high for the family and penalizes wives' employment (Esping-Andersen 1999). Today, most European countries have introduced individual taxation and provide some incentives toward a more equal sharing of paid work between men and women, France and Germany being exceptions (OECD 2010a). Nevertheless, there are persistent differences with regard to the level of taxation effects on households' income, dependent upon the level of both spouses' labor-market participation. These differences are used here as a measure for support for the dual-earner model through the tax system.

The measure uses the difference in net transfers to the government. It compares the average payment of a single-earner couple (in which the husband earns 200% of the average wage and the wife earns nothing) with the average payment of an equal dual-earner couple (in which both partners earn 100% of the average worker's wage). The resulting numbers indicate the tax advantage or disadvantage (in percent) between the two prototypical household models (single-earner couples versus equal dual-earner couples) both of which have two dependent children, ages 6 and 11. Hence, this indicator is in fact a continuous measure ranging from general family support (i.e., negative tax incentives for an equal sharing of paid work between the spouses) to dual-earner support (i.e., positive tax incentives for an equal sharing of paid work between the spouses). Tax incentives were calculated and provided by the OECD (2010a).

The indicators used to capture the dimension of general family support are thus 1) (effective) parental leave entitlements (either unpaid or remunerated flat-rate); 2) childcare services for children between three years of age and compulsory school age; and 3) the level of child allowances. The dimension of dual-earner support is represented by 1) effective maternity-, paternity-, and parental leave (only income-related benefits); 2) childcare services for children under age three; and 3) tax incentives for an equal sharing of paid work between spouses.

Table 3.4 presents the country-specific values for the final family-policy indicators and gives a first impression of variation of family-policy design among the 15 countries included in the analysis. Effective paternity leave varies between as much as two weeks in Spain and Denmark and two days in Luxembourg, the Netherlands, and Greece, and is not at all available in several other countries. Effective maternity leave varies between 18 weeks in Denmark and Ireland and 8 weeks in Sweden and the UK. What is striking here is the fact that both Ireland and the UK provide a very long period of maternity leave (i.e., 42 weeks in Ireland and 52 weeks in the UK). These leaves were introduced instead of parental leave because they were easier for employers to accept (Lewis et al. 2008b). However, these leaves are scarcely compensated financially. The calculation of the effective leave indicators (which took into account both length of leave and payment) results in a low amount of effective maternity leave in both countries. Most other countries provide much shorter periods of maternity leave but remuneration equals mostly 100% of former earnings (see Table 3.2).

With regard to parental leave, most countries provide either a flat-rate benefit (Austria, Belgium, France, and Luxembourg) or an income-related compensation (Sweden, Denmark, and Italy), while some countries provide solely uncompensated time rights (Greece, Italy, Spain, Portugal, the Netherlands, Ireland, and the UK). Additionally, a few countries provide a mix of different types of leave. Germany provides a 12-month, income-related leave, which can be prolonged without any further financial compensation, while Finland provides an income-related benefit that can be prolonged with a leave that is compensated flat-rate. Great variation is also apparent when looking at the weekly hours young children (under the age of three) spend in formal childcare. On average, children in Austria spend less than 1.5 hours per week in formal childcare, indicating low availability of care services, whereas children in Denmark spend an average of 25 hours per week in childcare services, indicating high availability. Differences in tax incentives for the dual-earner model are also striking. While Germany provides strong negative incentives of -20%, positive incentives are especially strong in Sweden, with 37%.

Table 3.4 Characteristics of family-policy systems, 2008

Country	Effective maternity leave (weeks)	Effective paternity leave (weeks)	Effective (flat-rate) parental leave (weeks)	Effective (income) parental leave (weeks)	Length of unpaid parental leave (weeks)
Austria	16.00	0.00	32.82	0.00	31
Belgium	11.53	8.74	6.06	0.00	0
Denmark	18.00	14.00	0.00	32.00	0
Finland	14.12	12.60	26.80	18.68	0
France	16.00	11.00	57.13	0.00	0
Germany	14.00	0.00	0.00	34.84	96
Greece	17.00	2.00	0.00	0.00	15
Ireland	18.20	0.00	0.00	0.00	14
Italy	16.00	0.00	0.00	7.80	0
Luxembourg	16.00	2.00	17.95	0.00	0
Netherlands	16.00	2.00	0.00	0.00	13
Portugal	17.14	5.00	0.00	0.00	13
Spain	16.00	15.00	0.00	0.00	150
Sweden	8.00	8.00	1.62	38.00	26
United Kingdom	8.12	0.82	0.00	0.00	13

Table continued on next page.

Table 3.5 Characteristics of family-policy systems, 2008 (continued)

Country	Childcare 0-2 years (hours/week)	Childcare 3-comp. school age (hours/week)	Child allowances (in PPPs/child.)	Tax incentives dual-earner model (in %)
Austria	1.30	17.20	12.83	11.30
Belgium	14.40	32.20	7.42	9.10
Denmark	24.70	32.70	4.58	14.70
Finland	8.90	26.30	4.11	26.50
France	12.20	28.00	7.17	-2.90
Germany	13.20	24.30	12.63	-20.60
Greece	3.50	18.20	2.48	25.00
Ireland	4.80	18.70	7.00	32.30
Italy	8.00	30.20	2.35	24.80
Luxembourg	7.60	17.10	20.74	12.10
Netherlands	8.10	18.20	3.34	17.90
Portugal	11.60	25.80	1.76	12.00
Spain	10.30	28.00	1.08	21.20
Sweden	14.30	30.00	4.07	37.10
United Kingdom	4.60	15.60	3.76	21.90

Source: Wendt et al. (2011: 77).
Data sources: Data on child allowances and childcare from Eurostat (2010b, 2010a). Information on maternity-, paternity-, and parental leave from Moss and Korintus (2008); for Luxembourg: Euraxess Luxembourg (2010) and Sellier and Mouris (2010); please refer to Table 3.2 for computational details. Data on tax incentives: OECD (2010a).

3.2 Methods

This section illuminates the method of cluster analysis (CA), which is applied in Section 3.3 to classify the 15 countries into different types of family policy. Cluster analysis (CA) generally aims to group cases (here, countries) by simultaneously taking a number of selected characteristics (here, family-policy indicators) into account. CA has already been applied in the comparison of welfare states as a whole (Obinger and Wagschal 1998; Kautto 2002; Powell and Barrientos 2004) as well as in specific policy fields, such as healthcare systems (Wendt 2009; Reibling 2010; Wendt et al. 2011), social-assistance schemes (Gough 2001; Wendt et al. 2011), and family policy (De Henau et al. 2006; Jensen 2008; Wendt et al. 2011). An important advantage of this method is that the number of resulting clusters is not predefined (e.g., by theoretical considerations) but rather remains an empirical issue. This approach thereby allows for capturing not only pluralistic policy orientations but also the whole variety of existing family-policy types.

This study applies the method of hierarchical cluster analysis (HCA) using Ward's method with the Euclidean dissimilarity measure, which is a standard technique for hierarchical cluster analysis (for an extended introduction to cluster analysis, see Everitt et al. 2001). HCA starts when each country forms a cluster of its own and then gradually joins similar countries to form new clusters until all cases finally come together within one group. Accordingly, the researcher has to determine the number of clusters that best represent the structure of the data. This is done here via a graphical approach, i.e., the dendrogram, presented in the following section. The cases are usually grouped such that both homogeneity within clusters as well as heterogeneity between clusters is maximized. Ideally, countries within a certain cluster should be more similar to each other than to any country of another cluster across all their characteristics.

Since the indicators described in Section 3.1 were measured on different scales, they have to be standardized prior to performing a cluster analysis (Milligan and Cooper 1988). Standardization of the input variables is necessary since the dissimilarity measure used in the analysis (Euclidean distance) is sensitive to differences in the magnitudes of the variables. Standardization furthermore serves the idea of equal weighting of all input variables.

Several approaches to the standardization of variables exist. The present study applies standardization through division by the range of the variable. In a simulation study, Milligan and Cooper (1988) have shown that this approach offers the best recovery of the underlying cluster structure across a variety of conditions (e.g., error conditions, separation distances, clustering methods, and coverage levels) and outperforms the traditional z-score transformation. The following calculation was used to obtain standardized values:

$$\text{Standardized Value } X_{std} = (X - \text{Min}(X)) / (\text{Max}(X)\text{-Min}(X))$$

Whenever possible, each variable's natural minimum and maximum value was used. As there was no natural benchmark, values were set at a level that was below or above the actual minimum or maximum value within the sample of EU countries. The final values range between 0 (low support) and 1 (high support) (for a similar approach, see De Henau et al. 2006; Plantenga et al. 2009).

3.3 Family-policy types: Results from the cluster analysis

The dendrogram below (Figure 3.1) graphically depicts the result of the hierarchical cluster analysis (HCA). This two-dimensional diagram illustrates the fusions made at each stage of the analysis. The y-axis indicates the distance or dissimilarity between two countries or groups of countries; the longer the vertical lines, the more dissimilar countries are to each other or to a group of countries merged at an earlier stage. The dendrogram suggests that four clusters best represent the structure of the data. Table 3.4 summarizes the clusters' characteristics, which are elaborated subsequently. It is important to note that it is never easy to distinctly classify all countries. Therefore, major differences between countries assigned to the same cluster are pointed out here as well.

Figure 3.1: Family-policy clusters - dendrogram resulting from hierarchical cluster analysis (Ward's method)

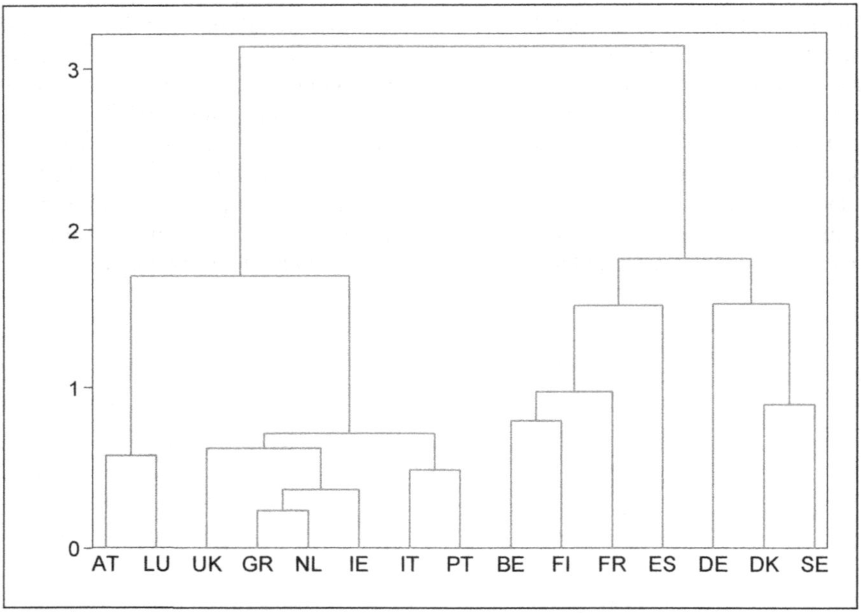

Note: AT=Austria; BE=Belgium; DE=Germany; DK=Denmark; ES=Spain; FI=Finland; FR=France; UK= United Kingdom; GR=Greece; IE=Ireland; IT=Italy; LU=Luxembourg; NL= the Netherlands; PT=Portugal; SE=Sweden.
Source: Wendt et al. (2011: 79).

Cluster 1, on the far left in Figure 3.1, consists of Austria and Luxembourg. This group is characterized by a high level of general family support and rather low dual-earner support and is labeled the *general family support cluster*. Both countries provide a high level of child allowances (which are especially high in Luxembourg) as well as extensive parental leave with monetary compensation paid as a flat-rate benefit (which is especially generous in Austria). Neither measure stimulates mothers' labor-market attachment. The tax system also does little to stimulate an equal sharing of paid work between spouses (the incentive is about 12%) and paternity leave is nonexistent in Austria and quite short in Luxembourg (two days). Moreover, childcare services are hardly available for the youngest age-group (1 hour in Austria, 7 hours in Luxembourg). The availability for older children lies at a medium position with 17 hours per week.

Cluster 2, also on the left of Figure 3.1, comprises the UK, Ireland, the Netherlands, and the Southern European countries of Greece, Italy, and Portugal. Cluster 2 contains the largest group of countries, all of which provide relatively little support for families in both dimensions, though Italy and Portugal do perform slightly better compared with the remaining countries in this group. This cluster is labeled the *low support cluster*. In this group, child allowances are at the lower end of the scale (the only exception is Ireland) and only Italy provides earnings-related compensation during parental leave, albeit at a very low level. No other countries provide any financial compensation at all. They have a very short period of unpaid parental leave (about 13 days), and paternity leave is either short or not at all available (as in Italy and Ireland). Compensating for the low support for families, strong tax incentives for the dual-earner model exist in several countries (highest in Ireland with 32% and lowest in Portugal with 12%), and childcare coverage is moderate, at least for somewhat older children. There are some notable differences among the countries regarding childcare services. For the youngest children, the availability centers around 4 hours per week in half of the countries and is twice as high in Italy and the Netherlands (8 hours) and tripled in Portugal (12 hours). The availability of services for children from three to compulsory school age centers around 18 hours in most countries and is again clearly higher in Italy (30 hours) and Portugal (26 hours). Overall, public support for families is low in this cluster, and balancing work and family life is tough and remains mainly a private responsibility. There is, however, some support for working parents in terms of taxation and childcare services (the latter especially in Italy and Portugal).

Cluster 3 includes Belgium, Finland, and France. This group, labeled the *pluralistic support cluster*, is quite heterogeneous and characterized by both general family support as well as dual-earner support. All three countries provide generous paternity leave (ranging from 9 days in Belgium to 13 days in Finland), and France and Finland also provide generous parental leave, though this leave is compensated flat-rate in France. In Belgium, parental leave benefits are also remunerated flat-rate, albeit humbly compared with the other two countries. A Finnish particularity is the combination of a parental leave entitlement, which is an income-related benefit with the provision of a flat-rate home-care allowance after the end of parental leave. After the end of parental leave, Finnish parents can choose between municipal daycare and this home-care allowance, which allows parents to stay at home to care for their child and receive a flat-rate benefit until the child is three years old (Kröger et al. 2003). This is in line with earlier studies indicating that all three countries advocate parental choice, supporting working mothers as well as emphasizing parents' right to provide care (Mahon 2002; Kremer 2007). This plurality in policy incentives is also mirrored in a medium level of child allowances (which is lowest in Finland) and the availability of childcare services. Availability of services for the youngest age group is at a medium level (ranging from 9 hours in Finland to 14 hours in Belgium) while at a high level for older children (ranging from 26 hours in Finland to 32 in Belgium). The level of tax incentives, in turn, considerably varies among the three countries. France provides a negative incentive of -3%, which promotes the traditional family model; Belgium provides a moderate positive tax incentive of 9%, whereas Finland provides a strong tax incentive for the dual-earner model of the family (with 27%). Within this Cluster, Finland clearly offers the strongest support for the dual-earner model of the family (especially in terms of income-related parental leave and tax incentives) and France the strongest support for the traditional model of the family (especially through a generous flat-rate remunerated parental leave and negative tax incentives).

Cluster 4, on the right of the figure, is made up of the Nordic countries of Denmark and Sweden. These two countries are characterized by a high level of dual-earner support combined with a moderate level of general family support, which is mirrored in the comparably low level of child allowances provided and a focus on income-related parental leave benefits. This cluster is labeled the *dual-earner support cluster*. Denmark and Sweden stand out with considerable incentives for fathers' involvement in care in terms of paternity leave (14 days in Denmark, 8 days in Sweden) and high childcare coverage rates for both age groups. Availability of childcare services for the youngest children is especially high in Denmark, with 25 hours (compared with 14 hours in Sweden). Moreover, both countries offer generous earnings-related parental leave. Sweden additionally offers some flat-rate and unpaid periods of leave to prolong the well-compensated parental leave period. Consequently, mothers' labor-market involvement and reconciliation of work and family life, as well as fathers' involvement in care work, are strongly supported publicly. High tax incentives (especially in Sweden) for the dual-earner model reveal this public support.

Two countries, namely Spain and Germany, are considered outliers that cannot be classified unambiguously. Figure 3.1 shows that Spain is fitted into the third cluster (with France, Belgium, and Finland), while Germany is grouped with the fourth cluster (with Denmark and Sweden), both at a very late stage of the clustering process. This classification is due to very specific characteristics of the two countries.

Spain's closeness to the pluralistic support cluster is due to comparably high values in both policy dimensions. However, a closer look at the countries' family-policy institutions reveals that existing support remains rudimentary in comparison with France, Belgium, and Finland. On the one hand, Spain provides a comparably high level of childcare services (i.e., 10 hours for the youngest children, 28 hours for older children), generous paternity-leave entitlements (15 days), and a long period of parental leave (150 weeks). On the other hand, Spain provides no financial compensation at all during the parental leave period. This fact reduces the likelihood of take-up and leaves families with considerable difficulties concerning income maintenance upon childbirth as well as during the following, most care-intensive period. Moreover, these entitlements do not stimulate female labor-market attachment. In line with these arguments, Spain is not subsumed under cluster 3 but rather assigned to cluster 2 consisting of the remaining Southern European countries as well as the UK, Ireland, and the Netherlands. Within this group, Spain remains a clear outlier with regard to paternity- and parental leave and resembles Portugal and Italy regarding the higher availability of childcare services compared with the other cluster members.

The main reason for Germany's proximity to the Nordic countries in Figure 3.1 is the strong dual-earner incentive in terms of income-related parental leave and a moderate availability of childcare services. Germany's parental leave regulations were reformed in 2007 in order to increase dual-earner support, and the formerly means-tested and flat-rate benefit was replaced by an income-related benefit (Wersig 2007; Henninger et al. 2008). Simultaneously, however, strong incentives supporting a traditional division of paid- and unpaid work between men and women persist, such as an additional period of unpaid parental leave (which can be used to prolong the paid period of parental leave) and strong negative tax incentives (-21%). Germany's tax system actually penalizes an equal sharing of paid work between spouses, promoting the traditional family model with a main wage earner. Moreover, paternity leave is nonexistent in Germany and child allowances are generous. The availability of childcare services lies at a medium position of 13 hours for the youngest children and 24 hours for older ones. However, Germany is a special case with regard to childcare services. Due to cultural and institutional differences originating from the division into East and West Germany (i.e., between the former German Democratic Republic and the Federal Republic of Germany), huge differences in the availability and use of childcare services persist between both parts of the country to the present day (Rosenfeld et al. 2004). The indicator used here includes information from both parts of the country, thereby underestimating usage in the East while overestimating usage in the West.

In contrast to Sweden and Denmark, Germany cannot be considered to be a country that provides clear incentives for the dual-earner model of the family. Instead, Germany's policy profile mainly promotes the traditional model of the family, which suggests that is should instead be assigned to cluster 1, which consists of Austria and Luxembourg. Within this cluster, Germany remains an outlier due to the generous and income-related parental-leave benefit and the higher availability of childcare services (these policies are in line with the dual-earner support dimension) on the one hand and the exceptionally strong negative tax incentive and additional unpaid parental leave entitlements (these policies are in line with the general family support dimension) on the other hand.

The family-policy typology resulting from the cluster analysis suggests four family-policy clusters and two outliers (i.e., Germany and Spain). Taking into account the specific policy profiles of these two cases and the inherent incentives and constraints for families' work- and care arrangements, the following cluster assignments are suggested: Germany's policy profile indicates compliance to cluster 1, whereas Spain's policy profile suggests proximity to cluster 2. The resulting clusters are comparably small (except cluster 2) but seem to represent a meaningful division. Eventually, the following 4 clusters are distinguished:

1. The *general family support cluster* with Austria, Luxembourg, and Germany. This cluster provides a high level of general family support and rather low dual-earner support. It is characterized by a high level of child allowances, extensive parental leave (mostly compensated flat-rate), limited or non-existing paternity leave, and limited availability of childcare services for the youngest age group.
2. The *low support cluster* with the UK, Ireland, the Netherlands, Greece, Italy, Portugal, and Spain. This cluster provides relatively little support for families in both dimensions. The level of child allowances is low, parental leave is short and/or scarcely compensated financially, and the provision of childcare services is moderate.
3. The *pluralistic support cluster* with France, Belgium, and Finland. This group is quite heterogeneous and combines both general family support as well as dual-earner support. It provides generous parental and paternity leave (though parental leave is partly compensated flat-rate) and a moderate to high level of childcare services.
4. The *dual-earner support cluster* with Denmark and Sweden. This group is characterized by a high level of dual-earner support combined with a moderate level of general family support. These countries provide generous

earnings-related parental- and paternity leave entitlements, a moderate level of child allowances, and well-established childcare facilities.

This cluster solution represents a rather flexible typology, and the classification of countries is subject to change relative to the inclusion of additional countries or indicators in the analysis or if the characteristics of family policies change as a result of policy reform. Table 3.4 summarizes the clusters' characteristics regarding all policy indicators included. For the two clusters containing the outliers (clusters 1 and 2), the table presents separate values for both outliers as well as the mean values for the respective cluster both with and without Germany and Spain.

Table 3.6: Description of the clusters

Cluster	Effective maternity leave (weeks)	Effective Paternity leave (days)	Effective parental leave (income) (weeks)	Effective parental leave (flat-rate) (weeks)	Parental leave (unpaid) (weeks)
Cluster 1 AT, LU, DE	Medium to high level (16/15.33)	No leave (exception: LU: 2) (1/0.67)	No benefits (exception: DE: 34.84) (0/11.61)	Medium to high level (exception DE: 0) (25.38/16.92)	Low level (exception: DE: 96) (15.5/42.33)
DE	14.00	0.00	34.84	0.00	96.00
Cluster 2 UK, GR, NL, IE, IT, PT, ES	Medium to high level (15.41/15.49)	No (IT, IE) / low level (exception: ES: 15) (1.64/3.55)	No benefits (exception IT: 7.8) (1.3/1.11)	No benefits	Low level (exception: ES: 150) (11.33/31.14)
ES	16.00	15.00	0.00	0.00	150.00
Cluster 3 FR, BE, FI	Medium level (13.88)	High level (10.78)	Mixed: No benefit in FI/BE High level in FI (18.7) Mean: 6.23	High level (30) (exception BE:6)	No unpaid leave
Cluster 4 SE, DK	Medium level (13)	High level (11)	High level (35)	No / low level (0.81)	Low level (13)

Note: see below.

Table 3.7: Description of the clusters (continued)

Cluster	Childcare 0-2 years (hours/week)	Childcare 3-comp. school age (hours/week)	Child allowances (pps/child)	Tax incentives (%)
Cluster 1 AT, LU, DE	Low level (4.45/7.37)	Low to medium level (17.15/19.53)	High level (16.79/15.4)	Medium incentive (exception: DE: -20.6) (11.7/0.93)
DE	13.20	24.30	12.63	-20.60
Cluster 2 UK, GR, NL, IE, IT, PT, ES	Low level (6.77/7.27)	Medium level (21.12/22.10)	Low level (3.45/3.11)	Strong incentive (22.32/22.16)
ES	10.30	28.00	1.08	21.20
Cluster 3 FR, BE, FI	Medium level (11.83)	High level (28.83)	Low to medium level (6.24)	Mixed: FR: -3; BE: 9; FI: 27 Mean: 10.9
Cluster 4 SE, DK	High level (19.5)	High level (31.35)	Low level (4.32)	Strong incentive (25.9)

Note: For Clusters 1 and 2: The two numbers indicate the mean values with and without the Outliers (i.e., with and without Germany in cluster 1, and with and without Spain in cluster 2). Country abbreviations: AT: Austria; BE: Belgium; DE: Germany; DK: Denmark; ES: Spain; FI: Finland; FR: France; UK: United Kingdom; GR: Greece; IE: Ireland; IT: Italy; LU: Luxembourg; NL: The Netherlands; PT: Portugal; SE: Sweden.
Source: Wendt et al. (2011: 81). For data sources, please refer to Table 3.3.

3.4 Conclusion

This chapter developed a family-policy typology in order to classify and describe empirically observed family-policy patterns in 15 countries belonging to the European Union. The typology-approach applied here is a useful means for reducing the complexity of reality; however, it necessarily implies the danger of neglecting important details of institutional variation (Korpi 2000: 144). Accordingly, the described family-policy typology provides a rough picture of family-policy diversity in Europe.

The following chapter uses the described typology of existing family-policy systems as a framework for the analysis and interpretation of differences in public attitudes toward family-policy issues. Several attitudinal patterns are expected to emerge. The dual-earner cluster represents a family-policy context that is highly supportive of the dual-earner model of the family. Such a context should nourish a societal consensus in favor of this family model. As a result, demand for government responsibility as well as the level of satisfaction with existing policies is expected to be high within this cluster. Skepticism toward the consequences of benefits and services, in contrast, is expected to be low.

A tradition of low state intervention in the sphere of the family, in contrast, could result in a public climate in which any type of government intervention is rejected. Skepticism toward the consequences of benefits and services is thereby expected to be high. Alternatively, it can be argued that a low level of support for families results in a climate of strong public demand for government responsibility, indicating disagreement with the status quo. Due to increasing female labor-market aspirations and participation rates, it is to be expected that support is especially strong for those policy measures that increase the compatibility of work and family life, such as parental leave and childcare services. Satisfaction with existing policies should then be low as should be the level of skepticism. The empirical analyses in the following chapters reveal, which of the described scenarios actually occur.

The general family support cluster and the pluralistic support cluster, finally, are likely to range in-between the dual-earner support and the low-support cluster with regard to all three attitudinal dimensions.

Compared with earlier research, the four family-policy clusters are only partly consistent with alternative classifications. It is critical to note, though, that the comparability of different classifications is limited because different studies include different countries and indicators and also focus on different points in time. Table 3.5 provides a brief summary of the country groupings suggested by Ferrarini (2006) and Bahle (2008a) as well as the current study. The main differences between these three classifications of family policies are discussed below.

Table 3.8: Classifications of family policies

Study	Analytical dimensions	Family-policy types	Countries
Ferrarini (2006)	Dual-earner support General family support	General FPM[a]	AT, BE, BE, FR, DE, IE, IT,NL
		Dual-earner FPM	DK, FI, NO, SE
		Market-oriented FPM	AU, CA, JP, UK, US
		Contradictory FPM	none
Bahle (2008)	State interference into the family-work relationship State-provided family income	Subsidiarity group	DE, LU, AT, HU, CZ, PL, LT, (SI)
		Universality model	DK, SE, FI, EE, LV
		Autonomy model	NL, UK, (IE)
		(France and Belgium)	FR, BE
		Familism	IT, PT, ES, GR, CY, MT
This study	Dual-earner support General family support	General family support CL[b]	AT, LU, DE
		Dual-earner support CL	DK, SE
		Pluralistic support CL	FR, BE, FI
		Low support CL	UK, IE, NL, GR, IT, PT, ES

Note: [a]: FPM = family-policy model; [b]: CL = cluster.

A first discrepancy with earlier typologies is the classification of Finland. Both Bahle (2008a) and Ferrarini (2006) classified Finland in the same group as the other two Nordic countries of Denmark and Sweden, whereas this study assigns Finland to the pluralistic support cluster (together with France and Belgium). Consistent with this distinction, Bahle also classified France and Belgium in a separate group. In the ideal-typical family-policy typology developed by Korpi (2000) and Ferrarini (2006), this group would coincide with the so-called contradictory family-policy model. However, this model was not identified in their empirical analyses and no country was assigned to this type. Both France and Belgium were instead allocated to the general family support type. The current typology assigns Germany, Luxembourg, and Austria to the general family support cluster; these countries also form their own group in Bahle's typology (together with other counties not included here).

An important question to consider was whether the Southern European countries form their own, distinct family-policy cluster, as suggested by Flaquer (2000) and Bahle (2008a). In contrast to their suggestion, this study reveals one low-support cluster, which includes the Southern European countries as well as the UK, Ireland, and the Netherlands. The common feature of this heterogeneous group of countries is a low level of government support in both dimensions and the absence of clear policy incentives for a certain family model. However, it is important to note that these countries differ with respect to important contextual features such as labor-market characteristics and female employment participation.

In comparison with earlier typologies, the low support cluster roughly corresponds with the market-oriented family policy model in Ferrarini's typology. It is critical to note, however, that Ferrarini did not include the Southern European countries in his study (except for Italy). Based on data from the year 2004, Bahle suggests a distinction between the Southern European countries of Portugal, Italy, Greece, and Spain on the one hand and the UK, Ireland, and the Netherlands on the other hand. He concludes that the Southern European countries provide even less support for families compared with the remaining three countries. An important peculiarity of the Southern European countries is furthermore the traditionally strong role of the Church, the late democratization (except in Italy), and the strong reliance on family solidarity or "familism" (Bahle 2008a: 104; see also Karamessini 2008).

It has been pointed out earlier in this study, that these historical, cultural, and political dimensions (e.g., family systems, religious traditions, the role of the Church, and the relationship between the Church and the state) have played a key role in the development of distinct family-policy systems and that they are mirrored in the institutional design of existing family-policy arrangements (Bahle 1995; Gauthier 1996; Pfau-Effinger 1996, 2005b; Kremer 2007; Strohmeier 2002).

This study assumes that the family-policy setup, as one element of the welfare arrangement (Pfau-Effinger 2005a), impacts public opinion toward family policy. The following chapter therefore investigates the link between the family-policy setup and public opinion. However, all other elements of the welfare arrangement play a role as well and differences in the degree of problem pressure (e.g., low fertility and child poverty) or labor-market characteristics and opportunities (e.g., the availability of part-time employment) are important factors that can be expected to modify public attitudes. Chapter Five elaborates on these issues and develops an adjusted version of the family-policy typology. The consideration of the broader social context suggests that the Southern European countries indeed split off into their own cluster and that Finland should be grouped with the Nordic countries of Denmark and Sweden.

4 Family policies and public opinion

There is currently very limited knowledge about the public's perception of family policies in a comparative perspective, which is due partly to a lack of adequate data. In the following three chapters, this study addresses this research gap and analyzes public attitudes toward family policy in the European Union.

This chapter adopts a macro-level perspective. The first part provides a brief description of differences in public attitudes at the country level, whereas the second part investigates the link between public attitudes toward family-policy issues and the family-policy context. The guiding question is whether and how attitudinal differences among countries are related to the current family-policy setup. The family-policy setup is thereby represented by the individual family-policy indicators as well as the family-policy typology developed in the previous chapter. The policy indicators as well as the family-policy clusters are used to explain country-level differences in public opinion toward the three attitudinal dimensions of responsibility (i.e., the evaluation of goals), satisfaction (i.e., the evaluation of means), and skepticism (i.e., the evaluation of consequences).

The subsequent chapter (5) broadens the perspective by taking into account not only the policy setup but also the broader social context in order to understand differences in attitudes. Thereafter, Chapter 6 adopts a micro-level perspective, analyzing patterns of polarization among social groups within family-policy regimes and in individual countries.

The micro-level data used in the following chapters stem from the European Social Survey (ESS) round 4, conducted in 2008/09 (European Social Survey 2008/09: see Chapter 1). Since the ESS included only 12 of the 15 EU member states analyzed in the previous chapter, this part of the study is restricted to a smaller country sample comprised of Belgium, Denmark, Finland, France, Germany, Greece, Ireland, the Netherlands, Portugal, Spain, Sweden, and the United Kingdom. The following three countries had to be excluded: Austria, Italy, and Luxembourg. Two of these countries belong to the general family support cluster. The only remaining representative of this cluster is thus Germany.

The research questions addressed in this chapter are the following:

- What do citizens expect from their governments in the field of family policy?
- How do Europeans perceive existing family policy institutions?
- Does the public anticipate the negative consequences of government intervention?
- How are the three attitudinal dimensions related to each other?
- What are the differences in terms of the level of public attitudes among the 12 countries?
- Can different types of family policies explain the country-level differences in public opinion?

4.1 The three dimensions of attitudes

Based on the distinction proposed by Roller (1992), three objects of evaluation are distinguished, namely the evaluation of goals, means, and the consequences of welfare-state intervention (see Chapter 2 for a discussion of these concepts).

Concerning the evaluation of goals, the focus is on the dimension of extensity. This dimension captures the extent to which the government is regarded as being responsible for a particular field of welfare-state intervention. This study analyzes the extent to which the state is regarded as responsible for the provision of family-policy measures and in particular childcare services. The following item was used to measure attitudes toward state responsibility: "People have different views on what the responsibilities of governments should or should not be. For each of the tasks I read out please tell me on a score of 0-10 how much responsibility you think governments should have. 0 means it should not be governments' responsibility at all and 10 means it should be entirely governments' responsibility. [....] How much responsibility do you think governments should have to ensure sufficient child care services for working parents?" This dimension is referred to as evaluation of extensity or responsibility.

In the multivariate analyses, the 11-point scale ranging from 0 to 10 is used. For descriptive purposes, an aggregated variable with three categories was also created. The first category combines answers ranging from 0 to 3 and indicates rejection of governments' responsibility for the provision of childcare services. The second category merges answers ranging between 4 and 6 and indicates a rather indecisive opinion or weak support of governments' responsibility. The third category, finally, contains values from 7 to 10 and represents strong support for governments' responsibility in the field of childcare service provision.

The second dimension, the evaluation of means, refers to the evaluation of specific institutions or programs of welfare-state intervention and captures public opinion about existing policy measures. This study focuses on the evaluation of existing childcare services. The question wording was, "In the next few questions we will be asking you how good or bad certain things are for different groups in [country] nowadays. What do you think about the provision of affordable child care services for working parents?" Respondents were asked to rank their opinion on a scale ranging from 0 (extremely bad) to 10 (extremely good). As above, an aggregated variable was created for descriptive purposes with three categories. The first category combines answers ranging from 0 to 3 and indicates a negative evaluation of existing childcare services. The second category merges answers ranging between 4 and 6 and indicates a medial position. The third category contains the values from 7 to 10 and represents a positive evaluation of existing services. This dimension is referred to as evaluation of means or satisfaction.

The third dimension, the evaluation of unintended consequences, measures the extent to which people anticipate the negative side effects of welfare-state benefits and services in terms of cheating or the undermining of norms of reciprocity. The level of skepticism toward the welfare state is captured using the following item: "And to what extent do you agree or disagree that social benefits and services in [country] make people less willing to look after themselves and their family?" Respondents were asked to use a 5-point scale to indicate to what extent they agreed with this statement. A higher score indicates a more positive evaluation of the effects generated by social benefits and services. Again, an aggregated version of the variable was created by merging the first and second category (i.e., "agree strongly" and "agree") as well as the fourth and fifth category (i.e., "disagree" and "disagree strongly"). The intermediate category, "neither agree nor disagree," remains as it was. In the multivariate analyses, the whole range of response categories is used for all dependent variables. This dimension is referred to as evaluation of unintended consequences or skepticism.

4.2 The link between family policies and public attitudes

According to the comparative welfare-state literature, welfare-state institutions represent institutionalized norms and values (e.g., in terms of solidarity and social justice beliefs) and, as such, impact citizens' normative beliefs and orientations (e.g., Esping-Andersen 1990). Along this line of thought, Mau (2003, 2004) uses the term "moral economies" of the welfare state in order to describe the fact that welfare-state institutions can be understood as sets of institutionalized normative assumptions about who should get what, for what reasons, and under what conditions.

These arguments imply that existing institutional structures (and in particular inherent values and normative beliefs) structure people's perception of what is just, what is a pressing societal problem, and what is the appropriate sphere for solving this problem (e.g., the state, the market, the community, the family, or the individual). Social policy institutions thereby do not causally determine orientations but rather have a mediating effect; "certain institutions tend to make some orientations more likely than others" (Svallfors 2007: 10).

Most research in this field assumes that attitudes toward the welfare state are dependent on an individual's position in societal hierarchies (e.g., income or status hierarchies) and on the design of existing social-policy arrangements, since these arrangements constitute the context in which citizens' attitudes are shaped (e.g., Svallfors 1997; Gelissen 2000: see also Chapter 2).

This study focuses on family-policy institutions, which structure gender relations and the division of paid and unpaid work between parents as well as between society and families. These institutions have important implications for men's and women's agency to realize a work-life balance as well as for orientations and living conditions of individuals and families (Korpi 2000; Ferrarini 2006; Hobson et al. 2006). The question of whether the state is actually held responsible for the provision of childcare services might thus be contingent upon the questions of whether 1) supporting the reconciliation of work and family life is actually viewed as an important and valuable goal and 2) whether the state is regarded as being responsible for mitigating the challenge of achieving a work-life balance that many families face. The question of whether the public is satisfied with existing childcare services, in turn, can be contingent upon the type of childcare that is actually preferred as well as upon the quality and quantity of available childcare options.

Hypotheses

Which patterns can be expected to emerge regarding the relationship between the family-policy clusters and public attitudes? The dual-earner support cluster is highly supportive of the dual-earner model of the family. Demand for government responsibility in the field of family policy as well as the level of satisfaction with existing family-policy measures is expected to be high within this cluster. Simultaneously, skepticism toward the consequences of benefits and service is expected to be low.

A tradition of low state intervention in the sphere of the family, in contrast, should go hand-in-hand with a public consensus of rejection of any type of government intervention. Skepticism toward the consequences of benefits and services is then expected to be high.

The general family support cluster and the pluralistic support cluster, finally, are likely to range in-between the dual-earner support and the low-support cluster with regard to all three attitudinal dimensions.

These scenarios suggest that the status quo of welfare-state intervention is broadly accepted and in accordance with public preferences, and that both policy context and public attitudes actually reinforce one another. Pfau-Effinger (2005a) described such a situation as a well-established welfare arrangement (i.e., the cultural and normative basis of the welfare arrangement is anchored in societal institutions as well as in the behavior of social actors). According to Pfau-Effinger, however, general processes of social and cultural change can result in a decline of the degree of the cultural and social integration of the welfare arrangement.

Currently, the situation many welfare states face is characterized by such processes of social and cultural change. For instance, a change in gender-role attitudes toward more egalitarian attitudes is taking place, and the massive increase in female participation in higher education since the 1960s (Schofer and Meyer 2005) has increased women's opportunities and aspirations to be gainfully employed and pursue careers. Consequently, female employment participation is increasing in many countries. Simultaneously, Western welfare states are facing urgent challenges in terms of new welfare needs related to new social risks, changing family structures, low fertility rates, and ageing societies. These challenges are accompanied by serious financing problems within the established branches of social security as well as discussions concerning the future viability of the welfare state (e.g., healthcare and pension systems) (e.g., Taylor-Gooby 2004; Bonoli 2005).

This situation could increase public awareness of the struggles faced by working parents and thus impacts the "perception of reality" in the broader population (Albrekt Larsen 2006: 22). In contrast to the ideal-typical scenarios described above, public debates and increased problem awareness might consequently yield broad public support for policies facilitating female labor-market participation and work-life balance, independent of the current policy setup. A currently low level of government support for families could then coincide with a climate of strong public demand for government responsibility, indicating disagreement with the status quo. Satisfaction with existing policies should then be low and the level of skepticism should be low as well. The empirical analyses in the following chapters reveal, which of the described scenarios actually occur.

4.3 Public attitudes in comparative perspective

Governments' responsibility for the provision of childcare services

With regard to the first dimension, responsibility, Figure 4.1 shows that a clear majority regards the state as being responsible in ensuring sufficient childcare services for working parents in all countries. This is in line with earlier studies, which show that European citizens essentially perceive the state as being responsible for the provision of social transfers and services in various fields of welfare-state intervention (e.g., Wendt et al. 2011: 155). Moreover, earlier research showed that "access to more flexible childcare arrangements" is the most broadly supported policy measure when people are asked which policies should receive priority in order to improve the quality of life for families (Wendt et al. 2011).

Despite a certain consensus about the role of the state, this study indicates some variation among the twelve countries in the extent to which the state is regarded responsible for the provision of childcare services. The strongest support for state responsibility is evident in Greece, where 93% of respondents say that it should be the state's responsibility to provide childcare services. However, Greece is not the only country with such a clear majority in favor of state intervention. In Finland, Spain, and Denmark, more than 85% agree, followed by Sweden, Portugal, and Germany, where still more than 80% agree. The lowest support for state responsibility, in contrast, is found in the Netherlands where 55% of the respondents regard the state as being responsible. Support for state intervention is also somewhat limited in Ireland, where 60% agree, and in the UK, where 63% support a strong role of the government in the field of childcare provision. The remaining two countries, France and Belgium, range in-between with 69% and 74% of respondents regarding the state as being responsible for the provision of childcare services, respectively.

The overall trend is that the strongest support for state responsibility is found in the Southern European (Greece, Spain, and Portugal) and Nordic countries (Finland, Denmark, and Sweden), as well as in Germany, whereas support is weakest in the Netherlands and the liberal countries (Ireland and the UK). France and Belgium range in-between.

Figure 4.1: Responsibility. Percentages per country

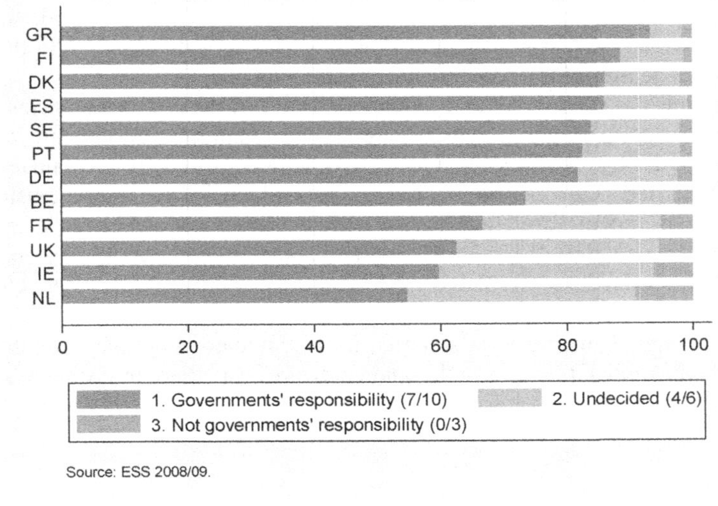

Note: Question wording: "How much responsibility do you think governments should have in ensuring sufficient childcare services for working parents?" Respondents were asked to rate their opinion on a scale ranging from 0 (not government's responsibility) to 10 (entirely government's responsibility). In the figure, category 1 summarizes the values 7 to 10, category 2 the values 4 to 6, and category 3 the values 0 to 3.

Country abbreviations: BE: Belgium, DE: Germany, DK: Denmark, ES: Spain, FI: Finland, FR: France, UK: United Kingdom, GR: Greece, IE: Ireland, NL: The Netherlands, PT: Portugal, SE: Sweden.

Satisfaction with childcare services

Regarding the second dimension, satisfaction, the results indicate that the overall public is not very satisfied with existing childcare services in most countries, though considerable differences exist in the degree of dissatisfaction. Based on Figure 4.2, it becomes apparent that respondents are least satisfied in the Southern European countries of Portugal, Spain, and Greece, as well as in Ireland. In these countries, at least 40% judge existing services as inadequate, while only 12% (in Portugal) to 18% (in Spain) are satisfied. Ordered by the degree of dissatisfaction, Germany and the UK follow with 36% and 34%, respectively. In both countries, about 17% of the respondents are satisfied. Next come France, with 30% dissatisfied, and Belgium with 26% dissatisfied. In these two countries, a quarter of the respondents are satisfied.

More people are satisfied than dissatisfied in four of the twelve countries. In Denmark and the Netherlands, about 35% assess the situation as good while 20% in Denmark and 14% in the Netherlands are dissatisfied. Only in two countries is a majority satisfied with existing services. In Finland, 60% assess existing services as good and in Sweden 53%. In both countries, only 5% are clearly unhappy with the situation. What is striking here is that 40 percent or more chose the intermediate category in almost all countries, indicating neither clear satisfaction nor discontent.

Overall, respondents are least satisfied in the Southern European countries (Portugal, Spain, and Greece) and Ireland and most satisfied in Sweden and Finland, two Scandinavian countries.

Figure 4.2: Satisfaction. Percentages per country

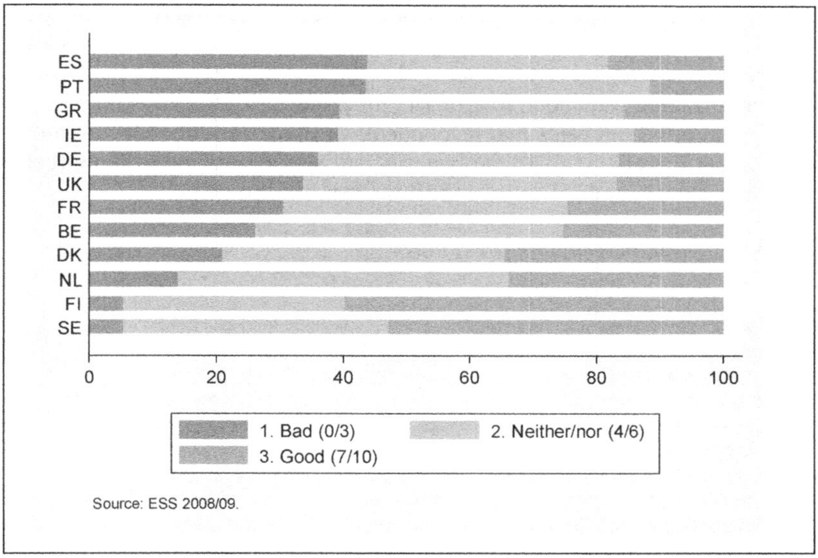

Note: Question wording: "What do you think about the provision of affordable childcare services for working parents?" Respondents were asked to give their opinion on a scale from 0 (extremely bad) to 10 (extremely good). The figure summarizes the values 0 to 3; 4 to 6; and 7 to 10.

Skepticism toward social benefits and services

Figure 4.3 shows that the level of agreement with the statement "Social benefits and services make people less willing to look after themselves and their families" considerably varies among the countries, ranging from 16% in Greece to 55% in France. Respondents in France and the UK are least optimistic about the effects of social benefits and services, with 55% and 50% agreeing with the statement, respectively. In both countries, only a quarter disagree. Belgium and Ireland follow, with almost 40% of respondents being skeptical and another 40% being optimistic. In Germany and Portugal, more people are undecided (category neither / nor). In the two countries, 40% are optimistic whereas 30% agree that social benefits and services make people less willing to look after themselves and their families. In contrast, a majority of respondents are optimistic about the effects of social benefits in three of the twelve countries. Disagreement with the statement is strongest in Spain and Greece, where 60% disagree, followed by Finland and Sweden, where 52% and 50% disagree, respectively. In all four countries, less than a quarter of those surveyed agree that benefits and services have negative consequences. Also rather optimistic are the Danes and the Dutch, 48% of whom disagree and about 30% of whom agree.

The general trend indicates that respondents in France and the UK are most pessimistic about the effects of social benefits and services, whereas the Greek, Spanish, Scandinavian, and Dutch respondents are most optimistic.

Figure 4.3: Skepticism. Percentages per country

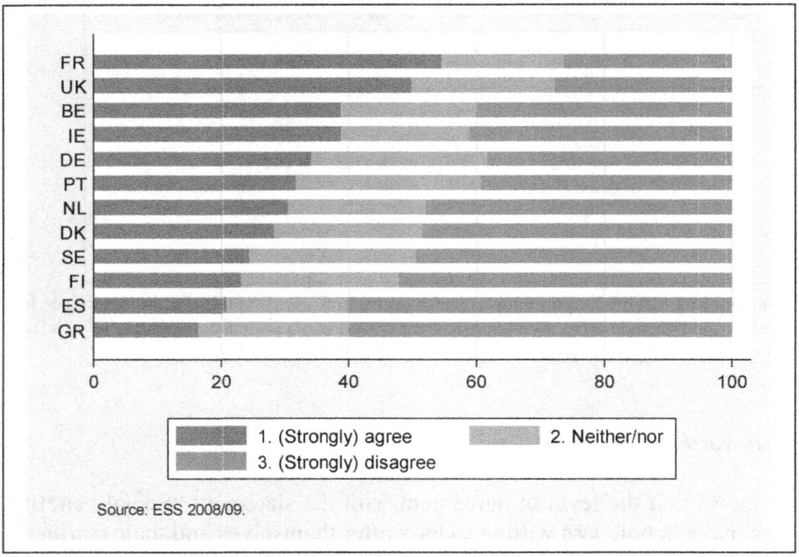

Note: Question wording: "To what extent do you agree or disagree that social benefits and services in [country] make people less willing to look after themselves and their family?" Respondents were asked to give their opinion on a scale ranging from 1 (strongly agree) to 5 (strongly disagree). In the table, values 1 and 2 are merged, as are values 4 and 5.

Responsibility, satisfaction, and skepticism

How are the three attitudinal dimensions of responsibility, satisfaction, and skepticism related to each other at the country level? The correlation coefficients depicted in Table 4.1 show that only two attitude dimensions are correlated to a statistically significant degree: Skepticism and responsibility (see also the scatter plots in Figure 4.4 to 4.6, which graphically display the relationship between the attitudinal dimensions). In those countries in which the level of skepticism toward the negative consequences of benefits and services is low, support for a strong role of the state in the provision of childcare services is strong. In contrast, in countries with a higher level of skepticism toward the negative consequences of benefits and services, support for a strong role of the state in the provisions of childcare services is lower (Figure 4.4). This result supports the idea that the anticipation of misuse of social benefits and services coincides with a lower demand of a strong role of the state for the provision of welfare (Edlund 1999). The strength of this relationship is -.65 and becomes even stronger (i.e., -.88) when excluding the only outlier, which is the Netherlands. In the Netherlands, respondents are least in favor of a strong role of the state but they are not especially skeptical regarding unintended negative side effects. The anticipation of negative side effects is thus not the reason for the low demand for state intervention in this country.

The degree of responsibility assigned to the government is uncorrelated to the level of satisfaction with existing childcare services. Several countries assign a high level of responsibility to the government (i.e., above the EU-12 mean). In about half of these countries, respondents are also satisfied with existing childcare services (i.e., the Nordic countries), whereas respondents in the remaining countries are mainly not satisfied (i.e., the Southern European countries and Germany). In another group of countries, respondents assign a lower level of responsibility to the government (i.e., below the EU-12 mean). In these countries, the level of satisfaction is low as well (e.g., the UK and Ireland). Except for the Netherlands, there is no country in which a low level of responsibility goes hand in hand with a high level of satisfaction (Figure 4.5). Assuming that higher satisfaction with childcare services equates to better actual provision of childcare services, this result suggests a mismatch between public preferences (or childcare service needs) and the actual provision in several countries. Therefore, this situation increases the demand for a strong role of the state in at least some of the countries.

Finally, the level of satisfaction and the degree of skepticism are not correlated either. There are several countries with a low level of skepticism (i.e., below the EU-12 mean). In most of these countries, a low level of skepticism goes hand in hand with a high level of satisfaction (i.e., the Nordic countries and the Netherlands) whereas it coincides with a low level of satisfaction in Greece and Spain. In the remaining countries, a higher level of skepticism goes hand in hand with a comparably low level of satisfaction. No country is found in the upper right cell of the plot (Figure 4.6) suggesting that a high level of skepticism does not coincide with a high level of satisfaction.

Table 4.1: The three attitudinal dimensions (correlations)

	Satisfaction Pearson r (p- value)	Responsibility Pearson r (p- value)	N
Responsibility	-0.040 (0.903)		12
Skepticism	-0.227 (0.479)	**-0.664 (0.019)**	12

Note: Bold coefficients are significant at p<=0.05.
Source: ESS 2008/09; own calculation.

Figure 4.4 Scatterplot: Responsibility and Skepticism

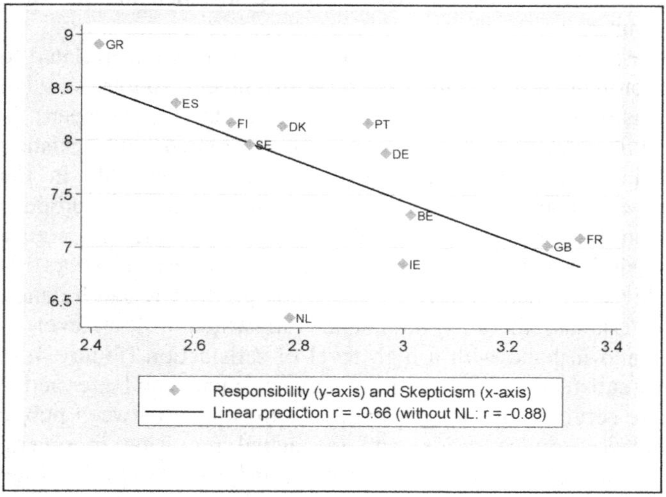

Source: ESS 2008/09; own calculation.

Figure 4.5 Scatterplot: Responsibility and Satisfaction

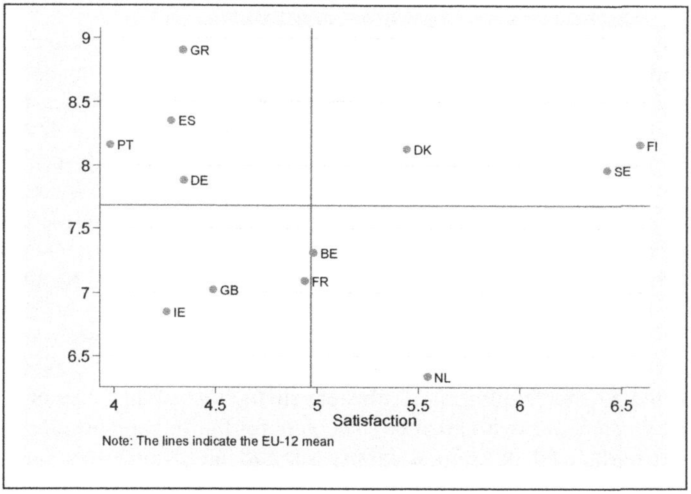

Source: ESS 2008/09; own calculation.

Figure 4.6 Scatterplot: Satisfaction and Skepticism

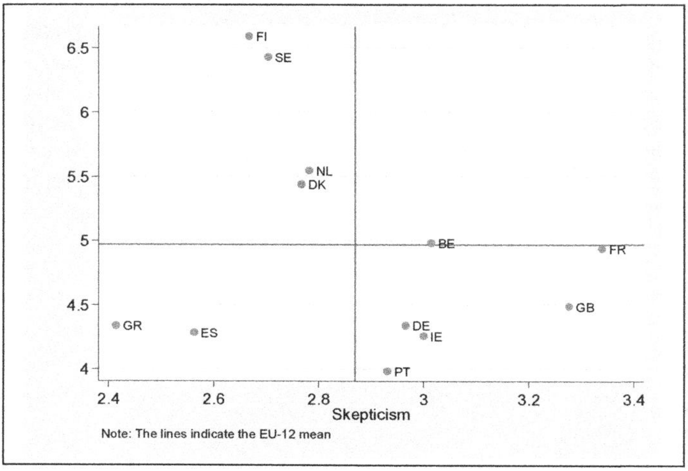

Source: ESS 2008/09; own calculation.

4.4 Research strategy and variables

The following analyses focus on the variability in public attitudes toward family policies at the macro level and investigate the impact of the family-policy setup on the three attitudinal dimensions. The first part of this section discusses the question of whether particular family-policy characteristics are systematically related to public attitudes and presents correlations between the family-policy indicators and the three attitudinal dimensions. The family-policy indicators thereby represent the dimensions of general family support and dual-earner support. It is crucial to note that these correlations do not indicate a causal relationship but rather crude associations between specific family-policy features and public attitudes.

The second part of this section then includes the family-policy clusters in a multi-level framework and tests whether differences in public attitudes are systematically related to the family-policy clusters distinguished in Chapter 3. The following four clusters are distinguished: The general family support cluster (characterized by a high level of general family support and rather low dual-earner support); the low support cluster (providing relatively little support for families in both dimensions); the pluralistic support cluster (combining both general family support as well as dual-earner support); and the dual-earner support cluster (characterized by a high level of dual-earner support combined with a moderate level of general family support). Table 4.2 (below) provides a brief overview of the family-policy indicators and family-policy clusters.

The question of whether social groups have divergent attitudes toward family policies is analyzed in Chapter 6. The following models also include individual-level characteristics, primarily in order to control for differences in the composition of the population in the twelve countries. Furthermore, the results provide a first but rough impression of existing social disparities in Europe.

Table 4.2: Family-policy characteristics

Concept	Indicators
Dual-earner support	Effective maternity leave (income-related benefits) Effective paternity leave (income-related benefits) Effective parental leave (income-related benefits) Childcare services for children under age three Tax incentives for an equal sharing of paid work between spouses
General family support	Effective parental leave (remunerated flat-rate) Duration of unpaid parental leave entitlements Childcare services for children between three years of age and compulsory school age Child allowances
Family-policy clusters	General family support cluster (DE) Low support cluster (IE, UK, NL, GR, PT, IT, ES) Pluralistic support cluster (FR, BE, FI) Reference category: Dual-earner support cluster (DK, SE)

Note: For coding information and data sources of the individual family-policy indicators as well as a detailed description of the family-policy clusters, please refer to Chapter 3.

The distinction between the calculus and the cultural approach (see Chapter 2) allows for the following individual-level characteristics to be taken into consideration: Gender, birth cohort, family situation, level of education, household income, labor-market status, public versus private sector employment, gender-role attitudes, religiosity, and place of living. All variables were coded as dummy variables with the exception of the religiosity scale. Table 4.3 (below) provides a brief overview of all individual-level variables and describes the included dummy variables and reference categories. For a detailed description of the variables and hypotheses, please refer to Chapter 6.

Table 4.3: Individual-level characteristics: Indicators and coding

Indicator	Coding
Gender	Female Reference category: Male
Birth cohort	Born between 1984 and 1994 Born between 1974 and 1983 Born between 1959 and 1973 Born between 1944 and 1958 Reference category: Respondents born before 1944
Family situation	Youngest child in the household is below age three Youngest child in the household is between age three and six Older children living in the household (i.e., above age 6) Respondent has children (not living in the same household) Reference category: Respondents without children
Education	Tertiary education (ISCED 5-6) Other upper and post-secondary education (ISCED 3-4) Reference category: ISCED 0 to 2 , i.e., lower secondary education and below
Income (subjective feeling)	Finding it (very) difficult on present income Reference category: Coping or living comfortably on present income
Labor-market status	Working Reference category: Not in the labor market (i.e., pensioners, the unemployed, students, and homemakers)
Public versus private sector	Public-sector employment Reference category: Private-firm employees, the self-employed, and others
Gender-role attitudes	Egalitarian gender-role attitudes Reference category: Traditional gender-role attitudes
Religiousness	Standardized, country-specific scale ranging from 0 to 1 (a higher value indicating stronger religiousness)
Place of living	Big city Countryside / village Reference category: Suburb / town

In order to account for the nested structure of the data (i.e., individuals within countries), a multi-level design is applied. This approach is theoretically and statistically most appropriate when combining different levels of analysis into a single framework (Langer 2010; Rabe-Hesketh and Skrondal 2008). In a first step, an empty model (i.e., a model without any explanatory variables) was estimated (not shown) for each attitudinal dimension. This model was calculated in order to decompose the variances between the micro level (here, individuals) and the macro level (here, countries). The intra-class correlation coefficient (ICC) thereby indicates the share of the total variance (in the dependent variable) that is explained by membership to a specific context (i.e., country). This coefficient was 13.1% for the responsibility dimension, 14.4% for the satisfaction dimension, and 6.6% for the skepticism dimension. These percentages indicate that there is substantial variation between countries regarding the demand for government responsibility as well as the level of satisfaction with existing childcare services; and to a lesser extent also regarding the degree of skepticism.

In a second step, micro-level variables (level-1) were added to the models (not shown). The intra-class correlation coefficients did not undergo any substantial changes during this step, indicating that the variation between the countries is not due to compositional effects. Due to the low number of level-two units (i.e., countries), random intercept models were run, which did not allow for random slopes. This means that the regression lines of the macro units (i.e., countries) are allowed to have different intercepts but are forced to have the same slopes. The estimated B coefficients, therefore, represent the mean slopes of the individual-level variables across the 12 countries. This procedure serves primarily the goal of controlling for compositional effects. It is important to note that the effects of the individual-level variables could differ between countries (this is analyzed in Chapter 6). The estimated differences among social groups give, therefore, only a rough impression of existing social cleavages and have to be interpreted carefully. Due to these limitations (i.e., the limited validity of the individual-level effects in the pooled models), this chapter only briefly describes the emerging patterns of social polarization, but it does not provide an interpretation of these patterns.

In a third step, the macro-level variables (level-2) were added to the regression model. These models are depicted in Table 4.5 and include both the micro-level and the macro-level characteristics. This part of the analysis uses the family-policy typology developed in Chapter 3 and investigates the question of whether membership to a certain family-policy cluster explains the differences in public opinion between countries. The estimated coefficients indicate the expected change in the dependent variable (i.e., the change in the level of responsibility, satisfaction, and skepticism) resulting from a change in cluster membership compared with the dual-earner support cluster (which serves as the reference group). Table 4.5 reports the intra-class correlation coefficients from the second model (including level-1 variables only) and the third model (including both level-1 and level-2 variables) in order to illustrate the change in the percentage of unexplained variance at the country level. The bigger this change, the bigger the share of the country-level variance that is explained by an individual's membership in a specific family-policy cluster.

4.5 The family-policy indicators and public attitudes

The correlation coefficients in Table 4.4 show that public attitudes are not systematically related to individual family-policy measures to a statistically significant degree. These results suggest that a single measure does not make any difference regarding public attitudes; rather, the particular combination of policy measures, the whole "family-policy package," needs to be taken into account.

The only exception is one measure representing the dual-earner support dimension, namely income-related parental leave, which is positively correlated with the level of satisfaction with existing childcare services. This type of leave, however, is only provided in four countries (i.e., Denmark, Finland, Sweden, and Germany). With the exception of Germany, these countries belong either to the dual-earner support cluster (Denmark and Sweden) or the pluralistic support cluster (Finland).

All three Nordic countries provide generous policy measures in line with the dual-earner model of the family (including the provision of childcare services) and have a long tradition of actively supporting female labor-market participation. Not surprisingly, the level of satisfaction with childcare services is high in these countries. The introduction of paid parental leave, however, does not guarantee a high level of satisfaction with childcare services, as is illustrated by the German case where satisfaction with existing services is rather low. Germany has recently reformed the parental leave legislation based on the Swedish model, introducing an income-related parental-leave entitlement in 2007. These changes promote mothers' labor-market participation as well as fathers' involvement in childcare and are therefore consistent with the dimension of dual-earner support. However, this policy shift is an exception within a family-policy context that is rather traditional in other respects. For instance, Germany's tax system continuously provides strong incentives for a traditional division of paid work between spouses, and Germany lacks sufficient childcare services, especially for children under the age of three. There is thus a care gap between the end of parental leave (after 12 to 14 months) and the entitlement to a place in public daycare, which comes into effect after the child turns three years old. And even then, most places are part-time places that do not facilitate the full-time employment of both parents (Sundström 1999, Wersig 2007, Henninger, Wimbauer and Dombrowski 2008).

The German case illustrates that the whole policy-package is important. A country may score high on a specific measure in line with the dimension of dual-earner support (e.g., income-related parental leave) but if important supplementary measures, such as comprehensive public childcare services, are lacking, satisfaction with this aspect remains low. Single policy measures and their statistical relationship with public attitudes, therefore, have to be interpreted very carefully.

Contrary to the expectations, even the childcare indicators are not correlated with the level of satisfaction with existing childcare services to a statistically significant degree. It is possible, that the chosen indicator is problematic and fails to capture the actual level of government involvement in the provision of childcare services. This assumption is based on the fact that reliable and internationally harmonized data on childcare service provision are scarce (Plantenga et al. 2008; Eurostat 2004). A common approach to overcome the lack of data is to use survey data that provide information on the actual use of childcare services as indicated by the parents themselves. In this study, data from the EU-SILC provided by Eurostat (2010a) are used. This indicator, however, has the disadvantage that it includes different types of formal childcare arrangements and does not strictly distinguish between services provided (or subsidized) by the (local) government and those provided by other organizations or private persons (e.g., registered caregivers). Furthermore, the chosen indicator does not capture any financial issues in terms of childcare fees or the quality of existing childcare options – both aspects could further reduce the satisfaction with childcare services, independently of the current level of usage.

Table 4.4: Correlations of the family-policy indicators and public opinion (Pearson r, p-values in parentheses)

Family-policy indicators (General family support)	Responsibility	Satisfaction	Skepticism	N
Parental leave (unpaid)	0.301 (0.341)	-0.351 (0.263)	-0.291 (0.359)	12
Childcare (age 3 to comp. school age)	0.322 (0.307)	0.358 (0.253)	-0.076 (0.815)	12
Child allowances	-0.284 (0.370)	-0.070 (0.829)	0.476 (0.117)	12
Effective parental leave (flat-rate)	-0.159 (0.621)	0.267 (0.402)	0.422 (0.172)	12
Family-policy indicators (Dual-earner support)	**Responsibility**	**Satisfaction**	**Skepticism**	**N**
Tax incentives	0.071 (0.826)	0.345 (0.272)	-0.433 (0.160)	12
Childcare (age 0 to under 3)	0.178 (0.580)	0.309 (0.329)	0.014 (0.966)	12
Effective parental leave (income-related)	0.316 (0.317)	**0.525 (0.080)**	-0.207 (0.520)	12
Effective maternity leave	0.142 (0.661)	-0.359 (0.251)	-0.249 (0.435)	12
Effective paternity leave	0.355 (0.257)	0.423 (0.171)	-0.227 (0.478)	12

Note: Bold coefficients are significant at $p<=0.1$.
Source: ESS 2008/09; own calculation. The family-policy indicators stem from various sources. For details, please refer to Chapter 3, Table 3.3.

4.6 The family-policy typology and public attitudes

This section presents the multi-level regression models, which test the impact of both individual-level and context variables on the three attitudinal dimensions: Responsibility, satisfaction, and skepticism. The family-policy clusters are included as dummy variables, indicating individuals' membership to a specific policy cluster. The dual-earner support cluster consisting of Denmark and Sweden is the reference group. The lower part of Table 4.5 reports the intra-class correlation coefficients (ICC) from the second model (including level-1 variables only) and the third model (including both level-1 and level-2 variables). As explained above, the ICC is a measure for the amount of unexplained variance at the country level. The difference in the amount of unexplained variance between the two models is used to evaluate the explanatory power of the family-policy clusters.

Compared with men, women are significantly more in favor of a strong role of the state and less satisfied with existing childcare services. Men and women do not differ regarding skepticism toward unintended consequences.

Birth cohorts differ with regard to all three attitudinal dimensions. Compared with the oldest birth cohort (those born before 1944), each of the younger cohorts, those born between 1944 and 1983, is significantly more in favor of a strong role of the state whereas the youngest birth cohort (those born between 1984 and 1994) does not differ significantly from the oldest one. Each of the younger cohorts is less satisfied with existing childcare services as well as less skeptical concerning unintended consequences (compared with the oldest birth cohort). Least satisfied are respondents born between 1974 and 1984. An exception is the youngest birth cohort (those born between 1984 and 1994). This group is more satisfied with existing services compared with the oldest birth cohort.

Respondents with children (particularly children below age three) are more in favor of a strong role of the state compared with childless respondents. Respondents with a child below age three are also significantly less satisfied with existing childcare services. In contrast, respondents with and without (young) children do not differ regarding skepticism toward unintended consequences.

With regard to education, the results indicate that more highly educated persons (i.e., persons with an upper secondary or a tertiary degree) are less in favor of a strong role of the state compared with lesser-educated persons (i.e., persons with lower secondary education and below). Moreover, a tertiary degree coincides with a lower level of skepticism toward the negative side effects of government intervention. The level of education has no impact on the level of satisfaction.[1]

Compared with higher-income groups, low-income groups (i.e., persons who report difficulties living on their present income) are more in favor of a strong role of the state in the provision of childcare services and are clearly more dissatisfied with existing childcare services. This group of respondents, though, is also slightly more pessimistic about negative side effects.

Public-sector employees are more in favor of government responsibility as well as less skeptical, compared with private-sector employees.

The employment status, in turn, has no effect on the level of support for government responsibility or satisfaction with childcare services. Regarding

---

[1] The country-specific models in Chapter 6 reveal that a higher level of education is associated with a higher level of satisfaction in some countries and with a lower level of satisfaction in others. In the pooled models, these converse effects cancel each other out.

skepticism, those working are slightly more skeptical compared with those outside the labor market.

The cultural approach was captured by including gender-role attitudes as well as religiousness. Those who possess more egalitarian gender-role attitudes are more in favor of state intervention, less satisfied with existing childcare services as well as less skeptical regarding unintended consequences. More-religious persons, in contrast, are less in favor of a strong role of the state, more satisfied with existing services, as well as slightly more skeptical.

Finally, the place of living was taken into account. Results suggest that respondents living in a big city (compared with respondents living in a town) demand a stronger role of the state and are slightly less skeptical toward unintended consequences.

The lower part of Table 4.5 (below) depicts the effects of the context variables - the family-policy clusters. The level of support for government responsibility for the provision of childcare services does not differ significantly between the dual-earner support cluster and each of the three remaining groups: The low support cluster, the general family support cluster, or the pluralistic support cluster. The family-policy clusters hardly reduce the percentage of unexplained variance among countries, indicated by the intra-class correlation coefficient (ICC). The percentages of unexplained variance change from 13.9% in the first model (controlling for micro-level effects only) to 12.8% in the second model (controlling for micro-level effects and cluster membership).

The results indicate that support for government responsibility for the provision of childcare services is strong in many countries and that a context of low government support for families does not necessarily coincide with a rejection of government's responsibility for childcare services. Existing differences in the level of support are thus not systematically related to the family-policy clusters. This result supports the idea that processes of social change have increased the demand for dual-earner policies in many countries independent of the current level and type of government intervention in the field of family policies. Remaining differences among countries are possibly related to other contextual features, such as cultural traditions or labor-market characteristics and opportunities as well as the degree of problem pressure, e.g., in terms of low fertility, low female employment participation or child poverty. Some of these aspects are addressed in Chapter 5.

The level of satisfaction with childcare services, in contrast, does systemically vary along the lines of the distinct family-policy clusters. Compared with respondents in the dual-earner support cluster (DK and SE), respondents are less satisfied in the remaining family-policy clusters. Differences are statistically significant for the low support cluster and the general family support cluster. Not surprisingly, the level of existing government support for the dual-earner model of the family has an impact on satisfaction with existing childcare services as an important aspect of the dual-earner family-policy package. The inclusion of the family-policy clusters reduces the amount of unexplained country-level variance in the level of satisfaction from 14.4% (in the first model) to 7% (in the second model). This is a reduction by almost 50%.

With regard to the degree of skepticism toward the effects of social benefits and services, the dual-earner support cluster does not differ significantly from the three remaining groups: The low support cluster, the general family support cluster, or the pluralistic support cluster. The percentage of unexplained variance among the 12 countries (indicated by the ICC) changes only slightly from 7.3% to 6.4%.

Table 4.5: Two-level models of factors affecting public attitudes toward family policy: Responsibility, satisfaction, and skepticism (random intercept models)

	Responsibility	Satisfaction	Skepticism
Individual-level variables			
Women (Ref.: Men)	0.22*** (0.00)	-0.10*** (0.00)	0.01 (0.44)
Birth cohorts (Ref.: Born before 1944)			
1984/1994	-0.06 (0.30)	0.24*** (0.00)	-0.20*** (0.00)
1974/1983	0.29*** (0.00)	-0.23*** (0.00)	-0.18*** (0.00)
1959/1973	0.15** (0.00)	-0.16** (0.01)	-0.19*** (0.00)
1944/1958	0.10* (0.02)	-0.14** (0.01)	-0.12*** (0.00)
Children (Ref.: No children)			
Children under age 3	0.26*** (0.00)	-0.21** (0.00)	0.03 (0.30)
Children age 3 to 6	0.18** (0.00)	-0.03 (0.65)	-0.01 (0.79)
Child (in hh)	0.20*** (0.00)	0.05 (0.22)	-0.03 (0.14)
Child (not in hh)	0.20*** (0.00)	0.00 (0.94)	0.01 (0.64)
Education (Ref.: ISCED 0-2)			
ISCED 3:Upper secondary	-0.09** (0.01)	-0.06 (0.10)	-0.02 (0.26)
ISCED 5:Tertiary	-0.16*** (0.00)	-0.04 (0.33)	-0.12*** (0.00)
Income Situation (Ref.: Comfort./coping)			
(Very) difficult	0.17*** (0.00)	-0.34*** (0.00)	0.04* (0.04)
Public sector (Ref.: Private)	0.13*** (0.00)	0.02 (0.53)	-0.06*** (0.00)
Working (Ref.: Not in the labor market)	0.01 (0.66)	-0.00 (0.97)	0.08*** (0.00)
Egalitarian GRA[1] (Ref.: Traditional GRA)	0.35*** (0.00)	-0.21*** (0.00)	-0.23*** (0.00)
Religiosity (scale)	-0.05*** (0.00)	0.17*** (0.00)	0.06*** (0.00)
Place of living (Ref.: Suburbs/town)			
Big city	0.07* (0.05)	0.05 (0.26)	-0.08*** (0.00)
Countryside/village	-0.01 (0.72)	0.01 (0.69)	-0.01 (0.66)
Context variables (level-2)			
Family-policy clusters (Ref.: Dual-earner support CL)			
Low support cluster	-0.44 (0.43)	-1.50** (0.00)	0.02 (0.93)
General family support cluster	0.10 (0.90)	-1.54* (0.03)	0.14 (0.67)
Pluralistic support cluster	-0.50 (0.42)	-0.45 (0.38)	0.24 (0.31)
Constant	7.38*** (0.00)	6.31*** (0.00)	3.12*** (0.00)
Variance (constant)	0.47 (0.07)	0.32** (0.01)	0.07*** (0.00)
Variance (residual)	3.21*** (0.00)	4.18*** (0.00)	0.98* (0.02)
ICC (level-1 only)	13.9%	14.4%	7.3%
ICC (level-1 and level-2)	12.8%	7%	6.4%
N	20625	20625	20625

Note: The sample consists of 12 EU countries (N=20,625). [1] GRA = gender-role attitudes. Ref. = Reference category. P-values in parentheses. * p <= 0.05, ** p <= 0.01, *** p <= 0.001.
Source: ESS 2008/09; own calculation.

4.7 Conclusion

Public attitudes toward family policies are only partly related to the four family-policy clusters in a systematic way. The level of demand for government responsibility for the provision of childcare services as well as the degree of skepticism toward the unintended side effects of benefits and services hardly vary along the lines of the distinct family-policy clusters. In contrast, the level of satisfaction with existing childcare services is clearly related to the current policy-setup. Not surprisingly, the public is more satisfied in the dual-earner support cluster, in which the policy-context actively supports parents in balancing work and family life. However, a considerable amount (about 50%) of the country-level differences in the level of satisfaction remains unexplained.

These results do not imply that the current policy setup does not matter. In line with arguments provided by Pfau-Effinger (2005a: 14), these results instead support the idea that policies represent only one aspect of the whole welfare arrangement. Public attitudes toward family policies can thus be assumed to not only interact with the design of existing family-policy measures but also with the broader social context, e.g., in terms of labor-market characteristics and opportunities or cultural norms and values. Processes of social change, indicated by a trend toward more egalitarian gender-role attitudes, increasing female labor-market aspirations and participation rates, changing family forms, and increased economic necessities to be gainfully employed, might have increased the needs and preferences of individuals to combine gainful employment and family life. As a consequence, the demand for government responsibility for the provision of childcare services is not only strong in countries that already provide policies supporting the dual-earner model of the family (e.g., Denmark and Sweden) but also in countries that lack such policy measures (e.g., the Southern European countries).

The following chapter takes up these arguments and analyzes the relationship between the family-policy context, other contextual features, and public attitudes. Thereafter, Chapter 6 elaborates on patterns of social polarization within countries and asks whether the patterns of polarization found in this chapter can be confirmed when analyzing the single countries.

5 Family policy, contextual features, and public opinion

It has been discussed before that Western welfare states face similar demographic and socio-economic challenges in terms of new welfare needs, low fertility rates, and ageing societies (see Chapter 1 and 2). These challenges are accompanied by serious financing problems within the established branches of social security (e.g., healthcare and pension systems) and discussions concerning the future viability of the welfare state (e.g., Taylor-Gooby 2004; Bonoli 2005). Accordingly, the European Union has formulated clear policy goals for all member states in order to meet current and future challenges and to achieve social inclusion and cohesion. Among these goals are increasing fertility, raising employment participation of men and women, increasing gender equality, and reducing (child) poverty (European Commission 2007). Public support for families and especially measures supporting the reconciliation of paid work and family life are seen as a powerful means in helping to achieve these goals. Furthermore, several studies have demonstrated a positive relationship between policies promoting the dual-earner model of the family and different social outcomes, such as fertility (Castles 2003; Ferrarini 2006), child well-being (Kamerman et al. 2003), and women's labor-market participation (Ferrarini 2006; Kangas and Rostgaard 2007).

These findings suggest that the dual-earner support cluster should perform best with regard to the aspired outcomes, whereas the other groups of countries, in particular the low-support cluster should perform worse. Furthermore, it could be argued that respondents, who live in countries that are shown to be in an unfavorable position regarding important outcomes, such as fertility rates, child poverty, and the labor-market inclusion of women, are especially dissatisfied with the status quo and demand government interventions in order to improve the situation. A high degree of problem pressure is likely to increase public demand for government responsibility in the provision of childcare services and decrease the level of satisfaction with the status quo.

The previous chapter showed that attitudinal differences at the country level are only partly related to the four family-policy clusters (distinguished in Chapter

3) in a systematic way. This does not imply, however, that the policy context does not matter for the explanation of public attitudes.

The welfare arrangement approach (Pfau-Effinger 2005a) highlights the interrelatedness of family-policy measures, public attitudes, and the wider social and cultural context (e.g., labor-market characteristics and opportunities, country-specific work and care preferences and practices, and policy traditions).

Based on these arguments, this chapter aims to capture the social context by a set of indicators, such as fertility, female employment participation, gender equality, and child poverty. The first part of this chapter investigates the relationship between the four family-policy clusters and these contextual indicators. This part includes all 15 countries that have been included in the cluster analysis in Chapter 3. The second part then analyzes the relationship between family policies, contextual features, and public attitudes. Due to lacking data for the attitudinal dimensions, only twelve countries can be taken into account in this part.[1] The aim of this approach is to characterize the wider social context in which family policies operate and simultaneously illuminate differences in the degree of problem pressure. This knowledge can provide important information about the individuals' life chances, e.g., in terms of work-family compatibility. Eventually, this knowledge is used to develop an adjusted version of the family-policy typology, which is then used to explain country-level differences in public attitudes toward family policy. The last section, finally, provides data on public expenditure for families and investigates whether the type and level of public spending is systematically related to public attitudes.

The attitudinal dimensions considered are again responsibility ("How much responsibility do you think governments should have in ensuring sufficient childcare services for working parents?"), satisfaction ("What do you think about the provision of affordable childcare services for working parents?"), and skepticism ("To what extent do you agree or disagree that social benefits and services in [country] make people less willing to look after themselves and their family?"). In short, this chapter addresses the following research questions:

- What are the differences in social context among both the family-policy clusters and the individual countries?
- How are the contextual features related to public attitudes?
- Is an adjusted version of the family-policy typology, i.e., one that takes into account the broader social context, better suited to explain country-level differences in public opinion?

---

1 Again, Germany is the only representative of the general family support cluster.

- Is the type and level of public spending for families systematically related to public attitudes?

5.1 Contextual indicators

In order to capture the social context, the following contextual indicators are taken into account: The fertility rate, the level of child poverty, female labor-market participation, and gender equality. The data mostly refer to the year 2008 and stem from highly comparable data sources (see Table 5.1 for a brief description). As pointed out previously, these indicators mirror the degree to which countries have adapted to the new challenges they face and succeeded to promote social inclusion and cohesion. Moreover, public support for families, and in particular measures supporting the reconciliation of paid work and family life, are seen as a powerful means of helping to achieve the goals of fertility, employment participation of men and women, gender equality, and child well-being (European Commission 2007; Castles 2003; Ferrarini 2006; Kamerman et al. 2003; Kangas and Rostgaard 2007).

Fertility is measured using the average number of children per woman (that is the total fertility rate (TFR)) (available via Eurostat 2011a).

Child poverty is measured using the risk-of-poverty rate for persons below age 18, i.e., the share of persons under age 18 with an equivalised disposable income below the risk-of-poverty threshold (which is set at 60% of the national median equivalised disposable income, after social transfers). Data stem from the EU-SILC project (i.e., Statistics on Income and Living Conditions) and is provided by Eurostat (2011a).

Low fertility threatens the viability of the welfare state and can be seen as an indicator for existing obstacles in the process of family formation. A high rate of child poverty indicates difficulties in financially maintaining a family and results in a lack of quality of life and reduced life chances for a huge part of the population, particularly the younger generation. Strong problem pressure in terms of low fertility and high incidents of child poverty is expected to increase the level of problem awareness among both politicians and the public. This increased awareness might lead to increased public demand for state intervention in order to attenuate these problems and potentially result in a decreased level of satisfaction with existing childcare services.

Female employment participation is captured using the **female economic activity rate** measured in full-time equivalents (FTE) in order to control for differences in the degree of labor-market participation with regard to working hours. The total hours worked were divided by the average number of hours worked in full-time jobs, calculated as the proportion of all women in the 15 to 64 age group. Additionally, **female part-time employment** is included in the analysis, measured as a percentage of total female employment. The **gender employment gap**, finally, captures the difference in employment rates between men and women in percentage points including all persons in the age group 15 to 64. All employment data stem from the European Union Labour Force Survey (EU-LFS) and were provided by the European Commission (2010).

Female employment participation indicates women's labor market opportunities and the degree to which women are actually participating in the labor market and is thus also an indicator for the gender-specific division of labor in society. Part-time employment can be viewed as a possibility of combining gainful employment and family life, even in a context of otherwise low government support for working parents. A high share of female part-time employment might therefore reduce the demand for childcare services. A high level of female full-time employment as well as a small gender employment gap, in turn, can be seen as an indicator for either a good compatibility of work and family life or a lack of part-time work combined with strong (economic) pressure to be gainfully employed despite low government support for working parents. Both situations are expected to result in a strong demand for government responsibility for the provision of childcare services.

Gender equality is measured using the Gender Equality Index calculated by Plantenga et al. for 25 EU countries (2009). This index has been constructed in such a way that the value indicates the actual distance from a theoretical situation of full equality. Four dimensions have been included, namely equal sharing of paid work (gender employment gap and gender unemployment gap), money (gender pay gap and gender poverty gap among single-headed households), decision-making power (the gender gap in parliament and in ISCO1), and time (the gender gap in caring time for children and in leisure time). Most data included in the index stem from the year 2005 and are accordingly not completely up-to-date. However, the included aspects need time to change and it can be assumed that they have remained at a similar level until the year 2008 (the year 2008 is the reference year for the policy indicators as well as the remaining contextual indicators).

Table 5.1: Contextual indicators

Indicator	Measurement	Notes / data sources
Fertility rate	Total fertility rate (TFR), i.e., the average number of children per woman	Year: 2008 Source: (Eurostat 2011a)
Child poverty	Risk-of-poverty rate for persons below age 18 (in percent)	Year: 2008 Definition: The share of persons under age 18 with an equivalized disposable income below the risk-of-poverty threshold (i.e., 60% of the national median equivalized disposable income, after social transfers). Source: EU-SILC (Statistics on Income and Living Conditions), provided by Eurostat (2011a)
Female employment rate in full-time equivalents	Female economic activity rate (in percent) in full-time equivalents (FTE)	Year: 2008 Definition: The total hours worked were divided by the average number of hours worked in full-time jobs, calculated as the proportion of all women in the 15 to 64 age group. Source: European Union Labour Force Survey (EU-LFS), provided by the European Commission (2010)
Female part-time employment	Female part-time employment as a percentage of total female employment	Year: 2008 Source: European Union Labour Force Survey (EU-LFS), provided by the European Commission (2010)
Gender employment gap	The difference in employment rates between men and women (in percent)	Year: 2008 Data refer to the age group 15 to 64. Source: Eurostat Labour Force Survey, European Commission (2010)
Gender equality	Gender Equability Index ranging from 0 (complete inequality) to 1 (full equality)	Year: Most data stem from 2005 Source: Calculated by Plantenga et al. (2009). Indicators included: Gender employment gap, gender unemployment gap, gender pay gap, gender poverty gap, gender gap in parliament and in ISCO1, gender gap in caring- and leisure time.

5.2 The family-policy clusters put into context

This section compares the four family-policy clusters distinguished in Chapter 3, and describes the social context in which family policies operate. Table 5.2 provides the cluster-specific means and standard deviations for all contextual indicators as well as the country-specific values.

Roughly speaking, the dual-earner support cluster performs best, followed by the pluralistic support cluster and the general family support cluster. The low support cluster performs least favorably. Overall, the results corroborate earlier findings suggesting that policies supporting the dual-earner model of the family are especially suited to achieve a range of desired outcomes (e.g., Castles 2003; Ferrarini 2006; Kamerman et al. 2003; Kangas and Rostgaard 2007). However, results are not completely clear cut and there exists huge within-cluster variation regarding some of the indicators (indicated by the standard deviation). Within-cluster variation is most pronounced in the low support cluster and in the pluralistic support cluster.

Looking at total fertility rates, the pluralistic support cluster and the dual-earner support cluster perform best with rates of 1.9. The low-support cluster follows with a rate of 1.66 and the general family support cluster is in the last position with a fertility rate of 1.46. Within the low support cluster, variation is huge. Fertility is very high in Ireland (2.1), the UK (1.96), and the Netherlands (1.77) and resembles the level found in the pluralistic support cluster and the dual-earner support cluster. In contrast, fertility is very low in the Southern European countries, especially in Spain (1.46), Italy (1.42), and Portugal (1.37) and comes close to the low level found in the general family support cluster.

The level of child poverty also varies considerably among the clusters. The percentage of children affected is lowest in the dual-earner support cluster (11%), followed by the pluralistic support cluster (15%) and the general family support cluster (16.6%). Within the pluralistic support cluster, Finland scores more favorably with a poverty rate of only 12%. Within the general family support cluster, Luxembourg stands out with a higher child-poverty rate of 19.8%. The low support cluster once more performs least favorably with a mean of 21%, and only one country, the Netherlands, stands out with a significantly lower child-poverty rate of 12.9%.

Looking at female labor-market participation measured in full-time equivalents, women's employment participation is highest in the dual-earner support cluster with a mean of 63%. The pluralistic support cluster follows with a mean of 55%; however, within-cluster variation is huge here. Female employment rates in Finland are as high as in Denmark and Sweden with a percentage of 64, whereas rates are significantly lower in France (54%) and in Belgium (48%). Both the general family support cluster and the low support cluster are located at the third position with a mean (full-time) employment participation of 49%. Regarding the variation among countries, only the latter group stands out. Within the low support cluster, female full-time employment rates vary between comparably high rates in Portugal (59%) followed by the UK (52%) and lower rates in the Netherlands (46%) and Greece (47%).

Part-time employment, in contrast, is most prevalent in the general family support cluster (41%), followed by the dual-earner support cluster (38%). The low support cluster holds the third position (32%), closely followed by the pluralistic support cluster (29%). Again, variation among countries is huge in the latter two groups of countries. Within the pluralistic support cluster, part-time employment is most prevalent in Belgium (41%), followed by France (29%); in Finland, only a minority of 18% work part-time. Within the low support cluster, differences among countries are even more pronounced. Part-time employment is hardly existent in Portugal (14%) and Greece (10%) and ranges between 23% in Spain and 28% in Italy. In contrast, part-time employment is widespread in Ireland (32%), the UK (41%), and the Netherlands (75%) in particular. Part-time employment is one way to deal with the work-family conflict in spite of lacking support for the dual-earner model of the family. The described numbers indicate that parents (and especially mothers) in the Southern European countries are confronted with a significantly different labor-market situation compared with their counterparts in the two English-speaking countries and the Netherlands. The low availability of part-time jobs in Southern Europe forces mothers to leave the labor-market upon childbirth if they wish to provide care for their new-born child. The low level of family-policy support potentially has more serious consequences in these countries, e.g., in terms of women's long-term labor-market attachment or families' alternatives to choose between different work- and care arrangements and eventually in terms of attitudinal patterns and families' quality of life. These results underscore the idea of considerable differences regarding the social context and life chances between on the one hand the two English-speaking countries of the UK and Ireland as well as the Netherlands, and on the other hand the Southern European countries of Portugal, Italy, Greece, and Spain.

The last performance indicator taken into account here is gender equality, which was measured using an additive index (ranging between 0 and 1) including several gender-relevant dimensions, such as the equal sharing of paid work, money, or decision-making power (for details see above). As expected, the dual-earner support cluster scores highest with a mean index value of 0.71, followed by the pluralistic support cluster (0.64) and the general family support cluster (0.55). The low support cluster scores lowest (0.46). Within-cluster variation is again most pronounced in the pluralistic support and the low support cluster. In the first group of countries (i.e., the pluralistic support cluster), Finland stands out with a high level of gender equality (0.74), again resembling the level found in the dual-earner support cluster. In contrast, France stands out with a low level of gender equality (0.56), resembling the level found in the general family support cluster. In the low support cluster, gender equality is comparatively high in the Netherlands (0.65), followed by the UK (0.56) and Portugal (0.55) and is especially low in Greece (0.26) and Spain (0.37). Ireland and Italy are located close to the cluster's mean with 0.41 (Italy) and 0.44 (Ireland).

Table 5.2: Contextual indicators for the family-policy clusters and the individual countries. Standard deviation (SD) in parentheses

	Fertility	Child poverty in %	Female LFP (FTE)[a] in %	Female PTE[b] in %	Gender gap LFP[c] in %	Gender equality
General family support cluster (AT, LU, DE)						
Mean (SD)	1.47 (0.13)	16.63 (2.75)	49.67 (3.21)	41.43 (3.41)	13.2 (2.98)	0.55(0.04)
AT	1.41	14.90	52.7	41.1	12.70	0.52
LU	1.61	19.80	46.3	38.2	16.40	0.53
DE	1.38	15.20	50	45	10.50	0.59
Low support cluster (UK, GR, NL, IR, IT, PT, ES)						
Mean (SD)	1.66 (0.29)	21.40 (4.38)	49.23 (5.49)	31.77 (21.87)	15.78 (5.83)	0.46 (0.13)
UK	1.96	24.00	52.2	41	11.5	0.56
GR	1.51	23.00	46.6	9.8	26.3	0.26
IE	2.1	18.00	50.8	32	14.7	0.44
IT	1.42	24.70	41.7	27.8	23.1	0.41
NL	1.77	12.90	45.7	75.2	12.1	0.65
PT	1.37	22.80	58.9	14	11.5	0.55
ES	1.46	24.40	48.7	22.6	18.6	0.37
Pluralistic support cluster (FR, BE, FI)						
Mean (SD)	1.91 (0.09)	15.23 (2.82)	55.13 (8.12)	29.30 (11.50)	8.57 (4.19)	0.64 (0.09)
BE	1.86	17.20	47.7	40.8	12.40	0.61
FI	1.85	12.00	63.8	17.8	4.10	0.74
FR	2.01	16.50	53.9	29.3	9.20	0.56
Dual-earner support cluster (SE, DK)						
Mean (SD)	1.90 (0.01)	11.00 (2.69)	63.00 (1.27)	38.50 (3.39)	6.25 (1.91)	0.71 (0.02)
DK	1.89	9.10	63.9	36.1	7.60	0.69
SE	1.91	12.90	62.1	40.9	4.90	0.72

Note: [a] Female labor-force participation in full-time equivalents (FTE). [b] Female part-time (PT) employment as percentage of total female employment. [c] Gender employment gap. Data sources: Fertility rates: Eurostat (2011a); child poverty: Eurostat (2011a); Female LFP (FTE, PT, gender gap): European Commission (2010); gender equality index: Plantenga et al. (2009).

An adjusted version of the family-policy typology

Based on the findings provided above as well as arguments provided in the literature (e.g., Flaquer 2000; Bahle 2008a), this chapter suggests a slightly adjusted version of the family-policy typology, which might be better suited for explaining public attitudes toward family policies (for a brief summary of the adjusted version, please refer to Table 5.3).

A first adjustment is the classification of Finland which was assigned to the pluralistic support cluster in the original family-policy typology. Within the pluralistic support cluster Finland stands out with a higher rate of full-time employment, a higher level of gender equality, and a lower incidence of child poverty compared with Belgium and France. With respect to the outcomes analyzed here, Finland resembles the other two Nordic countries of Denmark and Sweden. All three Nordic countries (Denmark, Finland, and Sweden) perform very well concerning female employment participation, fertility, gender equality, and child poverty. Furthermore, Chapter 3 revealed that Finland provides the highest level of dual-earner support within the pluralistic support cluster (see Chapter 3). These findings indicate a high level of work-family compatibility in all three Nordic countries and allow for assuming a high level of public support for and satisfaction with existing family-policy institutions. Together with the other two Nordic countries of Denmark and Sweden, Finland is therefore reallocated to the group of dual-earner support / Nordic countries. The pluralistic support cluster is consequently reduced to the two remaining countries of France and Belgium. This reallocation is supported by earlier studies in this field (e.g., Bahle 2008a; Ferrarini 2006).

The second adjustment concerns the low support cluster, in which the within-cluster variation with regard to the contextual features was most pronounced. This group of countries is split up distinguishing between on the one hand the low support / Southern European countries of Spain, Greece, Italy, and Portugal and on the other hand the low support / liberal countries of the UK, Ireland, and the Netherlands.

The Southern European countries are characterized by low part-time employment and low fertility rates suggesting a lack of work-family compatibility and limited labor-market opportunities and thus a strong degree of problem pressure. In the UK, Ireland, and the Netherlands, in contrast, a more flexible labor-market and a higher availability of private-sector solutions seem to absorb the lack of family policies, at least partly.

However, the suggested split between the Southern European countries and the liberal countries of the UK, Ireland, as well as the Netherlands is not unambiguous. Among the Southern European countries, Portugal stands out with a higher rate of female full-time employment and a higher level of gender equality compared with the remaining Southern European countries. And the Netherlands stands out with extremely high female part-time employment, a higher level of gender equality, and a lower level of child poverty compared with the UK and Ireland.

Nevertheless, the suggested distinction between a group of low support / Southern European countries and a group of low support / liberal countries, is clearly supported by earlier studies conducted by authors, such as Flaquer (2000) and Bahle (2008a). These authors emphasized important peculiarities of the Southern European countries, such as the traditionally strong role of the church, the late democratization (except in Italy), and the strong reliance on family solidarity or familism (Bahle 2008a: 104).

The UK, Ireland, and the Netherlands, in contrast, have a long tradition of liberal principles of public non-intervention (Bahle 2008a: 104). Furthermore, the UK in particular has a history of early industrialization and urban married women's employment. These developments have potentially created a favorable climate for mothers' labor-market participation despite the fact that a range of policies actually discourage married women's employment (Knudsen and Wærness 2001b).

Table 5.3: The original and the adjusted family-policy typology

Family-policy typology	Adjustment	Adjusted family-policy typology
General family support cluster: AT, LU, DE	No adjustment	General family support cluster: AT, LU, DE
Low support cluster: ES, IE, IT, UK, GR, NL, PT	Split between the Southern European countries of Italy, Greece, Portugal, and Spain and the liberal countries of the UK, Ireland, as well as the Netherlands	Low support / Southern European countries ES, IT, GR, PT Low support / liberal countries: IE, UK, NL
Pluralistic support cluster: BE, FI, FR	Exclusion of Finland	Pluralistic support cluster: BE, FR
Dual-earner support cluster: DK, SE	Finland added	Dual-earner support / Nordic countries: DK, SE, FI

5.3 Family policies, contextual features, and public attitudes

The first part of this section correlates the contextual indicators and the three attitudinal dimensions. The second part then provides multilevel regression models and investigates the question of whether differences in public attitudes among countries are systematically related to the adjusted family-policy clusters.

As explained in more detail in the previous chapter, the procedure in the multivariate part of the analysis is as follows: In a first step, an empty model (i.e., a model without any explanatory variables) was estimated (not shown) for each attitudinal dimension in order to decompose the variances between the micro-level and the macro-level units. In a second step, only the micro-level variables (level-1) were added to the models (not shown). Eventually, the macro-level variables (level-2) were added to the regression models. These models are depicted in Table 5.5 and include both the micro-level and the macro-level characteristics. The effects of the individual-level (level-1) characteristics have already been described in the previous chapter and are therefore not discussed here. Instead, this chapter focuses on the effects of the context variables addressing the question of whether the membership to a certain adjusted family-policy cluster explains the differences in public opinion at the country level. The estimated coefficients indicate the expected change in the dependent variables resulting from a change in cluster membership. The reference category is the dual-earner support / Nordic countries cluster containing Denmark, Sweden, and Finland. Table (5.5) reports the intra-class correlation coefficients from the second model (including level-1 variables only) and the third model (including both level-1 and level-2 variables) in order to illustrate the change in unexplained variance at the country level between these two models. The higher this change, the better the explanatory power of the context variables (i.e., the adjusted family-policy clusters).

Correlations

Table 5.4 depicts the correlations between the contextual indicators and the three attitudinal dimensions. These correlations have to be interpreted with caution and it is critical to note that they do not indicate causal relationships but rather crude associations between specific contextual features and public attitudes. They can be understood as reflecting the characteristics of the countries in which certain attitudes prevail (Castles 2003).

The demand for state responsibility in the provision of childcare services is negatively correlated with fertility and female part-time employment. The higher the fertility rate and the higher the level of female part-time employment in a country, the lower is the demand for a strong role of the state in the provision of childcare services.

Looking at the second item, the level of satisfaction with existing childcare services, several correlation coefficients are significant. Child poverty and the employment gap between men and women are negatively correlated with the level of satisfaction. In countries with a high incidence of child poverty as well as a huge gender gap in employment participation, the level of satisfaction is low. In contrast, a high share of female full-time employment as well as a high level of gender equality is positively associated with the level of satisfaction.

The level of skepticism toward the negative consequences of benefits and services, finally, does not correlate with any of the contextual features.

Table 5.4: Correlations between contextual features and public opinion (Pearson r, p- values in parentheses)

Contextual features	Responsibility	Satisfaction	Skepticism	N
Fertility	**-0.59 (0.043)**	0.438 (0.155)	0.446 (0.146)	12
Child poverty	0.185 (0.564)	**-0.759 (0.004)**	0.052 (0.873)	12
Female LFP (FTE)[a]	0.320 (0.311)	**0.569 (0.054)**	-0.041 (0.899)	12
Female PTE[b]	**-0.747 (0.015)**	0.256 (0.422)	0.266 (0.403)	12
Gender employment gap	0.263 (0.408)	**-0.678 (0.015)**	-0.364 (0.245)	12
Gender equality index	-0.29 (0.362)	**0.76 (0.005)**	0.24 (0.450)	12

Note: Bold coefficients are significant at p<=0.1. [a] Female LFP = Female labor-force participation in full-time equivalents (FTE). [b] Female PTE = Female part-time employment as percentage of total female employment.
Data sources: ESS 2008/09; own calculation. Contextual indicators: Female LFP (FTE, PT and gender employment gap): European Commission (2010); fertility rates: Eurostat (2011a); gender equality index: Plantenga et al. (2009); child poverty Eurostat (2011a).

Overall, these findings support the argument that the chosen context indicators mirror the degree of problem pressure as well as existing opportunities to combine gainful employment and family life. The stronger the degree of problem pressure, the higher the demand for a strong role of the state and the lower the level of satisfaction with the status quo. In contrast, gender equality and a high level of female employment participation indicate compatibility of work- and family-life and coincide with a higher level of satisfaction.

Public attitudes in the adjusted family-policy clusters

Table 5.5 provides the results of the multilevel regression models for all three attitudinal dimensions. In contrast to the original family-policy clusters used in the previous chapter, the adjusted family-policy clusters used here are better suited to explain country-level differences in public attitudes toward family policies. Compared with the reference group, which is the dual-earner support / Nordic countries cluster, support for a strong role of the state is lower in the pluralistic support cluster (i.e., France and Belgium) and in the low support / liberal countries cluster. The latter group is least in favor of a strong role of the state, compared with the dual-earner / Nordic countries cluster. The group of low support / Southern European countries as well as Germany, in contrast, does not differ significantly from the dual-earner / Nordic countries cluster. The results clearly support the assumption that a similar family-policy context (e.g., low support for families) can coincide with opposing attitudes due to differences in the broader social context these policies operate in or differences in cultural and political traditions. In the liberal countries, the public prefers a low level of state intervention suggesting approval of the status quo. In contrast, the Southern European countries are clearly in favor of a strong role of the state. This situation indicates a considerable discrepancy between the status quo and public preferences in the latter group of countries.

The explanatory power of the adjusted version of the family-policy clusters is high. The percentage of unexplained variance among the countries (indicated by the intra-class correlation coefficient) is reduced from 13.9% (in the model including only the micro-level variables) to 1.7% (in the model including both individual-level variables and the adjusted family-policy clusters). This means that membership to a specific cluster explains 88% of the country-level variance in public attitudes toward state responsibility.

Looking at the second question – the level of satisfaction with the provision of affordable childcare services for working parents – the adjusted clusters are again very well suited to explain attitudinal variation at the country level. The following patterns emerge: The level of satisfaction is highest in the dual-earner / Nordic countries cluster and significantly lower in the other four groups of countries. Compared with the reference group, the level of satisfaction is lowest in the low support / Southern European countries, followed by the general family support cluster (represented by Germany), the low support / liberal countries, and finally, the pluralistic support cluster. The inclusion of the adjusted family-policy clusters reduces the percentage of unexplained variance among the countries from 14.4% (in the model including only the micro-level variables) to 3.3% (in the model including both individual-level variables and the adjusted family-policy clusters). This is a reduction by 77%. The adjusted family-policy clusters thus explain a high share of the county-level differences in the level of satisfaction.

This result roughly mirrors the actual availability of childcare services as indicated by the childcare indicators used in the cluster analysis (see Chapter 3). An interesting case, though, is Finland where the availability of childcare services is lower compared with the remaining Nordic countries. However, the level of satisfaction with existing childcare services is high in Finland. A Finnish particularity is the combination of a parental leave entitlement (which is an income-related benefit) with the provision of a flat-rate home-care allowance after the end of parental leave. After the end of parental leave, Finnish parents can choose between municipal daycare and this home-care allowance, which allows parents to stay at home to care for their child and receive a flat-rate benefit until the child is three years old (Kröger et al. 2003). This regulation advocates parental choice, supporting working mothers as well as emphasizing parents' right to provide care (Mahon 2002; Kremer 2007) and it reduces the needs for pubic childcare options. Simultaneously, Finnish mothers are well integrated in the labor-market which is mirrored in a high share of female full-time employment (64%) and a very low gender gap in overall employment (4%). The comparably high level of satisfaction in Finland, suggests that this arrangement is popular and meets families' care preferences. The Finnish example illustrates that different policy solutions can work as functional equivalents (for examples in the field of pension systems, see Ebbinghaus 2006) and achieve similar outputs, e.g., in terms of work-family compatibility and satisfaction. Furthermore, this example corroborates the argument that family-policy characteristics and contextual features (e.g., in terms of culture or labor-market characteristics) interact and have to be taken into account when analyzing public attitudes.

The third question, finally, addresses skepticism toward the consequences of benefits and services. The share of variance at the country-level amounts to 7.3% (in the model including only the micro-level variables), which is much lower compared with the other two attitudinal dimensions. The inclusion of the adjusted family-policy clusters reduces this amount to 2.4%, which represents a reduction of the country-level variance by 67%, i.e., the adjusted family-policy clusters explain a considerable share of the county-level differences in the level of skepticism.

Neither the low support / Southern European countries nor the general family support cluster differ from the group of dual-earner support / Nordic countries in the level of skepticism. Two country clusters, however, differ from the reference group to a statistically significant degree. The highest level of skepticism is found in the pluralistic support cluster, followed by the group of low support / liberal countries. The two country groups with the highest level of skepticism (i.e., the low support / liberal countries and the pluralistic support cluster) also exhibit the lowest levels of public demand for a strong role of the state in the provision of childcare services. A high level of skepticism toward the negative side effects of social benefits and services thus coincides with a low demand for a strong role of the state in the provision of services, which was already pointed out in the previous chapter.

The group of low support / liberal countries consists of the UK, Ireland, and the Netherlands. These countries have a tradition of liberal principles of non-intervention by the government (Bahle 2008a) and this tradition has potentially nourished a climate of skepticism toward social benefits and services. More surprising, however, is the high level of skepticism in Belgium and France. Additionally, there is one interesting exception to the described pattern. The descriptive statistics in the previous chapter have revealed that the Dutch public is very optimistic about the effects of social benefits and services. Nevertheless, demand for state intervention is limited in this country. The questions of why the Dutch are not skeptical and why, in contrast, the French and the Belgium public is skeptical, have to remain unanswered in this study and might be addressed in future studies.

The low level of skepticism in the dual-earner support / Nordic countries corroborates the findings provided by Kumlin and Rothstein, who showed that "universal welfare-state institutions tend to increase social trust, whereas experiences with need-tested social programs undermine it" (Kumlin and Rothstein 2005: 339). Based on these findings, the high share of means-tested cash benefits in the French system could offer a preliminary explanation for high level of skepticism toward the negative side effects of welfare-state benefits and services in France (Fagnani and Math 2008). In the Southern European countries, in turn, the low level of skepticism could result from the strong tradition of familism in these countries (Jensen and Svendsen 2009).

Table 5.5: Two-level models of factors affecting public attitudes toward family policy: Responsibility, satisfaction, and skepticism (random intercept models)

	Responsibility	Satisfaction	Skepticism
Individual-level variables			
Women (Ref.: Men)	0.22*** (0.00)	-0.10*** (0.00)	0.01 (0.44)
Birth cohorts (Ref.: Born before 1944)			
1984/1994	-0.06 (0.30)	0.24*** (0.00)	-0.20*** (0.00)
1974/1983	0.29*** (0.00)	-0.23*** (0.00)	-0.18*** (0.00)
1959/1973	0.15** (0.00)	-0.16** (0.01)	-0.19*** (0.00)
1944/1958	0.10* (0.02)	-0.14** (0.01)	-0.12*** (0.00)
Children (Ref.: No children)			
Children under age 3	0.26*** (0.00)	-0.21** (0.00)	0.03 (0.30)
Children age 3 to 6	0.18** (0.00)	-0.03 (0.65)	-0.01 (0.79)
Child (in hh)	0.20*** (0.00)	0.05 (0.22)	-0.03 (0.14)
Child (not in hh)	0.20*** (0.00)	0.00 (0.94)	0.01 (0.64)
Education (Ref.: ISCED 0-2)			
ISCED 3:Upper secondary	-0.09** (0.01)	-0.06 (0.10)	-0.02 (0.26)
ISCED 5:Tertiary	-0.16*** (0.00)	-0.04 (0.33)	-0.12*** (0.00)
Income Situation (Ref.: Comfort./coping)			
(Very) difficult	0.17*** (0.00)	-0.34*** (0.00)	0.04* (0.04)
Public sector (Ref.: Private)	0.13*** (0.00)	0.02 (0.53)	-0.06*** (0.00)
Working (Ref.: Not in the labor market)	0.01 (0.66)	-0.00 (0.97)	0.08*** (0.00)
Egalitarian GRA[1] (Ref.: Traditional GRA)	0.35*** (0.00)	-0.21*** (0.00)	-0.23*** (0.00)
Religiosity (scale)	-0.05*** (0.00)	0.17*** (0.00)	0.06*** (0.00)
Place of living (Ref.: Suburbs/town)			
Big city	0.07* (0.05)	0.05 (0.26)	-0.08*** (0.00)
Countryside/village	-0.01 (0.72)	0.01 (0.69)	-0.01 (0.66)
Context variables (level 2)			
Adjusted family-policy clusters (Ref.: Dual-earner support/Nordic)			
Low support/Southern Europe	0.37 (0.06)	-2.02*** (0.00)	-0.20 (0.13)
Low support/liberal countries	-1.34*** (0.00)	-1.42*** (0.00)	0.29* (0.02)
General family support cluster	0.06 (0.82)	-1.76*** (0.00)	0.16 (0.37)
Pluralistic support cluster	-0.85*** (0.00)	-1.22*** (0.00)	0.44** (0.00)
Constant	7.42*** (0.00)	6.52*** (0.00)	3.09*** (0.00)
Variance (constant)	0.06*** (0.00)	0.14*** (0.00)	0.02*** (0.00)
Variance (residual)	3.21*** (0.00)	4.18*** (0.00)	0.98* (0.02)
ICC (level-1 variables only)	13.9%	14.4%	7.3%
ICC (level-1 and level-2 variables)	1.7%	3.3%	2.4%
N	20625	20625	20625

Note: The sample consists of 12 EU countries (N=20,625).
[1] GRA = gender-role attitudes. P-values in parentheses. * p <= 0.05, ** p <= 0.01, *** p <= 0.001.
Source: ESS 2008/09; own calculation.

5.4 Public expenditures for families

In times of "permanent austerity," welfare states face severe budgetary strain, which instigates debates concerning restructuring and retrenchment (P. Pierson 1998, 2001). However, in the field of family policy and particularly in social services, public commitment and spending levels are expanding in most countries (Bahle 2008b; Jensen 2009; Fagnani and Math 2008). Despite a general increase in public spending for families, Western welfare states differ with respect to both their total amount of financial resources spent and the type of benefits provided. Indicators that capture these differences can therefore provide useful information about spending priorities and the organization of modern welfare states (Castles 2009).[2]

This section investigates what governments actually do for families in terms of monetary input and whether this input is related to public attitudes. How much do the countries spend for families and which types of benefits are primarily provided? Does a high level of public spending for families and childcare services coincide with a high level of satisfaction? And does a low level of spending coincide with a low level of satisfaction?

The following four indicators are used to describe the level and type of public spending for families: First, the level of public expenditure for childcare services; second, the level of public expenditure for cash benefits (e.g., child payments and allowances and parental leave benefits); third, the level of expenditure for tax benefits; and fourth, the sum of public spending, including public expenditure for services, tax benefits, and cash benefits (i.e., the sum of the previous three measures). These indicators capture governments' efforts in terms of financial resources, measured as a percentage of the gross domestic product (GDP). These expenditures concern public spending that is exclusively for families (e.g., child payments and allowances, parental leave benefits, and childcare support). Spending recorded in other social policy areas (e.g., health and housing support) also assists families, but not exclusively, and is not included here (OECD 2010b).

---

2 Esping-Andersen (1990) has often been cited in his criticism of aggregate social spending as a measure for comparing welfare states. However, the recently developed databases (e.g., the OECD Social Expenditure Database) provide disaggregated, comparable expenditure data at program level, which are well suited for comparing the spending priorities of welfare states (Castles 2009).

In addition to the indicators covering type and level of public expenditures for families, the gross domestic product (GDP) is provided as a measure for the overall size of the countries' economies and as an indicator for differences in the standard of living among the countries. The indicator used here measures the GDP per capita as a percentage of the EU-27 average (EU-27=100), adjusted for differences in price levels (by means of purchasing power parities (PPS)). Table 5.6 briefly describes the monetary indicators and data sources.

Table 5.6: Economic indicators

Indicator	Coding
Public expenditure for childcare services	In % of GDP
Public expenditure for cash benefits for families	In % of GDP
Public expenditure for tax benefits for families	In % of GDP
Total public expenditure for families	The sum of public spending for services, tax benefits, and cash benefits in % of GDP
Gross domestic product (GDP)	GDP per capita as a percentage of the EU-27 average (EU-27=100), adjusted for differences in price levels

Source: Data on public expenditure (for services, cash, and tax benefits) refer to the year 2007 and stem from the OECD Social Expenditure Database (OECD 2010b). Data on tax benefits were not available for DK, FI, GR. GDP data refer to the year 2008 and stem from Eurostat (2011b).

The level of total public spending for families (in % of the GDP) is highest in the pluralistic support countries (the percentage is especially high in France), followed by the Nordic countries (the highest value is found in Denmark). The general family support cluster is located at the third position, closely followed by the group of low support / liberal countries (with comparatively high spending levels in the UK). The amount of total public spending for families is lowest in the low support / Southern European countries (see Table 5.7, below).[3]

Regarding the type of spending, public expenditure for childcare services is highest in the group of dual-earner / Nordic countries, followed by the pluralistic

[3] Spending data for Italy, Luxembourg, and Austria are also depicted in the table for completeness. However, since data on public attitudes were not available for these countries, they could not be included in the correlation analysis and their expenditure patterns are not discussed in detail.

support cluster (mainly driven by the high percentage in France) and the group of low support / liberal countries (mainly driven by the high spending level in the Netherlands). The general family support cluster and the group of low support / Southern European countries spend the lowest share of their GDP for childcare services.

With regard to spending on cash benefits, the general family support cluster has a leading position (due to the high share of cash benefits provided in Austria and Luxembourg), followed by the low support / liberal countries. The pluralistic support cluster is located at the third position, followed by the group of dual-earner / Nordic countries. The least spending countries are again the group of low support / Southern European countries.

Concerning the level of tax benefits, data for several countries are missing, which limits the comparability of this indicator among the country groups or individual countries. The highest amount of tax benefits (in % of the GDP) is found in the pluralistic support cluster and the general family support cluster (driven by the high percentage in Germany). At a much lower level the group of low support / Southern European countries and the group of low support / liberal countries follows. Data for the Nordic countries is mainly missing and Sweden provides no tax benefits.

The GDP, finally, indicates the general wealth of a nation in a certain year. In 2008, the wealthiest countries were found in the general family support cluster (due to the exceptionally high value in Luxembourg). It follows the group of low support / liberal countries and the dual-earner support / Nordic countries. The pluralistic support cluster ranks at the fourth position, and the GDP is lowest in the group of low support / Southern European countries.

Table 5.7: Economic indicators: Public spending for families and GDP per capita Cluster means with standard deviation (SD) in parentheses as well as country-specific values

	Services (% GDP)	Cash (% GPD)	Taxes (% GDP)	Total (% GDP)	GDP (per Capita)[a]
General family support cluster					
Mean (SD)	0.73 (0.24)	1.94 (0.77)	0.47 (0.61)	2.99 (0.18)	173 (91.81)
DE	0.79	1.09	0.90	2.78	116
AT	0.93	2.16	0.04	3.13	124
LU	0.47	2.58	-	3.05	279
Low Support / Southern European countries					
Mean (SD)	0.62 (0.24)	0.61 (0.10)	0.20 (0.05)	1.33 (0.28)	94.5 (12.37)
ES	0.85	0.52	0.24	1.6	104
GR	0.39	0.55	-	0.94	92
PT	0.45	0.74	0.17	1.36	78
IT	0.80	0.63	-	1.43	104
Low support / Liberal countries					
Mean (SD)	0.94 (0.55)	1.65 (0.90)	0.17 (0.17)	2.75 (0.74)	126.3 (12.42)
UK	0.95	2.26	0.34	3.55	112
IE	0.38	2.07	0.15	2.59	133
NL	1.48	0.61	0.01	2.1	134
Pluralistic support cluster					
Mean (SD)	1.29 (0.52)	1.45 (0.23)	0.60 (0.18)	3.33 (0.47)	111.5 (6.36)
BE	0.92	1.61	0.47	2.99	116
FR	1.65	1.29	0.72	3.66	107
Dual-earner support / Nordic countries					
Mean (SD)	1.75 (0.43)	1.36 (0.12)	-	3.11 (0.51)	122.67 (3.21)
DK	2.19	1.48	-	3.67	125
SE	1.73	1.24	0	2.97	124
FI	1.34	1.35	-	2.69	119

Note: [a] GDP per capita as a percentage of the EU-27 average (EU-27=100), adjusted for differences in price levels. Data on tax benefits was not available for LU, GR, IT, DK, and FI. "Total (% GDP)" indicates the sum of expenditures for services, cash benefits, and tax benefits.
Source: OECD (2010b); Eurostat (2011b).

Table 5.8 (below) depicts the correlations between the economic indicators and the three attitudinal dimensions. As discussed above, these correlations mirror associations between public attitudes and the economic characteristics of the countries, but they do not indicate causal relationships (Castles 2003).

The GDP is negatively associated with the level of demand for government responsibility. This result suggests that the demand for government responsibility is weaker the richer a country is. Similar results have been found in earlier studies and have been attributed to a saturation effect. This effect describes a situation in which highly redistributive institutions (or welfare states) generate resistance against further redistribution (Kumlin and Svallfors 2007; Pfeifer 2009). In this study, however, the negative correlation is strongly influenced by two groups of countries, namely 1) the group of low support / southern European countries, which have the lowest GDP values but strongly demand government responsibility and 2) the group of low support / liberal countries, which have the highest GDP values but simultaneously a low demand for state responsibility, particularly the Netherlands and Ireland. In contrast, both spending levels and support for a strong role of the state in the provision of childcare services are high in the dual earner support / Nordic countries.

In contrast, the GDP is positively correlated with the level of satisfaction. The Southern European countries, on the one hand, have the lowest GDP, and are the least satisfied with existing childcare services. In these countries, the low standard of living increases economic needs to be gainfully employed. Simultaneously, the government hardly supports working parents. The Nordic countries, on the other hand, are among the rich nations and invest in public daycare which results in a comparably high level of satisfaction in these countries. In the remaining countries, a higher standard of living potentially enables individuals to purchase private solutions for existing childcare needs and reduces the economic pressure to be gainfully employed, particularly, when the children are young.

Not surprisingly, the level of satisfaction is significantly and positively correlated with the level of expenditure for childcare services. This positive association between a strong role of the state and the level of satisfaction is corroborated by a study conducted by Wendt et al. (2010), who investigated public attitudes toward the healthcare system.

An interesting case is found in the Netherlands, which spends a comparably high share of the GDP for childcare services. This commitment, however, was not mirrored in a high level of usage of childcare services measured in hours per week (see Chapter 3). The high costs of childcare in the Netherlands are partly due to high staff-to-child ratios as well as limited usage of home-based (but regulated) family daycare (2002).[4] Dutch children thus spend rather short hours in daycare places. In combination with a high share of female part-time employment, this arrangement seems to be popular in the Netherlands.

---

4 Home-based (but regulated) family daycare is widely used in countries, such as Denmark, and has lower cost structures for staff and space (OECD 2002).

The level of skepticism toward unintended consequences, finally, is positively associated with the share of cash benefits as well as with the level of total spending. The higher the overall level of spending and the higher the share of cash benefits (measured in % of the GDP), the more skeptical is the public. This association is strongly driven by the UK, France, and Belgium, which are countries with a high level of total spending and a high level of skepticism toward benefits and services. Cash benefits are most prone to misuse. This fact potentially generates a higher level of skepticism toward benefits and services in those countries that support families primarily by means of cash benefits. Corroborating these arguments, Fagnani and Math showed that especially the UK and France (as well as Ireland) are characterized by a large proportion of mean-tested cash benefits for families (Fagnani and Math 2008: 62).

Table 5.8: Correlations between economic indicators and public opinion (Pearson r, p- values in parentheses)

	Responsibility	Satisfaction	Skepticism	N
Services (% GDP)	-0.147 (0.650)	0.729 (0.007)	0.0611 (0.850)	12
Cash (% GDP)	-0.453 (0.139)	0.068 (0.835)	0.637 (0.026)	12
Taxes (% GDP)	0.107 (0.785)	0.356 (0.348)	0.542 (0.132)	9
Total (% GDP)	-0.451 (0.141)	0.379 (0.225)	0.658 (0.020)	12
GDP (per Capita)	-0.584 (0.046)	0.525 (0.080)	0.086 (0.791)	12

5.5 Conclusion

This chapter combined an analysis of the family policy setup with an analysis of the broader social and cultural context in which these policies operate. The insights gained from this approach were then used to explain country-level differences in public opinion toward family policies. The findings corroborate the welfare arrangement approach, which emphasizes the interrelatedness of public attitudes and all elements of the welfare arrangement (Pfau-Effinger 2005a).

It is crucial to note that the choice of contextual indicators taken into account in this study inevitably provides a limited picture of reality. Further research is needed in order to deepen our understanding of the interrelatedness of the relevant elements of the welfare arrangement and their specific impact on public opinion. Case studies focusing on individual countries or smaller groups of countries are thereby valuable sources of information that can help shed light on country-specific characteristics and interdependencies.

Furthermore, the findings of this chapter clearly corroborate that the Southern European countries should be grouped into their own, distinct family-policy cluster, as has been suggested by Flaquer (2000) and Bahle (2008a). This group of countries faces not only considerable economic problems but also serious challenges due to processes of social and cultural change, e.g., in terms of very low fertility rates, increasing numbers of women attaining higher education, and growing female labor-market participation. Sjöberg (2010) has argued that the growth of female educational attainment has outpaced the growth in female labor-market participation in the Southern European countries, resulting in a mismatch between women's aspirations to pursue a career and the structural possibility of realizing those aspirations. Not surprisingly, this situation generates extremely low levels of satisfaction with the status quo as well as a strong demand for government intervention. Simultaneously, the low level of economic wealth in these countries (indicated by the GDP per capita) limits the potential scope for government intervention. The current financial and economic crisis has worsened this situation.

Chapter 6 analyzes public attitudes from a micro-level perspective and investigates whether the same patterns of social polarization emerge in all countries or whether cluster- or even country-specific patterns emerge. Moreover, several questions are addressed that are specific to a group of countries or refer to a particular dimension.

Regarding the dimension of responsibility, it is asked whether the rejection of a strong role of the state is widespread among all respondents belonging to the low-support / liberal countries or whether certain groups of the population prefer a higher level of government responsibility in the provision of childcare services.

An interesting case regarding the level of satisfaction with existing childcare services is found in Finland. An effort is made to determine whether the Finnish policy arrangement is popular among all groups of the population or whether it generates social distinctions in the level of satisfaction. It has been argued that the Finnish home-care allowance (a flat-rate benefit) is more attractive to women with lower levels of education (and who have lower labor-market prospects in terms of job quality and income), whereas women with higher educational degrees (who have better labor-market chances) prefer a place in public daycare (OECD 2001; Salmi 2006). Depending on families' actual choices and experiences, satisfaction with existing childcare services could thus vary among socio-economic groups. Social distinctions in the level of satisfaction would then indicate social inequalities in the quality of life.

An interesting question regarding the degree of skepticism toward the negative consequences of social benefits and services is whether the same groups of the population are critical in all countries, or whether country-specific patterns emerge.

Appendix

Table A 5: Responsibility, satisfaction, and skepticism. Cluster- and country means, standard deviation in parentheses

	Responsibility		Satisfaction		Skepticism		N
General family support cluster							
DE	7.89	(1.89)	4.34	(2.02)	2.97	(0.97)	2302
Low support / Southern Europe							
Cluster mean	8.50	(1.68)	4.21	(2.23)	2.62	(1.04)	5297
ES	8.35	(1.59)	4.28	(2.42)	2.56	(1.01)	1802
GR	8.91	(1.56)	4.34	(2.23)	2.41	(1.03)	1800
PT	8.16	(1.79)	3.98	(2.03)	2.93	(1.00)	1695
Low support / liberal countries							
Cluster mean	6.74	(2.06)	4.75	(2.06)	3.02	(1.00)	4818
UK	7.02	(2.04)	4.49	(2.05)	3.28	(0.97)	1890
IE	6.85	(2.03)	4.26	(2.05)	3.00	(1.02)	1523
NL	6.34	(2.04)	5.54	(1.85)	2.78	(0.94)	1405
Pluralistic support cluster							
Cluster mean	7.20	(1.88)	4.96	(2.18)	3.18	(1.11)	3374
BE	7.31	(1.72)	4.98	(2.06)	3.01	(1.03)	1501
FR	7.09	(2.02)	4.94	(2.28)	3.34	(1.15)	1873
Dual-earner support / Nordic countries							
Cluster mean	8.09	(1.67)	6.15	(1.97)	2.71	(0.96)	4834
DK	8.13	(1.73)	5.44	(2.13)	2.77	(0.98)	1384
SE	7.96	(1.75)	6.43	(1.81)	2.70	(0.92)	1452
FI	8.17	(1.52)	6.59	(1.75)	2.67	(0.98)	1998
EU 12	7.67	(1.95)	4.99	(2.22)	2.87	(1.04)	20625

Note: Higher values indicate a stronger demand for state responsibility; a higher level of satisfaction; and a higher level of skepticism. The number of observations in each country was standardized to 1,000. Data weighted.
Source: ESS 2008; own calculation.

6 Social cleavages within European welfare states

This chapter analyzes public attitudes from a micro-level perspective and focuses on attitudinal differences among social groups within both the adjusted family-policy clusters and the individual countries. This step is crucial in order to investigate whether the patterns of social polarization that were found at the aggregate level (in the previous chapters) can be confirmed for all countries included in the analysis. Only country-specific models can reveal the country-specific patterns of social polarization. A high level of attitudinal polarization among social groups is thereby regarded as an indicator for societal conflicts and social inequalities in life chances and opportunities. Again, the three dimensions of attitudes are analyzed, namely responsibility, satisfaction, and skepticism.

Chapter 4 has shown that two dimensions of attitudes, namely responsibility and skepticism, are correlated at the country level. This result indicates that the demand for a strong role of the state in the provision of childcare services is systematically lower in those countries in which skepticism toward the negative side effects of government intervention is high. This chapter investigates whether this patterns is also found at the individual level, i.e., whether those individuals who are skeptical toward social benefits and services are also less in favor of a strong role of the state. In order to test the relationship between all three attitudinal dimensions at the individual level, this chapter conducts a series of correlation analyses.

Moreover, this chapter addresses several questions that have been raised in the preceding chapters. One example is the question of whether the rejection of a strong role of the state, which was found in the group of low-support / liberal countries, is widespread among all respondents belonging to this cluster, or whether particular groups of the population would prefer a higher level of state intervention.

In the Finnish case, results revealed a comparatively high level of satisfaction with existing childcare services despite a lower level of childcare service provision as compared with the other two Nordic countries of Sweden and Denmark. A Finnish particularity is the choice between a place in public daycare and a home-care allowance (as a flat-rate benefit) after the end of parental leave. It has been argued that this home-care allowance might be more attractive to women with lower levels of education (due to lower labor-market prospects in terms of job quality and income), whereas families with higher educational degrees prefer a place in public daycare (due to better labor-market prospects) (OECD 2001). Strong patterns of polarization regarding the level of satisfaction with existing childcare services, e.g., between educational- or income groups, would corroborate these arguments.

Regarding the degree of skepticism toward the negative side effects of social benefits and services, this chapter investigates whether the same groups are skeptical toward benefits and services in all countries or whether country-specific patterns emerge.

This chapter addresses the following research questions:

- To what extent are the three attitudinal dimensions related at the individual-level?
- What are the differences regarding social polarization of public attitudes among the twelve countries?
- To what extent are public attitudes structured along the lines of self-interest and different cultural values?
- Are the patterns of polarization uniform among countries or instead country-specific?
- Do the attitudinal patterns differ along the line of the five adjusted family-policy clusters distinguished in the previous chapter?

Due to data limitations, this part of the study is again restricted to a smaller country sample comprised of Belgium, Denmark, Finland, France, Germany, Greece, Ireland, the Netherlands, Portugal, Spain, Sweden, and the United Kingdom. The data used stem from the European Social Survey (ESS), which was described in Chapter 1.

This chapter proceeds as follows: In a first step, the three attitudinal dimensions of responsibility, satisfaction, and skepticism are correlated at the micro level in order to investigate the question of whether the three dimensions are related in a systematic way. In a second step, multivariate regression models are presented for both the adjusted family-policy clusters and the single members of each cluster. This approach allows for the investigation of whether the patterns of social polarization that emerged at the aggregate level (in the previous chapters) can be confirmed for all countries included in this study.

Before presenting the empirical results, the following section briefly describes the micro-level variables used in the analyses, coding decisions, and the hypotheses regarding expected social cleavages.

6.1 Independent variables and hypotheses

Based on the comparative welfare-state literature and institutional theory, this study argues that existing institutions have an impact on attitude formation and might generate not only different levels of support but also differences in the level and pattern of social polarization (see, e.g., Lewin-Epstein et al. 2000; Svallfors 2006; Esping-Andersen 1990; Korpi and Palme 1998; Svallfors 2007). This argument implies that the following analyses are likely to reveal country-specific differences among social groups. The hypotheses provided below, however, state in very general terms which group differences are expected based on the self-interest and the cultural approaches. Due to an assumed lack of quality and availability of existing services in most countries, it is hypothesized that those groups that are supportive of a strong role of the state for the provision of childcare services are also more critical regarding the current quality of these services as well as less skeptical regarding the perception of the negative side effects of social benefits and services.

In order to test if the theoretically expected differences among social groups can be confirmed empirically, country-specific multivariate regression models are conducted for the twelve countries (Section 6.3). The socio-economic and demographic variables capturing the distinct social groups were mostly coded as dummy variables. The following section presents these individual-level variables as well as the hypotheses regarding their effect on the three attitudinal dimensions. Both aspects have already been discussed in the theory chapter (Section 2.9) and are repeated here for convenience. Table 6.1 provides a brief summary of the individual-level variables; Table 6.2 summarizes the hypotheses.

Gender. Compared with men, women are expected to demand stronger state intervention in the field of family policy and to be less satisfied with existing childcare services as well as less skeptical toward the negative side effects of social benefits and services. From a self-interest perspective, it can be argued that women are more likely to be dependent on family policy and other welfare benefits and services (e.g., Svallfors 1997; Gelissen 2000). From the cultural perspective, it has been argued that women have different socialization experiences than men and are more likely to embrace a "rationality of caring" (Svallfors 1997; e.g., d'Anjou et al. 1995; Andreß and Heien 2001). In the multivariate models, females were coded as 1 and male respondents comprised the reference category.

The **family situation** indicates the past or actual need for family-policy measures and childcare services and is therefore a measure of self-interest. It is expected that all parents, especially those with young children, are more in favor of government responsibility for the provision of childcare services compared with individuals. Parents are furthermore expected to be less satisfied with the status quo as well as less skeptical toward unintended side effects. Four dummy variables are included to capture whether respondents have children (including step-, adopted-, foster-, and partner's children) as well as the age of the youngest child currently living in the household. Three age groups are distinguished, namely those of children below age three, children between three and six, and older children. Additionally, a dummy variable is included that indicates whether or not respondents ever had children living in the same household. The reference group is thus composed of respondents without children.[1]

With respect to **birth cohorts**, it is argued that members of the younger generations are more supportive of a strong role of the state as well as less satisfied and less skeptical compared with members of older generations due to a higher probability of being affected personally by family policies and the work-family conflict. Furthermore, the cultural approach suggests that younger age groups and the middle-aged are more likely to have internalized post-materialistic values, such as solidarity and social justice, and should therefore more strongly support government intervention compared with older birth cohorts (Inglehart 1977; Andreß and Heien 2001). Six different birth cohorts are distinguished. The oldest birth cohort (including respondents born before 1944) is the reference group, which is contrasted with the five remaining cohorts (see Table 6.1 for details).

Education. Both approaches (i.e., the self-interest and the cultural approach) suggest that more highly educated persons are more in favor of public support for families. More highly educated persons are furthermore expected to be less satisfied and less skeptical. In order to test these hypotheses, two dummy variables are included in the multivariate models, one representing tertiary education (ISCED 5-6) and the other upper and post-secondary education (ISCED 3-4). Both groups were compared with ISCED 0 to 2 (lower secondary education and below).

Household income. The economic situation of the household is a further indicator of self-interest, and lower-income groups are expected to be more in favor of a strong role of the state in the provision of childcare services as well as less satisfied and less skeptical. In order to capture respondents' income situations, a subjective income measure was used, namely the perception of the

1 An exception is Denmark: Due to a filter error, respondents who are not currently living with children were not asked if they had ever had children. Denmark's reference group is therefore composed of respondents without children or with older children who have already left their parents' household.

household's income situation. The question was formulated as follows: "Which of the descriptions on this card comes closest to how you feel about your household's income nowadays?" In the multivariate models, those who face difficulties (i.e., moderate or extreme difficulty living on present income) are contrasted with the reference group, which is composed of those respondents who face no difficulties (i.e., coping or living comfortably on present income).

The actual **employment status** is often used to control for current dependency on welfare benefits. On the one hand, it can be argued that the transfer classes (such as the unemployed or pensioners) might have a strong preference for state involvement in the different fields of welfare-state intervention. On the other hand, those working are more in need of family-policy benefits and services, such as employment protection or childcare services, especially if both partners are employed.[2] It can also be argued that those working are more aware of what it means to combine gainful employment and family life, even though they might not face this challenge personally. It is therefore expected that those currently working are more in favor of family-policy benefits and services, less satisfied with the status quo, and less skeptical compared with persons who are not involved in the labor market. In the models, those working are compared with those not working (including pensioners, the unemployed, those currently in education, and homemakers).

Public-sector employment. Both the self-interest approach and the cultural approach suggest that public-sector employees are more in favor of government intervention than employees in the private sector. From a self-interest perspective, public-sector employees have an interest in safeguarding their employment conditions (e.g., in terms of wages or job security); from a cultural perspective, this group shares a specific socialization experience involving solidarity with other public-sector employees as well as their clients or patients (e.g., Svallfors 1995, 1997; Hoel and Knutsen 1989; Müller 1998, 2000). Consequently, public-sector employees are expected to be more in favor of family polices, less satisfied with existing childcare services, and less critical concerning the unintended consequences of welfare-state intervention. The coding of the employment sector is based on the responses to the following question: "Which of the types of organization on this card do / did you work for?" The models contrast public-sector employees with the reference group, which is composed of private-firm employees, the self-employed, and others.

---

[2] Unfortunately, the employment status of the partner could not be included in the models due to data limitations. Since the labor-market participation of the household as a whole is a crucial indicator of actual childcare needs, this aspect should be taken into account in future studies.

Finally, the cultural approach is captured by including **gender-role attitudes** as well as **religiousness**. Traditional gender-role attitudes reinforce a strict division of paid and unpaid work between men and women in which routine household maintenance and childcare responsibilities are delegated to women (DeMaris et al. 2011; Voicu et al. 2009). Consequently, it is hypothesized that those who possess more traditional gender-role attitudes prefer the traditional male-breadwinner model of the family, whereas individuals with more egalitarian gender-role attitudes are more in favor of the dual-earner model of the family and therefore more supportive of policies promoting this model. Those holding egalitarian gender-role attitudes are furthermore expected to be less satisfied with existing services as well as less skeptical regarding negative side effects.

In order to assess gender-role attitudes, respondents were asked to give their opinion on the statement, "When jobs are scarce, men should have more right to a job than women." Responses covered a scale ranging from 1 (agree strongly) to 5 (disagree strongly) so that a higher value indicates more egalitarian attitudes. In the regression models, individuals with more egalitarian gender-role attitudes (i.e., those who disagree or disagree strongly with the statement) are compared with those who possess more traditional gender-role attitudes (i.e., the reference category). This item has the advantage that it captures normative beliefs toward both gender equality and female labor-market participation (Jensen 2009).

Regarding **religiousness**, it is argued that more-religious persons might regard public family policies as an infringement upon the private sphere of the family (Lewin-Epstein et al. 2000). Furthermore, it has been shown empirically that religiousness increases support for traditional gender-role attitudes (Bolzendahl and Myers 2004; Crompton et al. 2005). More-religious persons are therefore expected to be less in favor of the dual-earner model of the family as well as of government policies supporting this model. Simultaneously, it is hypothesized that more-religious persons are more satisfied with existing childcare services as well as more skeptical toward unintended side effects. In order to assess religiousness, a country-specific, standardized additive index was calculated from the following three items: "How religious are you?" "How often to you attend religious services apart from special occasions?" and "How often do you pray apart from at religious services?" These three items capture an overall religious tendency as well as activities through which religiousness may be expressed (see also Wolf 2005).

The main advantage of using an index instead of the responses to the individual questions is that information can be effectively summarized and different dimensions of a specific object are captured. Additionally, measurement problems on any particular item, such as those regarding the item formulation, disturb the results to a lesser degree.

Place of living. Respondents' place of living is included as a control variable. Previous research has not only shown variation within countries in the levels of childcare service provision across municipalities and regions (Melhuish and Moss 1991; OECD 2001) but also between rural and urban areas (OECD 2001: 57). As this study is interested in attitudes toward childcare services, diverging levels of service provision within countries might play an important role in explaining variation in public attitudes. Due to data limitations, differences across specific regions cannot be analyzed, but it is possible to examine differences between rural and urban areas. Respondents' place of living was measured based on responses to the question, "Which phrase on this card best describes the area where you live?" In the regression models, persons living in a big city as well as those living in a village or in the countryside are each contrasted with persons living in the suburbs of a big city or in a town or small city.

For Germany, the multivariate regression models additionally control for the interview location and distinguish between **East and West Germany** (West Germany is the reference category). Chapter 2 highlighted several important differences between the two parts of the country; both in terms of existing institutional arrangements and public opinion (see Section 2.9). Regarding institutional differences, childcare coverage rates are higher in the East, and childcare facilities operate mainly on a full-time basis (European Commission 2005; OECD 2006). With respect to attitudinal differences, several studies showed that East Germans are more in favor of a strong role of the state (Edeltraut Roller 2002; Lewin-Epstein et al. 2000; Mau 2003) and both public childcare and mothers' labor-market participation is much more accepted (Rosenfeld et al. 2004). Considering these differences, East German respondents are expected to be more in favor of government responsibility for the provision of childcare services, more satisfied with existing childcare services, and less critical regarding the negative side effects of government intervention compared with their West German counterparts.

Table 6.1: Summary of the individual-level characteristics

Indicator	Coding
Gender	Female Reference category: Male
Family situation	Youngest child in the household is below age 3 Youngest child in the household is between age 3 and 6 Older children living in the household (i.e., above age 6) Respondent has children (not living in the household) Reference category: Respondents without children
Birth cohort	Born between 1984 and 1994 Born between 1974 and 1983 Born between 1959 and 1973 Born between 1944 and 1958 Reference category: Respondents born before 1944
Education	Tertiary education (ISCED 5-6) Other upper and post-secondary education (ISCED 3-4) Reference category: ISCED 0 to 2 , i.e., lower secondary education and below
Income (subjective feeling)	Finding it (very) difficult on present income Reference category: Coping or living comfortably on present income
Labor-market status	Working Reference category: Not in the labor market (i.e., pensioners, the unemployed, students, and homemakers)
Public versus private sector	Public-sector employment (i.e., central or local government, other public sector, state-owned enterprise) Reference category: Private-firm employees, the self-employed, and others
Gender-role attitudes	Egalitarian gender-role attitudes (i.e., categories 4 and 5) Reference category: Traditional gender-role attitudes (i.e., categories 1 to 3)
Religiousness	Standardized, country-specific scale ranging from 0 to 1 (a higher value indicating stronger religiousness)
Place of living	Big city; Countryside / village (i.e., "A country village" or "A farm or home in the countryside") Reference category: Suburb / town (i.e., "The suburbs or outskirts of a big city" or "A town or a small city")
East versus West Germany	East Germany Reference category: West Germany

To sum up, the following attitudinal cleavages among the different social groups are expected: Families (especially those with young children), women, more highly educated persons, and lower-income groups should have a stronger self-interest in government intervention in the field of family policies, be less satisfied with existing childcare services and be less skeptical regarding the negative side effects of welfare-state intervention. Furthermore, public-sector employees and those currently working (in contrast to pensioners, the unemployed, students, and homemakers) are expected to be more supportive as well as less satisfied and less skeptical. Regarding the cultural approach, those who possess more egalitarian gender-role attitudes as well as less-religious persons are expected to be more supportive of government intervention, less satisfied with the status quo, and less skeptical toward negative side effects. Table 6.2 summarizes the hypotheses concerning attitudinal differences among social groups.

Table 6.2: Hypotheses regarding attitudinal differences among social groups

	Dimensions of attitudes		
Social groups	Responsibility	Satisfaction	Skepticism
Self-Interest			
Women vs. men	+	-	-
Families vs. individuals	+	-	-
Young birth cohorts versus older cohorts	+	-	-
High vs. low education level	+	-	-
Low vs. high income	+	-	-
Public vs. private sector	+	-	-
Working vs. not in the labor market	+	-	-
Normative beliefs			
Egalitarian gender-role attitudes	+	-	-
Religiousness	-	+	+
Control variables			
Place of living (city / town / countryside)			
East vs. West Germany (relevant only in DE)	+	+	-

Note: + indicates a positive effect, – a negative effect comparing the first group with the respective reference group. Reading example: Compared with individuals, families are expected to be more in favor of government responsibility (+), less satisfied with existing services (-), and less critical regarding negative side effects (-).

6.2 Correlations

Chapter 4 has shown that responsibility and skepticism are correlated to a statistically significant degree at the country level: The higher the level of skepticism in a country, the lower the demand for a strong role of the state in the provision of childcare services. This paragraph correlates the three attitudinal dimensions in order to investigate to what extent the three dimensions of attitudes are related at the individual level.

The results in Table 6.3 show that the macro-level relationship between the degree of skepticism and the demand for a strong role of the state is confirmed at the individual level in most countries. The only exceptions are the two pluralistic support countries of France and Belgium as well as the Netherlands.[3] In all other countries, those respondents who demand a strong role of the state are also less skeptical regarding the negative consequences of benefits and services.

In many countries, responsibility is also correlated with the level of satisfaction. In the countries belonging to the group of low support / Southern European countries (except Greece) and the group of low support / liberal countries, this association is negative, which implies that those who are demanding a strong role of the state are less satisfied with existing services. This corroborates the finding that the current level of government support for families is low in both groups of countries. Consequently, those who demand a strong role of the state are less satisfied with the status quo. In contrast, the association between responsibility and satisfaction is positive in the group of dual-earner support / Nordic countries (except in Denmark). The high level of government support for the dual-earner model of the family in these countries goes hand in hand with a high level of satisfaction with existing services among those respondents who regard the state as being responsible for the provision of childcare services.

Spain, finally, is the only country in which those respondents who are skeptic toward the negative consequences of benefits and services are also more satisfied with the status quo. In all other countries, the degree of skepticism is uncorrelated with the level of satisfaction with existing childcare services.

---

[3] Interestingly, France and Belgium are the only countries in which all three items are uncorrelated at the micro level.

Table 6.3: Correlations between responsibility, satisfaction, and skepticism (Pearson r, p-value in parentheses)

Country	Responsibility / Satisfaction	Responsibility / Skepticism	Satisfaction / Skepticism	N
General family support cluster				
DE	-0.042 (0.045)	**-0.104 (0.000)**	-0.016 (0.451)	2,302
Low support / Southern				
ES	**-0.117 (0.000)**	**-0.105 (0.000)**	**0.105 (0.000)**	1,802
GR	-0.072 (0.002)	**-0.225 (0.000)**	0.007 (0.755)	1,800
PT	**-0.148 (0.000)**	**-0.108 (0.000)**	0.005 (0.823)	1,695
Low support / Liberal countries				
UK	**-0.097 (0.000)**	**-0.144 (0.000)**	0.040 (0.081)	1,890
IE	**-0.126 (0.000)**	**-0.107 (0.000)**	0.053 (0.038)	1,523
NL	**-0.098 (0.000)**	-0.050 (0.060)	0.016 (0.548)	1,405
Pluralistic support cluster				
FR	0.053 (0.021)	-0.061 (0.009)	0.039 (0.088)	1,873
BE	-0.067 (0.010)	-0.052 (0.046)	0.010 (0.704)	1,501
Dual earner / Nordic countries				
SE	**0.104 (0.000)**	**-0.107 (0.000)**	-0.040 (0.128)	1,452
DK	-0.063 (0.019)	**-0.187 (0.000)**	0.036 (0.186)	1,384
FI	**0.093 (0.000)**	**-0.075 (0.001)**	-0.037 (0.102)	1,998

Note: Bold coefficients are significant at $p<=0.001$.

6.3 Cluster- and country-specific regression models

The following sections analyze the differences among social groups for each attitudinal dimension (i.e., responsibility, satisfaction, and skepticism). Each section provides the following three tables: 1) A table depicting the pooled regression models for the five adjusted family-policy clusters, 2) a table containing the pooled models and the twelve country-specific models, and 3) a table summarizing the hypotheses and the main findings.

The evaluation of extensity

The first item captures attitudes toward the goals of government intervention (or the evaluation of extensity) by asking how much responsibility governments should have in ensuring sufficient childcare services for working parents.

Table 6.4 shows the pooled regression models for the five adjusted family-policy clusters. The results show that the cleavage patterns are diverse among the five clusters and differ from the patterns found in the pooled models, which included all twelve countries (see Chapter 4). The most widespread patterns are the following: 1) In all country groups (except for the low support / Southern European countries), women are more in favor of a strong role of the state than men; and 2) egalitarian gender role attitudes coincide with a stronger preference for government responsibility in all country groups except for Germany.

The remaining patterns are only present in a few clusters. Younger birth cohorts are more in favor of government responsibility in Germany, in the low support / liberal countries, and in the low support / Southern European countries. These differences are less pronounced in the latter group of countries. In contrast, the youngest birth cohort is less in favor of a strong role of the state both in the pluralistic support cluster and in the dual-earner support / Nordic countries. Parents with small children (below age three or between age three and six) demand a higher level of state responsibly compared with childless respondents in three country clusters, namely in the low support / liberal countries, the pluralistic support cluster, and the dual-earner support / Nordic countries. Education matters only in the low support / liberal countries, where those with a higher level of education (i.e., with an upper secondary or tertiary degree) are less in favor of a strong role of the state compared with those who have a lower educational degree. A difficult income situation increases the demand for government intervention in the low support clusters (i.e., in the Southern European countries and the liberal countries). Public-sector employers demand a stronger role of the state in the low support / liberal countries and in the dual-earner support / Nordic countries. Religiosity, finally, is associated with a weaker preference for government responsibility in Germany and in the low support / Southern European countries and has a converse effect in the low support / liberal countries.

Table 6.4: Responsibility: Is it the governments' responsibility to provide childcare services? (Pooled OLS Regression models for the adjusted family-policy clusters)

	DE (general family support)	Low support/ Southern Europe	Low support/ liberal countries	Pluralistic support	Dual-earner support/ Nordic countries
Women (Ref.: Men)	0.22*	0.11+	0.20**	0.14*	0.34***
Birth cohorts (Ref.: Born before 1944)					
1984/1994	0.57**	-0.08	0.65***	-0.69***	-0.28**
1974/1983	0.66***	0.33**	0.73***	-0.19	0.02
1959/1973	0.53**	0.21*	0.35*	-0.27+	0.05
1944/1958	0.37**	0.03	0.17	-0.11	0.21*
Children (Ref.: No children)					
Children under age 3	0.32+	-0.02	0.40**	0.37*	0.22*
Children age 3 to 6	0.17	-0.16	0.36**	0.20	0.33**
Child (in hh)	0.14	0.24**	0.11	0.17	0.28***
Child (not in hh)	0.17	0.10	0.25*	0.05	0.24**
Education (Ref.: ISCED 0-2)					
ISCED 3:Upper secondary	0.19	0.05	-0.31**	-0.06	0.04
ISCED 5:Tertiary	0.10	0.10	-0.21**	-0.11	-0.01
Income Situation (Ref.: Comfort./coping)					
(Very) difficult	0.05	0.16**	0.46***	0.17+	0.04
Public sector (Ref.: Private)	0.17+	-0.13+	0.15*	0.05	0.14**
Working (Ref.: Not in the labor market)	-0.05	0.01	-0.06	0.13	0.03
Egalitarian GRA[1] (Ref.: Traditional GRA)	0.07	0.26***	0.33***	0.17*	0.34***
Religiosity (scale)	-0.12*	-0.09**	0.09*	-0.07	-0.05
Place of living (Ref.: Suburbs/town)					
Big city	0.31**	0.42***	0.00	-0.06	-0.13+
Countryside/village	0.06	0.11+	-0.11	-0.07	-0.02
East Germany	0.90***	-	-	-	-
Constant	6.82***	7.80***	5.98***	7.09***	7.32***
N	2302	5297	4818	3374	4834
adj. R^2	0.070	0.034	0.038	0.022	0.044

Note: Reference categories in brackets. [1] GRA = Gender role attitudes.
The number of observations in each country was standardized to 1,000 so that each country enters the pooled regressions with the same weight. Data weighted; robust standard errors. +p <= 0.10 *p <= 0.05 **p <= 0.01 ***p <= 0.001. Source: ESS 2008; own calculation.

In the next step, the results of the country-specific models are described (see Table 6.5). Overall, the results show that the patterns of social polarization are diverse among the twelve individual countries. The emerging patterns can thereby be only poorly structured by the adjusted family-policy clusters, i.e., the patterns found in the pooled cluster models (see above) are not confirmed for each of the countries belonging to a specific cluster. This finding confirms the necessity of conducting country-specific analyses in order to detect which patterns of social polarization are indeed universal and which of the patterns are cluster- or even country specific.

In accordance with the hypothesis, women are clearly more in favor of a strong role of the state in eight of the twelve countries; however, gender differences are not significant in Greece, the UK, Ireland, or France.

Regarding birth cohorts, it has been argued that younger respondents should be more in favor of a strong role of the state due to a higher probability of being personally affected by family policies and the work-family conflict (i.e., self-interest) as well as due to different value orientations in line with post-materialistic values, such as solidarity and social justice. The results provided here show that this hypothesis is not confirmed unequivocally for all the countries included. Polarization among birth cohorts is strongest in Germany and the UK. The hypothesized pattern thus emerges in these two countries. In the Nordic countries as well as in the Netherlands and Portugal, in contrast, no polarization among birth cohorts emerged. In the Nordic countries, this result can be explained by the long tradition of both working mothers and government support for the dual-earner model of the family.

Contrary to the hypotheses, the youngest respondents are even less in favor of a strong role of the state in three countries, namely Spain, France, and Belgium. Longitudinal data are needed in order to analyze the question of whether the described differences among birth cohorts are due to attitudinal differences in the life cycle or whether true cohort effects are present. Are the youngest respondents in Spain, France, and Belgium for instance "not yet" in favor of a strong role of the state or do these results indicate a trend toward a lower demand of state intervention among younger generations in these countries?

In several countries, respondents with children demand stronger state responsibility for the provision of childcare services than respondents without children. In the Netherlands and Finland, parents with children under the age of three as well as those with children between three and six years demand a stronger role of the state. In France, only parents with young children (under age three) significantly differ from the reference group, whereas parents in the UK with children between three and six are more demanding. In Portugal, Denmark, and Sweden, in contrast, only those parents with older children demand more government responsibility. These differences are potentially related to the level of the actual provision of childcare services for different age groups (and the organization of the pre-school system) as well as to country-specific care ideals regarding the best type of childcare for children in different age groups (Kremer 2007).

Contrary to the expectations, education has no effect on attitudes toward government responsibility in most countries. In four countries, however, a higher level of education reduces the demand for a strong role of the state. This negative effect of education is found in Portugal (the effect is only significant for ISCED 3), the UK (significant for ISCED 3 and ISCED 5), Belgium (only significant for ISCED 5), and Finland (only significant for ISCED 5). These results suggest that the more highly educated are better able to find a satisfying childcare solution either with government support (e.g., Finland) or without it (e.g., in the UK), whereas lesser-educated persons might be more dependent on public solutions. This finding corroborates earlier studies in the field of comparative welfare-state research, which have shown that a higher level of education is associated with a lower level of support for the welfare state (e.g., Jæger 2006b; Andreß and Heien 2001; Linos and West 2003; Jæger 2009; Arts and Gelissen 2001). These authors have argued that persons with a higher level of education have better labor-market opportunities and are therefore less likely to become dependent on welfare-state benefits. Consequently, this situation results in a lower level of support for the welfare state. However, this finding contradicts the results provided by Lewin-Epstein et al. (2000), who compared public attitudes toward family policy in Germany and Israel. The researchers found a higher level of support for family-policy measures among the more-highly educated groups.

The economic situation of the household plays a minor role almost everywhere. This result contradicts the argument that lower-income groups are particularly in need of public childcare services due to their lack of financial means to purchase private solutions. This situation was expected to result in a higher level of demand for a strong role of the state among the poor. Solely in two countries, namely in France and the UK, do poorer households demand stronger responsibility of the government in the provision of childcare services compared with more affluent households. In the UK, this result can be explained by the fact that the first public childcare services were introduced for the poor in order to support "at risk" children (Lewis et al. 2008b: 270; Del Boca et al. 2005). Moreover, family-policy benefits are mainly provided for poor families, in particular those classed as working poor (Fagnani and Math 2008). In accordance with the status quo, poorer households thus exhibit a stronger demand for government responsibility in the provision of childcare services in the UK.

Differences between public- and private-sector employees appear only in Finland and the Netherlands, where those working in the public sector are more in favor of government responsibility for the provision of childcare services.

The labor-market status has no effect on attitudes toward government responsibility except in Belgium, where those working are more in favor of government responsibility.

In half of the countries, egalitarian gender-role attitudes increase demand for a strong role of the state. This is the case in Spain, Portugal, the Netherlands, France, Finland, and Denmark.

Religiousness, in contrast, has a more ambiguous effect: More-religious persons are less in favor of a strong role of the state in Germany and Portugal, whereas this group demands more government intervention in the UK. In the remaining countries, religiousness has no significant effect.

Finally, the place of living matters in some of the countries, though again, the effect is far from uniform among these countries. In Belgium and Finland, those living in a big city are significantly less in favor of a strong role of the state, whereas this group in Germany and Greece demands more government responsibility compared with those living in the suburbs of a big city or in a town. In Spain, Greece, and Ireland, in turn, those living in the countryside demand stronger state intervention compared with the reference group. For Germany, the place of the interview has been additionally included. The results confirm that East Germans are indeed more supportive of a strong role of the state compared with West Germans.

Overall, the results support the idea that both self-interest (in terms of gender and the presence of children) and normative beliefs (i.e., gender-role attitudes) play a role in the formation of attitudes toward government responsibility for the provision of childcare services. However, it has also been confirmed that only a few group differences are virtually universal (e.g., differences between men and women or respondents with and without children), whereas most other polarization tendencies among social groups are country specific and can only be understood by taking the national particularities into account.

The previous chapters raised the question of whether the rejection of a strong role of the state, which was found in the group of low-support / liberal countries, is widespread among all respondents belonging to this cluster, or whether particular groups of the population would prefer a higher level of state intervention. The results described above show that the patterns of social polarization are diverse in this group of countries and not typical to the cluster as whole. Instead, several country-specific patterns emerge. Gender matters only in the Netherlands, where women show a stronger preference for government responsibility compared with men. The parents with young children (i.e., children under the age of three and between three and six) are significantly more supportive of a strong role of the state compared with respondents without children. Furthermore, respondents working in the public sector (compared with private-sector employees) and those with egalitarian gender-role attitudes (compared with respondents with traditional gender-role attitudes) are more in favor of government responsibility in the Netherlands. In the Dutch system, employers and unions play an important role in financing centre-based childcare (OECD 2002; Rostgaard 2002).[4] This situation might explain the stronger demand of government responsibility among those working for the government (i.e., in the public sector).

In Ireland, in contrast, the variables included in the model hardly matter, which indicates a high level of homogeneity in public opinion. The only exceptions are the following: Respondents born between 1974 and 1983 are more supportive compared with respondents born before 1944, and respondents living in the countryside prefer a stronger role of the state compared with respondents living in the suburbs of a city or in a small town.

In the UK, finally, the following patterns emerge: Most of the younger birth cohorts (i.e., respondents born after 1958) are more in favor of a strong role of the state compared with the oldest birth cohort. This pattern resembles the one found in Germany and suggests a trend toward a stronger demand of government intervention in the family-policy field among younger cohorts. With regard to children, parents with children between three and six as well as parents with older children (who are not living in the household) demand a higher level of state intervention. A higher level of education, in contrast, reduces the demand for state responsibility. Moreover, respondents who face a difficult income situation (compared with more affluent households) and more-religious persons are more in favor of a strong role of the state. The latter result contradicts the hypothesis, otherwise confirmed in the case of Germany and Portugal, that suggests a negative impact of religiosity. In all other countries, religiosity has no

---

4 This situation arose during a time in which employers faced labor shortages and (together with unions) addressed childcare needs to encourage women to remain at work, whereas the Dutch government was reluctant to be involved (OECD 2002).

significant impact at all. Table 6.6 summarizes the hypotheses as well as the patterns of social polarization in the individual countries.

Table 6.5: Responsibility. Country- and cluster-specific OLS Regression models

	DE (General family support)	Low support / Southern Europe	ES	GR	PT
Women (Ref.: Men)	0.22*	0.11^{+}	0.28**	-0.10	0.25*
Birth cohorts (Ref.: Born before 1944)					
1984/1994	0.57**	-0.08	-0.44*	-0.00	-0.28
1974/1983	0.66***	0.33**	0.01	0.48*	0.09
1959/1973	0.53**	0.21*	-0.03	0.34*	-0.06
1944/1958	0.37**	0.03	-0.09	0.12	-0.14
Children (Ref.: No children)					
Children under age 3	0.32^{+}	-0.02	0.23	-0.26	0.18
Children age 3 to 6	0.17	-0.16	-0.06	-0.18	-0.14
Child (in hh)	0.14	0.24**	0.06	0.11	0.27*
Child (not in hh)	0.17	0.10	-0.32^{+}	0.04	0.39**
Education (Ref.: ISCED 0-2)					
ISCED 3:Upper secondary	0.19	0.05	-0.07	-0.07	-0.39*
ISCED 5:Tertiary	0.10	0.10	-0.21^{+}	0.03	-0.32^{+}
Income Situation (Ref.: Comfort./coping)					
(Very) difficult	0.05	0.16**	0.12	-0.09	0.14
Public sector (Ref.: Private)	0.17^{+}	-0.13^{+}	0.12	-0.16	-0.15
Working (Ref.: Not in the labor market)	-0.05	0.01	-0.07	0.03	0.04
Egalitarian GRA[1] (Ref.: Traditional GRA)	0.07	0.26***	0.48***	0.16^{+}	0.90***
Religiosity (scale)	-0.12*	-0.09**	-0.09	-0.07	-0.19**
Place of living (Ref.: Suburbs/town)					
Big city	0.31**	0.42***	0.14	0.45***	0.02
Countryside/village	0.06	0.11^{+}	0.22*	0.32*	-0.20^{+}
East Germany	0.90***		-	-	-
Constant	6.82***	7.80***	7.86***	8.39***	7.44***
N	2302	5297	1802	1800	1695
adj. R^2	0.070	0.034	0.044	0.026	0.086

Table continued on next page.

Table 6.5 Responsibility (continued)

	Low support / liberal countries	UK	IE	NL
Women (Ref.: Men)	0.20**	0.07	0.19	0.36**
Birth cohorts (Ref.: Born before 1944)				
1984/1994	0.65***	1.12***	0.33	0.36
1974/1983	0.73***	1.07***	0.74**	0.23
1959/1973	0.35*	0.57*	0.46+	-0.03
1944/1958	0.17	0.27	0.28	-0.09
Children (Ref.: No children)				
Children under age 3	0.40**	0.09	0.29	0.92***
Children age 3 to 6	0.36**	0.46*	-0.03	0.73**
Child (in hh)	0.11	0.10	0.16	-0.03
Child (not in hh)	0.25*	0.32*	0.15	0.20
Education (Ref.: ISCED 0-2)				
ISCED 3:Upper secondary	-0.31**	-0.36*	-0.04	-0.22
ISCED 5:Tertiary	-0.21**	-0.28*	-0.22	-0.21
Income Situation (Ref.: Comfort./coping)				
(Very) difficult	0.46***	0.50***	0.31+	0.24
Public sector (Ref.: Private)	0.15*	0.18	0.06	0.25*
Working (Ref.: Not in the labor market)	-0.06	-0.08	-0.16	0.14
Egalitarian GRA[1] (Ref.: Traditional GRA)	0.33***	0.16	0.30+	0.64***
Religiosity (scale)	0.09*	0.17**	0.12	-0.04
Place of living (Ref.: Suburbs/town)				
Big city	0.00	0.03	0.28	0.15
Countryside/village	-0.11	-0.19	0.33**	-0.16
East Germany		-	-	-
Constant	5.98***	6.25***	5.92***	5.44***
N	4818	1890	1523	1405
adj. R^2	0.038	0.047	0.025	0.055

Table continued on next page.

Table 6.5 Responsibility (continued)

	Pluralistic support cluster	FR	BE
Women (Ref.: Men)	0.14*	-0.01	0.32***
Birth cohorts (Ref.: Born before 1944)			
1984/1994	-0.69***	-1.02***	-0.38*
1974/1983	-0.19	-0.38	-0.08
1959/1973	-0.27+	-0.33	-0.20
1944/1958	-0.11	-0.12	-0.08
Children (Ref.: No children)			
Children under age 3	0.37*	0.53**	0.31
Children age 3 to 6	0.20	0.27	0.19
Child (in hh)	0.17	0.08	0.23
Child (not in hh)	0.05	0.01	0.07
Education (Ref.: ISCED 0-2)			
ISCED 3:Upper secondary	-0.06	0.06	-0.19+
ISCED 5:Tertiary	-0.11	0.04	-0.31*
Income Situation (Ref.: Comfort./coping)			
(Very) difficult	0.17+	0.42**	-0.08
Public sector (Ref.: Private)	0.05	-0.08	0.14
Working (Ref.: Not in the labor market)	0.13	-0.02	0.27*
Egalitarian GRA[1] (Ref.: Traditional GRA)	0.17*	0.29*	0.08
Religiosity (scale)	-0.07	-0.08	-0.06
Place of living (Ref.: Suburbs/town)			
Big city	-0.06	0.10	-0.31*
Countryside/village	-0.07	-0.12	-0.17+
East Germany		-	-
Constant	7.09***	7.08***	7.23***
N	3374	1873	1501
adj. R^2	0.022	0.029	0.025

Table continued on next page.

Table 6.5 Responsibility (continued)

	Dual-earner Support / Nordic countries	FI	DK	SE
Women (Ref.: Men)	0.34***	0.27***	0.27**	0.46***
Birth cohorts (Ref.: Born before 1944)				
1984/1994	-0.28**	-0.32+	-0.32	-0.06
1974/1983	0.02	0.03	0.11	-0.01
1959/1973	0.05	0.06	0.21	-0.19
1944/1958	0.21*	0.17	0.38*	-0.11
Children (Ref.: No children)				
Children under age 3	0.22*	0.40**	0.12	0.08
Children age 3 to 6	0.33**	0.52***	0.15	0.32+
Child (in hh)	0.28***	0.16	0.34**	0.54**
Child (not in hh)	0.24**	0.20+		0.55**
Education (Ref.: ISCED 0-2)				
ISCED 3:Upper secondary	0.04	0.00	0.05	-0.08
ISCED 5:Tertiary	-0.01	-0.20*	0.10	-0.10
Income Situation (Ref.: Comfort./coping)				
(Very) difficult	0.04	-0.00	-0.07	0.21
Public sector (Ref.: Private)	0.14**	0.16*	0.16	0.07
Working (Ref.: Not in the labor market)	0.03	-0.04	0.14	0.21
Egalitarian GRA[1] (Ref.: Traditional GRA)	0.34***	0.40***	0.61**	0.16
Religiosity (scale)	-0.05	-0.05	-0.02	-0.05
Place of living (Ref.: Suburbs/town)				
Big city	-0.13+	-0.23*	0.01	-0.24
Countryside/village	-0.02	0.04	-0.09	-0.14
East Germany		-	-	-
Constant	7.32***	7.55***	6.95***	7.19***
N	4834	1998	1384	1452
adj. R^2	0.044	0.050	0.059	0.040

Note: Reference categories in brackets. [1] GRA = gender-role attitudes. Data weighted; robust standard errors. +p <= 0.10 *p <= 0.05 **p <= 0.01 ***p <= 0.001.
Source: ESS 2008; own calculation.

Table 6.6: Hypotheses and results regarding attitudinal differences among social groups: Responsibility

Social groups	Hypo-theses	Significant in the pooled model	Confirmed at the country level	Significant at country level / opposite direction	Not significant at the country level
Women vs. men	+	+	DE ES, PT NL BE FI, DK, SE		GR UK, IE FR
Parents vs. individuals	+	+	PT UK, NL FR FI, (DK, SE)		DE ES, GR IE BE
Young birth cohorts vs. older cohorts	+	+	DE GR UK, (IE)	ES (FR, BE)	PT NL FI, (DK), SE
High vs. low education level	+	-	PT (-) UK (-) BE (-) FI (-)		DE ES, GR IE, NL FR DK, SE
Low vs. high income	+	+	UK FR		DE ES, GR, PT IE, NL BE FI, DK, SE
Public vs. private sector	+	+	NL FI		DE ES, GR, PT UK, IE DK, SE

Table continued on next page.

Table 6.6: Responsibility. Hypotheses and results (continued)

Social groups	Hypo-theses	Significant in the pooled model	Confirmed at the country level	Significant at country level / opposite direction	Not significant at the country level
Those working vs. those not in the labor market	+	n.s.	BE (+)		DE ES, GR, PT UK, IE, NL FR FI, DK, SE
Egalitarian gender-role attitudes	+	+	ES, PT NL FR FI, DK		DE GR UK, IE BE SE
Religiousness	-	-	DE PT	UK	ES, GR IE, NL FR, BE FI, DK, SE
Place of living (big city / town (Ref.) / countryside)			Big city (+) DE GR Big city (-) BE FI Countryside (+) ES, GR IE		PT UK, NL FR DK, SE
East vs. West Germany (relevant only in DE)	+	n.a.	DE		

Note: + indicates a positive effect, – a negative effect comparing the first group with the respective reference group. Reading example: Compared with individuals, families are expected to be more in favor of government responsibility (+), less satisfied with existing services (-), and less critical regarding negative side effects (-).

The evaluation of means

The second item ("What do you think about the provision of affordable child care services for working parents?") captures the level of satisfaction with a specific family-policy institution (i.e., evaluation of means).

Table 6.7 depicts the cluster-specific models. Religiosity is associated with a higher level of satisfaction with existing childcare services in all five clusters, and those who face a difficult income situation are less satisfied (except for the pluralistic support cluster). With regard to education, a higher level of education is associated with a lower level of satisfaction in a majority of clusters. However, in the dual-earner support / Nordic countries, those with a tertiary education are more satisfied. Education has no significant effect in the general family support cluster (i.e., Germany). Other patterns of social polarization are again cluster specific or significant in a few clusters only. Compared with men, women are less satisfied in the two low support clusters and in the pluralistic support cluster. Parents with children under age three are less satisfied than childless respondents in Germany and in the dual-earner support / Nordic countries, and those with egalitarian gender-role attitudes are less satisfied in the low support / Southern European countries.

Table 6.7: Satisfaction with the provision of affordable child care services (Pooled OLS Regression models for the adjusted family-policy clusters)

	DE (general family support)	Low support / Southern Europe	Low support / liberal countries	Pluralistic support	Dual-earner support / Nordic countries
Women (Ref.: Men)	-0.08	-0.25***	-0.18**	-0.26**	0.03
Birth cohorts (Ref.: Born before 1944)					
1984/1994	0.71***	0.62***	0.26^{+}	0.05	0.39***
1974/1983	0.03	0.06	-0.03	-0.51**	0.05
1959/1973	0.02	-0.05	-0.12	-0.25	0.07
1944/1958	-0.05	-0.23*	-0.03	0.04	-0.17^{+}
Children (Ref.: No children)					
Children under age 3	-0.56*	-0.24	-0.16	-0.16	-0.39**
Children age 3 to 6	-0.14	0.07	-0.10	-0.24	0.25^{+}
Child (in hh)	0.30*	-0.04	-0.19^{+}	-0.05	0.51***
Child (not in hh)	0.21	-0.18	-0.18*	-0.19	0.99***
Education (Ref.: ISCED 0-2)					
ISCED 3:Upper secondary	-0.15	-0.09	0.15^{+}	-0.27**	0.10
ISCED 5:Tertiary	-0.18	-0.36***	-0.37***	-0.34**	0.51***
Income Situation (Ref.: Comfort./coping)					
(Very) difficult	-0.28*	-0.51***	-0.52***	-0.17	-0.30**
Public sector (Ref.: Private)	0.11	0.04	-0.02	-0.00	-0.04
Working (Ref.: Not in the labor market)	-0.06	-0.03	0.01	-0.00	-0.00
Egalitarian GRA (Ref.: Traditional GRA)	-0.08	-0.46***	-0.12	-0.16^{+}	0.12
Religiosity (scale)	0.34***	0.32***	0.19***	0.16**	0.20***
Place of living (Ref.: Suburbs/town)					
Big city	-0.01	0.34***	0.30**	-0.19	0.05
Countryside/village	-0.07	0.16^{+}	0.21**	0.15^{+}	-0.13*
East Germany	0.65***				
Constant	4.26***	4.78***	5.17***	5.65***	5.47***
N	2302	5297	4818	3374	4834
adj. R^2	0.037	0.050	0.042	0.029	0.053

Note: Reference categories in brackets. [1] GRA = Gender role attitudes.
The number of observations in each country was standardized to 1,000 so that each country enters the pooled regressions with the same weight. Data weighted; robust standard errors. +p <= 0.10 *p <= 0.05 **p <= 0.01 ***p <= 0.001.
Source: ESS 2008; own calculation.

Table 6.8 depicts the country-specific models, which again reveal distinct patterns of social polarization among the twelve individual countries. However, two variables have a universal impact in almost all countries. The first is religiousness, the second is income.

More-religious respondents are more satisfied everywhere except in France. It has been argued that religiousness promotes a traditional gendered division of labor with respect to childcare, meaning that the mother is regarded as being responsible for the provision of care (e.g., DeMaris et al. 2011). These beliefs can result in a low level of actual service usage among more-religious persons and in the view of facilities as being only a supplementary option not frequently needed. Moreover, the Church as well as confessional parties has played a major role in the development of different family policies in many countries (Bahle 1995; Kremer 2007; Pfau-Effinger 2005b; Strohmeier 2002; Bahle 2003, 2008a; Korpi 2000). In some countries, these groups served as important political actors that advocated social norms, values, and policies promoting the maintenance of the traditional family model. It can be argued that this (ideological) impact is mirrored in the actual institutional design of existing childcare facilities and that this design is rather consistent with the (ideological) preferences of more-religious persons. Moreover, religious institutions in many countries offer childcare services, which potentially meet the preferences of their members. These factors could explain the higher level of satisfaction with existing childcare services among more-religious persons despite rather rudimentary childcare facilities in some countries. However, they hardly explain why more-religious persons are also more satisfied in the three countries belonging to the group of dual-earner support / Nordic countries.

The economic situation of the household also has a clear impact on attitudes almost everywhere. In nine of the twelve countries, poorer households are less satisfied with existing services compared with wealthier households. The exceptions are the UK, France, and Sweden. These differences among income groups might be due to the fact that the wording of the question explicitly denotes the affordability of childcare services. Nevertheless, the findings corroborate the argument that childcare fees are an important issue and that (high quality) childcare might not be affordable for low-income groups in many countries.

Moreover, education has an impact in seven countries – though the effects are converse. In Finland, Denmark, and Sweden, the more highly educated groups are more satisfied with existing services compared with the lesser-educated groups. In Spain, Portugal, the UK, and Belgium, in contrast, more-highly educated persons are less satisfied with the status quo. This finding indicates that existing childcare facilities serve the preferences of the more highly educated groups in the Scandinavian countries, whereas facilities in the other four countries are insufficient to meet the needs of this group. Due to these converse effects, education had no significant effect on the level of satisfaction in the pooled models in the previous chapters (4 and 5).

With regard to birth cohorts, no unequivocal patterns emerge. In a few countries, namely Germany, Greece, Ireland, and Denmark, the youngest birth cohort (those born between 1984 and 1994) is significantly more satisfied with existing services compared with the oldest cohort (those born before 1944). In contrast, the youngest birth cohort is less satisfied in Sweden. Moreover, the second-oldest birth cohort (those born between 1944 and 1958) is significantly less satisfied in Spain, Portugal, and Denmark, and birth cohorts make no difference at all in the UK, the Netherlands, and Finland.

For the evaluation of childcare services, the remaining variables seem to make no difference, yet there are several exceptions in single countries. The presence of children, e.g., has an impact in a few countries. In Germany and Finland, parents with very young children in the household (i.e., below age three) are particularly dissatisfied. In contrast, German parents with older children in the household are significantly more satisfied compared with respondents without children. In Ireland, those respondents with older children who have already left their parents' households are less satisfied with childcare services.

Gender-role attitudes matter in four countries. In Spain, Greece, and Ireland, those with egalitarian gender-role attitudes are less satisfied than respondents with traditional gender-role attitudes. In Finland, the opposite effect arises. Here, respondents with egalitarian gender-role attitudes are more satisfied.

Furthermore, men and women hardly differ in their evaluation of existing services; however, in three countries, namely the UK, Ireland, and Belgium, women are significantly less satisfied than man. Neither the employment sector nor the labor-market status has a significant effect on satisfaction.

Finally, the place of living impacts satisfaction with existing childcare services in three countries. In Greece, two groups, namely those living in a big city and those living in the countryside or a village, are more satisfied with existing childcare services compared with persons living in the suburbs of a big city or in a town. In Belgium, those living in the countryside or a village are more satisfied as well. In Finland, in turn, this group is less satisfied compared with respondents living in the suburbs of a big city or in a town.

In the German case, East German respondents are more satisfied with existing childcare services compared with West Germans, which is in line with the expectations.

Overall, the expectations have been confirmed with regard to the income situation and religiousness. Poorer households are less satisfied in almost all countries (except in the UK, France, and Sweden), and more-religious respondents are more satisfied in all countries except for France. Both self-interest (income) and normative beliefs (religiousness) thus play a role in the evaluation of existing services. However, results are far from universal, and several differences among social groups are country specific or even have obverse effects in different countries. The gender effect, e.g., is confirmed in the UK, Ireland, and Belgium only; and the presence of young children (below age three) decreases satisfaction in Germany and Finland but not in the other countries.

Egalitarian gender-role attitudes, in turn, have a positive effect in Finland but reduce satisfaction in Spain, Greece, and Ireland. Moreover, a tertiary education increases satisfaction in Denmark, Finland, and Sweden, but decreases satisfaction in Spain, Portugal, the UK, and Belgium. Assuming a stronger labor-market attachment of the more highly educated groups combined with a preference to be able to combine family life with gainful employment in both groups of countries, these results show that existing childcare services better serve the more highly educated groups in the Nordic countries, where comprehensive childcare services exist, whereas the situation is difficult for these groups in Spain, Portugal, the UK, and Belgium.

These findings corroborate the idea that attitudinal differences across social groups are country specific and related to country-specific characteristics of the welfare program in question. This observation might be especially relevant when examining the public's evaluation of means (such as existing childcare services). Attitudinal patterns cannot be exclusively explained with reference to either self-interest or normative beliefs but have to be understood in the broader context of the institutional design, expectations, and experiences as well as other country-specific particularities. Table 6.8 depicts the country-specific regression models; Table 6.9 provides a brief summary of the hypotheses and results.

Table 6.8: Satisfaction. Country- and cluster-specific OLS Regression models

	DE (General family support)	Low support / Southern Europe	ES	GR	PT
Women (Ref.: Men)	-0.08	-0.25***	-0.24+	-0.21	-0.23+
Birth cohorts (Ref.: Born before 1944)					
1984/1994	0.71***	0.62***	0.19	1.17***	0.37
1974/1983	0.03	0.06	-0.40	0.45+	-0.09
1959/1973	0.02	-0.05	-0.32	0.17	-0.06
1944/1958	-0.05	-0.23*	-0.63**	0.21	-0.35*
Children (Ref.: No children)					
Children under age 3	-0.56*	-0.24	-0.31	-0.14	-0.19
Children age 3 to 6	-0.14	0.07	-0.13	0.34	-0.18
Child (in hh)	0.30*	-0.04	-0.29	0.22	-0.21
Child (not in hh)	0.21	-0.18	-0.43+	0.00	-0.26
Education (Ref.: ISCED 0-2)					
ISCED 3:Upper secondary	-0.15	-0.09	-0.32*	-0.02	-0.22
ISCED 5:Tertiary	-0.18	-0.36***	-0.49**	-0.30	-0.38*
Income Situation (Ref.: Comfort./coping)					
(Very) difficult	-0.28*	-0.51***	-0.64***	-0.44***	-0.41***
Public sector (Ref.: Private)	0.11	0.04	0.04	-0.08	0.24
Working (Ref.: Not in the labor market)	-0.06	-0.03	-0.16	-0.03	0.19
Egalitarian GRA[1] (Ref.: Traditional GRA)	-0.08	-0.46***	-0.41**	-0.69***	-0.21+
Religiosity (scale)	0.34***	0.32***	0.34***	0.36***	0.18*
Place of living (Ref.: Suburbs/town)					
Big city	-0.01	0.34***	0.28+	0.66***	-0.09
Countryside/village	-0.07	0.16+	-0.05	0.55**	0.07
East Germany	0.65***		-	-	-
Constant	4.26***	4.78***	5.65***	4.01***	4.62***
N	2302	5297	1802	1800	1695
adj. R^2	0.037	0.050	0.064	0.069	0.028

Table continued on next page.

Table 6.8: Satisfaction (continued)

	Low support / liberal countries	UK	IE	NL
Women (Ref.: Men)	-0.18**	-0.26*	-0.29*	0.01
Birth cohorts (Ref.: Born before 1944)				
1984/1994	0.26+	0.32	0.58*	0.13
1974/1983	-0.03	0.08	0.25	-0.16
1959/1973	-0.12	-0.28	-0.08	-0.06
1944/1958	-0.03	-0.19	0.04	0.06
Children (Ref.: No children)				
Children under age 3	-0.16	-0.36	-0.32	-0.03
Children age 3 to 6	-0.10	-0.26	-0.39	-0.03
Child (in hh)	-0.19+	-0.12	-0.26+	0.07
Child (not in hh)	-0.18*	-0.14	-0.40*	-0.06
Education (Ref.: ISCED 0-2)				
ISCED 3:Upper secondary	0.15+	-0.11	0.07	0.02
ISCED 5:Tertiary	-0.37***	-0.36**	-0.12	-0.12
Income Situation (Ref.: Comfort./coping)				
(Very) difficult	-0.52***	-0.15	-0.35*	-0.54*
Public sector (Ref.: Private)	-0.02	-0.02	-0.19	-0.12
Working (Ref.: Not in the labor market)	0.01	0.05	-0.17	-0.12
Egalitarian GRA[1] (Ref.: Traditional GRA)	-0.12	-0.18	-0.29*	0.04
Religiosity (scale)	0.19***	0.18**	0.26***	0.16*
Place of living (Ref.: Suburbs/town)				
Big city	0.30**	0.03	0.05	-0.08
Countryside/village	0.21**	0.08	0.09	0.21+
East Germany		-	-	-
Constant	5.17***	5.13***	4.96***	5.60***
N	4818	1890	1523	1405
adj. R^2	0.042	0.031	0.052	0.012

Table continued on next page.

Table 6.8 Satisfaction (continued)

	Pluralistic support cluster	FR	BE
Women (Ref.: Men)	-0.26**	-0.19	-0.35**
Birth cohorts (Ref.: Born before 1944)			
1984/1994	0.05	-0.18	0.27
1974/1983	-0.51**	-0.80**	-0.21
1959/1973	-0.25	-0.45+	-0.05
1944/1958	0.04	-0.08	0.17
Children (Ref.: No children)			
Children under age 3	-0.16	0.03	-0.39
Children age 3 to 6	-0.24	-0.16	-0.33
Child (in hh)	-0.05	0.07	-0.19
Child (not in hh)	-0.19	-0.23	-0.16
Education (Ref.: ISCED 0-2)			
ISCED 3:Upper secondary	-0.27**	-0.22	-0.28*
ISCED 5:Tertiary	-0.34**	-0.27	-0.39*
Income Situation (Ref.: Comfort./coping)			
(Very) difficult	-0.17	0.05	-0.31*
Public sector (Ref.: Private)	-0.00	-0.19	0.19
Working (Ref.: Not in the labor market)	-0.00	0.07	-0.11
Egalitarian GRA[1] (Ref.: Traditional GRA)	-0.16+	-0.21	-0.13
Religiosity (scale)	0.16**	0.07	0.25***
Place of living (Ref.: Suburbs/town)			
Big city	-0.19	-0.20	-0.18
Countryside/village	0.15+	-0.01	0.29*
East Germany		-	-
Constant	5.65***	5.76***	5.55***
N	3374	1873	1501
adj. R2	0.029	0.016	0.050

Table continued on next page.

Table 6.8 Satisfaction (continued)

	Dual-earner support / Nordic countries	FI	DK	SE
Women (Ref.: Men)	0.03	0.13	0.03	0.03
Birth cohorts (Ref.: Born before 1944)				
1984/1994	0.39***	0.04	0.46*	-0.66**
1974/1983	0.05	-0.34+	-0.39	-0.32
1959/1973	0.07	-0.13	-0.43+	0.19
1944/1958	-0.17+	0.02	-0.80***	0.29
Children (Ref.: No children)				
Children under age 3	-0.39**	-0.72***	-0.11	0.08
Children age 3 to 6	0.25+	-0.02	0.49+	0.43+
Child (in hh)	0.51***	0.21	0.04	0.33+
Child (not in hh)	0.99***	0.08		0.21
Education (Ref.: ISCED 0-2)				
ISCED 3:Upper secondary	0.10	0.20*	0.27	0.22+
ISCED 5:Tertiary	0.51***	0.67***	0.62***	0.77***
Income Situation (Ref.: Comfort./coping)				
(Very) difficult	-0.30**	-0.66***	-0.62*	-0.02
Public sector (Ref.: Private)	-0.04	-0.07	-0.18	0.19+
Working (Ref.: Not in the labor market)	-0.00	-0.09	0.15	-0.21
Egalitarian GRA[1] (Ref.: Traditional GRA)	0.12	0.33**	0.32	0.05
Religiosity (scale)	0.20***	0.20***	0.23**	0.17**
Place of living (Ref.: Suburbs/town)				
Big city	0.05	0.05	-0.27	0.04
Countryside/village	-0.13*	-0.19*	-0.12	-0.20+
East Germany		-	-	-
Constant	5.47***	6.19***	5.18***	5.96***
N	4834	1998	1384	1452
adj. R2	0.053	0.065	0.037	0.101

Note: Reference categories in brackets. [1] GRA = gender-role attitudes. Data weighted; robust standard errors. +p <= 0.10 *p <= 0.05 **p <= 0.01 ***p <= 0.001. Source: ESS 2008; own calculation.

Table 6.9: Hypotheses and results regarding attitudinal differences among social groups: Satisfaction

Social groups	Hypotheses	Significant in the pooled model	Confirmed at the country level	Significant at the country level / opposite direction	Not significant at the country level
Women vs. men	-	-	UK, IE BE		DE ES, GR, PT NL FR FI, DK, SE
Parents vs. individuals	-	-	Child < 3 (-) DE FI Child >6 (+) DE Not in hh (-) IE		ES, GR, PT BE, FR DK, SE UK, NL
Young birth cohorts vs. older cohorts	-	-	1984/1994 vs. oldest cohort (-) SE 1944/1958 vs. oldest (-) ES, PT DK 1974/1983 vs. oldest (-) FR	1984/1994 vs. oldest (+) DE GR IE DK	UK, NL FI
High vs. low education level	-	n.s.	ES, PT UK BE	FI, DK, SE (+)	DE GR IE, NL FR

Table continued on next page.

Table 6.9: Satisfaction. Hypotheses and results (continued)

Social groups	Hypotheses	Significant in the pooled model	Confirmed at the country level	Significant at country level / opposite direction	Not significant at the country level
Low vs. high income	-	-	DE ES, GR, PT IE, NL BE FI, DK		UK FR SE
Public vs. private sector	-	n.s.			n.s. in any country
Working vs. not in the labor market	-	n.s.			n.s. in any country
Egalitarian gender-role attitudes	-	-	ES, GR IE	FI (+)	DE PT UK, NL FR, BE DK, SE
Religiousness	+	+	DE ES, GR, PT UK, IE, NL BE FI, DK, SE		FR
Place of living (big city / town (Ref.) / countryside)			Big city (+) GR Countryside (+) GR, BE Countryside (-) FI		DE ES, PT UK, IE, NL DK, SE
East vs. West Germany (relevant only in DE)	+	n.a.	DE (+)		

Note: + indicates a positive effect, – a negative effect comparing the first group with the respective reference group. Reading example: Compared with individuals, families are expected to be more in favor of government responsibility (+), less satisfied with existing services (-), and less critical regarding negative side effects (-).

The evaluation of unintended consequences

The third item ("Social benefits and services make people less willing to look after themselves and their family") analyzes attitudes toward the unintended consequences of government intervention and captures the public's perception of the unintended negative side-effects of welfare-state benefits and services.

Table 6.10 shows the pooled models for the five adjusted family-policy clusters. In all five clusters, those with egalitarian gender-role attitudes are less skeptical and religiosity is associated with an increase in skepticism (except for the pluralistic support cluster). Moreover, younger birth cohorts are less skeptical in most clusters compared with the oldest birth cohort, except for the general family support cluster (i.e., Germany). The more highly educated groups are less skeptical in three clusters, namely in the low support / Southern European countries, the pluralistic support cluster, and the dual-earner support / Nordic countries. The remaining variables only have an impact in individual clusters. Public-sector employees are less skeptical in the pluralistic support cluster and in the dual-earner support / Nordic countries, and those currently working are more skeptical in the low support / liberal countries and in the dual-earner support / Nordic countries.

Table 6.10: Skepticism: Benefits and services make people less willing to look after their families (Pooled OLS Regression models for the adjusted family-policy clusters)

	DE (general family support)	Low support / Southern Europe	Low support / liberal countries	Pluralistic support	Dual-earner support / Nordic countries
Women (Ref.: Men)	-0.03	0.03	0.06^{+}	0.03	-0.02
Birth cohorts (Ref.: Born before 1944)					
1984/1994	-0.16	-0.09	-0.23**	-0.29**	-0.33***
1974/1983	-0.01	-0.20**	-0.11	-0.28**	-0.34***
1959/1973	-0.02	-0.17**	-0.25***	-0.24**	-0.29***
1944/1958	-0.01	-0.11*	-0.12*	-0.18**	-0.25***
Children (Ref.: No children)					
Children under age 3	-0.01	0.01	0.09	0.00	0.08
Children age 3 to 6	-0.11	-0.01	0.05	-0.07	0.08
Child (in hh)	-0.04	-0.09^{+}	-0.02	0.10	-0.10*
Child (not in hh)	0.02	-0.04	0.05	0.18**	-0.10*
Education (Ref.: ISCED 0-2)					
ISCED 3:Upper secondary	-0.10	-0.15***	-0.11*	-0.01	-0.04
ISCED 5:Tertiary	-0.14^{+}	-0.29***	-0.07^{+}	-0.17**	-0.16***
Income Situation (Ref.: Comfort./coping)					
(Very) difficult	0.02	0.03	0.00	0.04	0.02
Public sector (Ref.: Private)	-0.08	0.05	-0.04	-0.13**	-0.06*
Working (Ref.: Not in the labor market)	-0.03	0.05	0.11**	0.06	0.17***
Egalitarian GRA[1] (Ref.: Traditional GRA)	-0.25***	-0.13***	-0.22***	-0.20***	-0.28***
Religiosity (scale)	0.06*	0.05*	0.07**	0.01	0.09***
Place of living (Ref.: Suburbs/town)					
Big city	-0.17**	-0.18***	-0.18***	-0.16*	-0.01
Countryside/village	-0.12*	0.02	-0.07^{+}	-0.15***	0.01
East Germany	-0.15**				
Constant	3.41***	2.96***	3.36***	3.56***	3.25***
N	2302	5297	4818	3374	4834
adj. R^2	0.036	0.038	0.031	0.038	0.032

Note: Reference categories in brackets. [1] GRA = Gender role attitudes.
The number of observations in each country was standardized to 1,000 so that each country enters the pooled regressions with the same weight. Data weighted; robust standard errors. +p <= 0.10 *p <= 0.05 **p <= 0.01 ***p <= 0.001.
Source: ESS 2008; own calculation.

Several patterns emerge regarding the degree of skepticism toward welfare-state interventions at the country level. Many patterns are again country specific, and the cleavages found in the pooled, cluster-specific models are not universally confirmed at the country level.

A common result is that there are no differences between men and women, except in Denmark, where women are less skeptical about the consequences of social benefits and services than men. Moreover, gender-role attitudes matter in almost all countries except in the Netherlands and Denmark. Individuals with more egalitarian gender-role attitudes are less skeptical regarding unintended consequences. Religiousness has the opposite effect: More-religious persons are more skeptical in six countries (i.e., Germany, Greece, Ireland, as well as the three Nordic countries of Finland, Denmark, and Sweden).

Birth cohorts also matter in several countries. Compared with the oldest birth cohort (those born before 1944), younger cohorts are less skeptical in the UK, France, Belgium, Finland, and Denmark. In Greece, only those born between 1974 and 1983 differ from the reference group. These finding suggests a trend toward a lower level of skepticism among younger birth cohorts. However, as pointed out above, longitudinal data is needed in order to verify this assumption.

The presence of children, in turn, makes no difference, except in Greece, the Netherlands, and Finland, where those who have older children are less skeptical compared with childless respondents. In contrast, Finnish parents with young children (below age three) are more skeptical toward unintended side effect.

In most countries, the level of education has no striking effect, though in a few countries, those with tertiary education are less pessimistic about the effects of social benefits (this is in line with the hypothesis). This is the case in Greece, France, Finland, and Denmark.

Regarding income, more pessimism emerges among the poorer households in Greece and Belgium, a result that is contrary to the expectations. In all other countries, the income situation has no impact on skepticism.

Public-sector employment matters in three countries only, though with diverging tendencies. In the UK and France, public-sector employment reduces pessimism, whereas it increases pessimism in Ireland.

Moreover, in three countries, i.e., the UK, Finland, and Sweden, those currently working are more critical compared with those not in the labor market.

The place of living, finally, makes a difference in several countries. In three countries (Germany, Greece, and France), those living in a big city are less skeptical compared with those living in the suburbs or in a town. Furthermore, in Germany and Spain, living in the countryside reduces skepticism. In contrast, in

Portugal, people living in the suburbs or a town are significantly less skeptical compared with people living in a big city or in the countryside. In Germany, the expected difference between East and West Germany can again be affirmed. Compared with West German respondents, those living in the East are significantly less critical toward public benefits and services.

Overall, most of the variables indicating self-interest have no or only a marginal effect regarding the public's evaluation of unintended consequences. Gender has an impact only in Denmark; the presence of children matters only in Greece, the Netherlands, and Finland; and income matters only in Greece and Belgium. In contrast, egalitarian gender-role attitudes and religiousness, both measuring normative beliefs, have an impact in many countries. Respondents with egalitarian gender-role attitudes are less skeptical in ten countries (all except the Netherlands and Denmark), and more-religious persons are more skeptical in six countries (namely Germany, Greece, Ireland, Finland, Denmark, and Sweden). These results suggest that the cultural approach is salient regarding attitudes toward the unintended side effects of welfare policies. This argument is corroborated by several results. Younger birth cohorts, e.g., are less skeptical in the UK, France, Belgium, Finland, and Denmark; and those with tertiary education are less pessimistic in Greece, France, Finland, and Denmark.

The survey question used to capture skepticism toward government intervention refers to social benefits and services in very general terms and addresses neither family policies nor a specific group of beneficiaries (e.g., working parents or children) exclusively. This fact potentially weakens the salience of self-interest and highlights normative beliefs.

Table 6.11: Skepticism. Country- and cluster-specific OLS Regression models

	DE (General family support)	Low support / Southern Europe	ES	GR	PT
Women (Ref.: Men)	-0.03	0.03	0.04	0.01	0.01
Birth cohorts (Ref.: Born before 1944)					
1984/1994	-0.16	-0.09	-0.18	-0.07	0.07
1974/1983	-0.01	-0.20**	-0.25+	-0.24*	0.03
1959/1973	-0.02	-0.17**	-0.23+	-0.13	0.01
1944/1958	-0.01	-0.11*	-0.18+	-0.11	0.03
Children (Ref.: No children)					
Children under age 3	-0.01	0.01	-0.08	0.15	-0.03
Children age 3 to 6	-0.11	-0.01	-0.03	0.07	-0.10
Child (in hh)	-0.04	-0.09+	0.00	-0.23**	0.05
Child (not in hh)	0.02	-0.04	0.09	-0.23*	0.02
Education (Ref.: ISCED 0-2)					
ISCED 3:Upper secondary	-0.10	-0.15***	-0.03	-0.02	-0.02
ISCED 5:Tertiary	-0.14+	-0.29***	-0.09	-0.21*	-0.14
Income Situation (Ref.: Comfort./coping)					
(Very) difficult	0.02	0.03	-0.05	0.17**	-0.03
Public sector (Ref.: Private)	-0.08	0.05	-0.07	0.04	0.02
Working (Ref.: Not in the labor market)	-0.03	0.05	0.05	0.06	0.02
Egalitarian GRA[1] (Ref.: Traditional GRA)	-0.25***	-0.13***	-0.16*	-0.21***	-0.28***
Religiosity (scale)	0.06*	0.05*	0.03	0.08*	0.06
Place of living (Ref.: Suburbs/town)					
Big city	-0.17**	-0.18***	-0.01	-0.26***	0.15*
Countryside/village	-0.12*	0.02	-0.12*	-0.01	0.28***
East Germany	-0.15**	-	-	-	-
Constant	3.41***	2.96***	2.91***	2.81***	2.94***
N	2302	5297	1802	1800	1695
adj. R^2	0.036	0.038	0.019	0.053	0.037

Table continued on next page.

Table 6.11: Skepticism (continued)

	Low support / liberal countries	UK	IE	NL
Women (Ref.: Men)	0.06^{+}	0.00	0.07	0.05
Birth cohorts (Ref.: Born before 1944)				
1984/1994	-0.23**	-0.52***	-0.07	-0.18
1974/1983	-0.11	-0.33**	-0.04	0.10
1959/1973	-0.25***	-0.48***	-0.23^{+}	0.02
1944/1958	-0.12*	-0.24**	0.03	-0.04
Children (Ref.: No children)				
Children under age 3	0.09	0.01	0.04	0.17
Children age 3 to 6	0.05	-0.03	0.14	0.02
Child (in hh)	-0.02	0.12	0.01	-0.20*
Child (not in hh)	0.05	0.01	-0.01	0.00
Education (Ref.: ISCED 0-2)				
ISCED 3:Upper secondary	-0.11*	0.00	-0.10	0.00
ISCED 5:Tertiary	-0.07^{+}	-0.07	-0.09	-0.11
Income Situation (Ref.: Comfort./coping)				
(Very) difficult	0.00	-0.06	-0.12	0.18^{+}
Public sector (Ref.: Private)	-0.04	-0.11*	0.15*	-0.10^{+}
Working (Ref.: Not in the labor market)	0.11**	0.15*	0.09	0.05
Egalitarian GRA[1] (Ref.: Traditional GRA)	-0.22***	-0.18**	-0.29***	-0.13^{+}
Religiosity (scale)	0.07**	0.06^{+}	0.11**	0.02
Place of living (Ref.: Suburbs/town)				
Big city	-0.18***	-0.20^{+}	-0.09	0.02
Countryside/village	-0.07^{+}	-0.03	0.09	0.04
East Germany	-	-	-	-
Constant	3.36***	3.71***	3.22***	2.95***
N	4818	1890	1523	1405
adj. R^2	0.031	0.044	0.050	0.014

Table continued on next page.

Table 6.11 Skepticism (continued)

	Pluralistic support cluster	FR	BE
Women (Ref.: Men)	0.03	0.07	-0.03
Birth cohorts (Ref.: Born before 1944)			
1984/1994	-0.29**	-0.42**	-0.26*
1974/1983	-0.28**	-0.29*	-0.34**
1959/1973	-0.24**	-0.32*	-0.23*
1944/1958	-0.18**	-0.15	-0.26**
Children (Ref.: No children)			
Children under age 3	0.00	-0.06	0.06
Children age 3 to 6	-0.07	-0.02	-0.16
Child (in hh)	0.10	-0.01	0.14+
Child (not in hh)	0.18**	0.06	0.17+
Education (Ref.: ISCED 0-2)			
ISCED 3:Upper secondary	-0.01	0.01	-0.02
ISCED 5:Tertiary	-0.17**	-0.19*	-0.08
Income Situation (Ref.: Comfort./coping)			
(Very) difficult	0.04	0.02	0.16*
Public sector (Ref.: Private)	-0.13**	-0.17*	-0.05
Working (Ref.: Not in the labor market)	0.06	0.14+	-0.02
Egalitarian GRA[1] (Ref.: Traditional GRA)	-0.20***	-0.18*	-0.25***
Religiosity (scale)	0.01	0.02	-0.01
Place of living (Ref.: Suburbs/town)			
Big city	-0.16*	-0.31***	0.06
Countryside/village	-0.15***	-0.07	-0.06
East Germany	-	-	-
Constant	3.56***	3.77***	3.37***
N	3374	1873	1501
adj. R2	0.038	0.043	0.042

Table continued on next page.

Table 6.11 Skepticism (continued)

	Dual-earner support / Nordic countries	FI	DK	SE
Women (Ref.: Men)	-0.02	0.02	-0.11*	0.01
Birth cohorts (Ref.: Born before 1944)				
1984/1994	-0.33***	-0.57***	-0.26*	-0.11
1974/1983	-0.34***	-0.67***	-0.10	-0.17
1959/1973	-0.29***	-0.48***	-0.23*	-0.15
1944/1958	-0.25***	-0.38***	-0.19*	-0.18+
Children (Ref.: No children)				
Children under age 3	0.08	0.23*	-0.07	0.03
Children age 3 to 6	0.08	0.05	0.16	0.06
Child (in hh)	-0.10*	-0.15*	-0.03	-0.13
Child (not in hh)	-0.10*	-0.07		-0.10
Education (Ref.: ISCED 0-2)				
ISCED 3:Upper secondary	-0.04	-0.06	-0.10	-0.01
ISCED 5:Tertiary	-0.16***	-0.14*	-0.24**	-0.09
Income Situation (Ref.: Comfort./coping)				
(Very) difficult	0.02	0.09	0.02	-0.02
Public sector (Ref.: Private)	-0.06*	-0.00	-0.09	-0.10+
Working (Ref.: Not in the labor market)	0.17***	0.19**	0.12	0.22**
Egalitarian GRA[1] (Ref.: Traditional GRA)	-0.28***	-0.25***	-0.14	-0.51***
Religiosity (scale)	0.09***	0.06*	0.07*	0.10***
Place of living (Ref.: Suburbs/town)				
Big city	-0.01	-0.05	0.03	0.02
Countryside/village	0.01	0.02	-0.02	0.04
East Germany	-	-	-	-
Constant	3.25***	3.28***	3.23***	3.29***
N	4834	1998	1384	1452
adj. R2	0.032	0.061	0.020	0.028

Note: Reference categories in brackets. [1] GRA = gender-role attitudes. Data weighted; robust standard errors. +p <= 0.10 *p <= 0.05 **p <= 0.01 ***p <= 0.001.
Source: ESS 2008; own calculation.

Table 6.12: Hypotheses and results regarding attitudinal differences among social groups: Skepticism

Social groups	Hypotheses	Significant in the pooled model	Confirmed at the country level	Significant at the country level / opposite direction	Not significant at the country level
Women vs. men	-	n.s.	DK		n.s. in all other countries
Parents vs. individuals	-	n.s.	(GR) (NL) (FI)	(FI)	DE ES, PT UK, IE FR, BE DK, SE
Young birth cohorts vs. older cohorts	-	-	(GR) UK FR, BE FI, DK		DE ES, PT IE, NL SE
High vs. low education level	-	-	GR FR FI, DK		DE ES, PT UK, IE, NL BE SE
Low vs. high income	-	+		GR (+) BE (+)	DE ES, PT UK, IE, NL FR FI, DK, SE
Public vs. private sector	-	n.s.	UK FR	IE (+)	DE ES, GR, PT BE FI, DK, SE

Table continued on next page.

Table 6.12: Skepticism. Hypotheses and results (continued)

Social groups	Hypotheses	Significant in the pooled model	Confirmed at the country level	Significant at the country level / opposite direction	Not significant at the country level
Those working vs. those not in the labor market	-	+		UK (+) FI, SE (+)	DE ES, GR, PT IE, NL FR, BE DK
Egalitarian gender-role attitudes	-	-	DE ES, GR, PT UK, IE FR, BE FI, SE		NL DK
Religiousness	+	+	DE GR IE FI, DK, SE		ES, PT UK, NL
Place of living (big city / town (Ref.) / countryside)			Big city (-) DE, GR, FR Big city (+) PT Countryside (-) DE, ES Countryside (+) PT		UK, IE, NL FI, DK, SE
East vs. West Germany (relevant only in DE)	-	n.a.	DE		

Note: + indicates a positive effect, – a negative effect comparing the first group with the respective reference group. Reading example: Compared with individuals, families are expected to be more in favor of government responsibility (+), less satisfied with existing services (-), and less critical regarding negative side effects (-).

6.4 Conclusion

The analyses in the previous chapter (4) have shown that the five adjusted family-policy clusters create different levels of support, satisfaction, and skepticism. This result is in line with earlier studies that suggest variation in the level of public attitudes toward the welfare state among different welfare-state regimes (see Svallfors 1997; Gelissen 2000; Arts and Gelissen 2001; Andreß and Heien 2001).

Earlier research results have been inconsistent regarding the polarization among social groups within countries. Some studies have confirmed different patterns of polarization among different welfare regimes (e.g., Andreß and Heien 2001; Linos and West 2003), whereas others find that most conflict lines are present in all welfare regimes (e.g., Svallfors 1997, 2010; Edlund 1999; Bean and Papadakis 1998; Svallfors 2003). The results presented here suggest that only the following cleavage patterns are virtually universal: Regarding the responsibility of the state, women and persons with children are more in favor of a strong role of the state almost everywhere. With respect to satisfaction with existing childcare services, lower-income groups are less satisfied, whereas more-religious persons are more satisfied in most countries. Concerning skepticism toward welfare-state intervention, finally, those with more egalitarian gender-role attitudes are predominantly less skeptical. It is critical to note, though, that these patterns are widespread, but none of them is significant in every single country.

Instead, many country-specific differences among social groups have emerged and been discussed above. Most of the hypotheses concerning the expected group differences have thus not been confirmed universally. These country-specific conflict lines among social groups can only be fully understood when taking the country-specific context as well as the specific institutional setup of existing policies into consideration. Doing such an in-depth analysis for twelve countries goes beyond the scope of this study, though a first attempt has been made in the previous chapters.

Regarding the five adjusted family-policy clusters distinguished in the previous chapter, no polarization patterns emerged that were specific to any of these clusters (i.e., none of the cluster-specific patterns was confirmed in all countries belonging to the cluster in question). The only exception is the group of dual-earner support / Nordic countries. In all three members of this cluster, tertiary education significantly increases satisfaction with existing childcare services. In contrast, tertiary education decreases satisfaction in Spain, Portugal, the UK, and Belgium. These results support the argument that existing childcare services better serve the more highly educated groups in the Scandinavian countries, where comprehensive childcare services exist.

Earlier studies analyzing attitudes toward the welfare state suggest that the employment sector (i.e., public- versus private-sector employment) is an important cleavage line in the Scandinavian countries (Esping-Andersen 1990; Svallfors 2004, 1997; Hoel and Knutsen 1989). The results of this study, however, are not corroborative. Regarding responsibility, public-sector employees are more in favor of government intervention in Finland and the Netherlands, but public-sector employment makes no difference in Denmark and Sweden. With regard to satisfaction, public sector employment makes no difference in any of the countries. Concerning skepticism, finally, public-sector employment hardly matters either. The only exceptions are the UK and France, where public-sector employees are less skeptical, as well as Ireland, where public sector employees are more skeptical.

A Finnish particularity is the choice between a place in public daycare and a home-care allowance (as a flat-rate benefit) after the end of parental leave. It has been argued that this home-care allowance might be more attractive to women with lower levels of education (due to lower labor-market prospects in terms of job quality and income), whereas families with higher educational degrees prefer a place in public daycare (due to better labor-market prospects) (OECD 2001; Salmi 2006). The previous chapters raised the question of whether this situation generates specific patterns of attitudinal polarization among social groups. The results provided above support this argument. Regarding satisfaction with existing services, parents with children below age three, poorer households, and persons living in the countryside or in a village were less satisfied with existing services. In contrast, those with a higher level of education as well as those with egalitarian gender-role attitudes were more satisfied. The Finnish arrangement might thus better serve those groups who have better labor-market prospects (e.g., in terms of educational degrees) and who are therefore better able to take advantage of the available childcare facilities. This result is in line with findings provided by Salmi (2006), who pointed out that the cash-for-care arrangement is generally quite popular among Finnish mothers of children under three; however, take-up and duration of take-up vary according to mothers' labor-market attachment (Salmi 2006).

Overall, the variables included in the regression models explain only a small proportion of the variance in welfare attitudes, which is a common result of empirical studies of welfare attitudes (Gelissen 2002: 159-160). To some degree, the results suggest a consensus toward family policies within the analyzed societies – at least with regard to differences across socio-economic and ideological groups (compare Edeltraud Roller 1992: 173).

A common approach in the field of comparative welfare-state research is the reliance on pooled regression models in order to detect patterns of polarization among social groups (e.g., Gelissen 2002; Blekesaune and Quadagno 2003; Jæger 2009). Only a few studies have analyzed patterns of social polarization within single countries, and these studies are often limited to a small number of countries when group differences are analyzed (e.g., Svallfors 2006, 1997; Lewin-Epstein et al. 2000). The results provided in this chapter clearly illustrate that country-specific models are a valuable and necessary extension of the pooled analyses and can reveal which patterns of social polarization are indeed universal and which are instead specific for single countries or certain groups of countries.

7 Summary and discussion

Economic and social pressures to be gainfully employed have increased during the last several decades, forcing women and mothers to enter the labor market. Moreover, women today are better educated, and their work-life preferences have evolved toward a stronger labor-market orientation, increasing their labor-market attachment (Daly and Klammer 2006; Lewis et al. 2008a; Sjöberg 2010; Esping-Andersen 1999). Not least, an overall rise in employment participation of both men and women is seen as crucial for the viability of the welfare state and economic prosperity as well as for the enhancement of social cohesion and inclusion. Policies enabling parents and mothers to combine work and family life are therefore regarded as the most appropriate to meet families' current needs and preferences for earning a living and caring for dependent children.

Despite a rife tendency in many countries to introduce or reform existing policies in order to support the dual-earner model of the family, family-policy variation in Europe is still enormous. Moreover, there is very limited knowledge about the publics' attitudes toward family-policy measures in a comparative perspective, though knowledge about the publics' opinion is an essential component and indicator of the legitimacy of modern democracies.

This study has addressed this research gap by combing a profound analysis of existing family-policy measures with a thorough analysis of public attitudes. Based on institutional theory, which argues that institutions structure the processes of orientation (Rothstein 1998; Lepsius 1997), the empirical analyses have shed some light on the relationship between the current family-policy setup, the social context, and public attitudes toward particular family-policy measures. From a macro-level perspective, this study has asked whether attitudinal differences among countries can be explained by county-level characteristics, such as the actual family-policy setup and other contextual features. From a micro-level perspective, this study has investigated patterns of social polarization among individuals or social groups.

The following paragraphs summarize the key findings chapter by chapter. The insights gained are discussed in reference to institutional theory and the comparative welfare-state literature. Additionally, limitations of this study and the applied methodological design are pointed out and implications for future research are highlighted.

Chapter 3, the first empirical chapter, explored different types of family policy in Europe and provided a profound analysis of existing family-policy institutions in the 15 member states of the European Union. Based on Korpi's (2000) family-policy typology (see also Ferrarini 2006), two dimensions of government support for families have been distinguished, namely general family support and dual-earner support. The general family support dimension includes measures that are either neutral with regard to their impact on mothers' labor-market participation or actively support a traditional male-breadwinner model of the family, whereas the dual-earner support dimension includes measures that actively support mothers' labor-market attachment and facilitate a more equal sharing of paid and unpaid work between men and women. The indicators used in order to capture the dimension of general family support are 1) (effective) parental leave entitlements (either unpaid or remunerated flat-rate); 2) childcare services for children between three and compulsory school age; and 3) the level of child allowances. The dimension of dual-earner support was represented by 1) effective maternity-, paternity-, and parental leave (only income-related benefits); 2) childcare services for children under age three; and 3) tax incentives for an equal sharing of paid work between spouses.

Based on the selected family-policy indicators, a cluster analysis was conducted, which revealed the following four distinct family-policy clusters:

1. A general family support cluster with Austria, Luxembourg, and Germany. This cluster is characterized by a high level of general family support and rather low dual-earner support.
2. A low support cluster with the UK, Ireland, the Netherlands, Greece, Italy, Portugal, and Spain. This cluster provides relatively little support for families in both dimensions.
3. A pluralistic support cluster with France, Belgium, and Finland. This group is quite heterogeneous and combines both general family support and dual-earner support.
4. A dual-earner support cluster with Denmark and Sweden. This group is characterized by a high level of dual-earner support combined with a moderate level of general family support.

The results of this chapter clearly demonstrated huge institutional variation within the family-policy field. European welfare states differ with regard to both the type and the level of benefits and services provided for families. Consequently, state support for the dual-earner model of the family is not a matter of course and in many countries parents (and particularly mothers) with young children have to find private solutions for the work-family conflict.

Compared with earlier research, the four family-policy clusters are only partly consistent with alternative classifications. The comparability of different classifications, however, is limited because the different studies included not only different countries and indicators but they also focused on different points in time. Discrepancies and similarities between the typology developed in this study and earlier classifications have been discussed extensively in Chapter 3.

This study advanced existing family-policy typologies by using updated family-policy indicators, thereby catching up with the recent developments in a rapidly changing policy field. Moreover, pluralistic policy orientations were captured and the inclusion of the Southern European countries (which were excluded in most previous studies) allowed for the investigation of whether these countries form their own distinct family-policy cluster, as suggested by Ferrara (1996) and Bahle (2008a). The cluster analysis conducted in this study did not reveal a separate group of Southern European countries. However, the consideration of the broader social context in Chapter 5 clearly demonstrates the distinctiveness of this group of countries.

The selected indicators inevitably represent a limited picture of the diversity in the family-policy field. The typology approach itself, as well as the limited choice of indicators, naturally implicates the danger of neglecting important details of institutional variation (Korpi 2000). Moreover, it has to be kept in mind that the obtained cluster solution represents a rather flexible typology. This implies that the classification of countries could change if additional countries or indicators are included in the analysis or if the characteristics of family policies change as a result of policy reform.

Chapter 4 analyzed the relationship between the family-policy setup and public attitudes and addressed the following questions: What do citizens expect from their governments in the field of family policy? How do Europeans perceive existing family-policy institutions? Does the public anticipate the negative side effects of government intervention? And, are public attitudes toward these issues systematically related to particular family-policy characteristics and the family-policy clusters distinguished in Chapter 3?

The micro-level data capturing public attitudes stem from the European Social Survey (wave 2008/09) and were used in this chapter as well as in subsequent chapters. Public opinion data were available for twelve member states of the European Union (Belgium, Denmark, Finland, France, Germany, Greece, Ireland, the Netherlands, Portugal, Spain, Sweden, and the UK). Three dimensions of attitudes were taken into account, namely: 1) "How much responsibility should governments have in ensuring sufficient childcare services for working parents?" (i.e., responsibility or the evaluation of extensity); 2) "What do you think about the provision of affordable child care services for working parents?" (i.e., satisfaction or the evaluation of means); and 3) "Social benefits and services make people less willing to look after themselves and their family" (i.e., skepticism or the evaluation of unintended consequences).

When asking "How much responsibility should governments have in ensuring sufficient childcare services for working parents?," the descriptive results show that a clear majority regard the state as being responsible for the provision of childcare services in all countries. The strongest support for state responsibility is found in the Southern European (Greece, Spain, and Portugal) and Nordic countries (Finland, Denmark, and Sweden), as well as in Germany, whereas support is weakest in the Netherlands and the liberal countries (Ireland and the UK). France and Belgium range in-between. The percentages of respondents who are clearly in favor of strong government responsibility range from 55% in the Netherlands to 93% in Greece. This result corroborates the findings provided by Wendt et al. (2011: 155), who concluded that European citizens essentially perceive the state to be responsible for the provision of social transfers and services in different fields of welfare-state intervention (such as health care, family policy, and unemployment benefits and social assistance). Moreover, previous research showed that "access to more flexible childcare arrangements" is the most broadly supported family-policy measure in all countries, and should receive political priority in order to improve the quality of life for families (Wendt et al. 2011). This result emphasizes the widespread need of (public) childcare services in several European countries.

Analyzing patterns of social polarization in the degree to which the state is perceived as being responsible for the provision of childcare services in the second part of this chapter, the following general patterns emerged: Women, younger cohorts, respondents with children, lesser-educated persons, low-income groups, and public-sector employees demand stronger state responsibility for the provision of childcare services compared with the respective reference groups. Furthermore, egalitarian gender-role attitudes (compared with traditional gender-role attitudes) and living in a big city are associated with a stronger demand for state-responsibility, whereas stronger religiosity has the opposite effect. These results suggest that both self-interest and cultural values matter for the degree to which certain groups regard the state as being responsible for the provision of childcare services. Those groups who are most in need of childcare services (e.g., women and families) as well as those groups who are most dependent on publicly provided (or subsidized) services (e.g., low income groups) are thus most in favor of a strong role of the state. Similar patterns have also been found in earlier studies and with regard to various policy fields (Wendt et al. 2011; Arts and Gelissen 2001; Jæger 2006b, 2009; Andreß and Heien 2001). However, it has to be kept in mind that the estimated effects of the individual-level indicators represent the mean effect of the individual-level variables across the twelve countries. The inclusion of these variables serves primarily the goal of controlling for compositional effects and it is important to note that the effects of the individual-level variables could differ between countries (this was analyzed in Chapter 6). Estimated differences among social groups, therefore, give only a rough impression of existing social cleavages and have to be interpreted carefully.

When the family-policy context was taken into account, the results show that the preferred level of government responsibility is not systematically related to the distinct family-policy clusters. This result supports the idea that processes of social change have increased the demand for a strong role of the state in many countries, resulting in a situation of non-coherence between the actual policy setup and the public's expectations toward the government (compare Pfau-Effinger 2005a). A policy context, which is characterized by a low level of support for families, can thus coincide with strong public demand for government responsibility in the provision of childcare services.

Looking at the second item ("What do you think about the provision of affordable child care services for working parents?"), the results show that the public is not especially satisfied with existing childcare services. Respondents are least satisfied in the Southern European countries (Portugal, Spain, and Greece), as well as in Ireland. In these countries, at least 40% judge existing services to be bad. The situation is slightly better in Denmark and the Netherlands, where 35% are satisfied. Only in two of the twelve countries, namely Finland and Sweden, is a clear majority satisfied with existing services, where 60% and 53% are satisfied respectively.

The multivariate results depicted the following patterns of polarization among social groups: Women, respondents with a child below age three, younger cohorts, low-income groups, and persons with egalitarian gender-role attitudes are significantly less satisfied with existing childcare services (compared with the respective reference groups). More-religious persons, in contrast, are more satisfied. These results suggest that those groups who are most in need of public childcare services (e.g., women, families with young children, low-income groups), are also least satisfied with the status quo. Again, both self-interest and cultural values seem to matter for the evaluation of existing childcare services.

Taking the family-policy context into account, the results show that respondents in the dual-earner support cluster (Denmark and Sweden) are most satisfied, whereas respondents in the low support cluster and the general family support cluster are significantly less satisfied with existing childcare services. Denmark and Sweden are characterized by a high availability of affordable childcare services, which is part of a coherent family-policy package supporting the dual-earner model of the family. This policy context facilitates parents to combine work and family life and generates a high level of satisfaction with the status quo. Hence, with regard to the evaluation of a specific family-policy institution (i.e., childcare services), public attitudes do to some extent vary along the lines of the four family-policy clusters. Nevertheless, a considerable amount of existing differences at the country level remained unexplained (i.e., about 50% of the total country-level variance).

The third item, finally, captured attitudes toward the unintended consequences of government intervention and analyzes the public's opinion toward the statement "Social benefits and services make people less willing to look after themselves and their family." The percentage of respondents agreeing with this statement varies considerably among the countries. It ranges between a minority of 16% in Greece and a majority of 55% in France. Respondents are most pessimistic about the effects of social benefits and services in France and the UK and most optimistic in Greece, followed by Spain, the Scandinavian countries, and the Netherlands.

Looking at the polarization among social groups, results show that younger cohorts, respondents with a tertiary degree, public-sector employees, and respondents living in a big city are less skeptical compared with the respective reference groups. In contrast, persons with a low income and those working are slightly more skeptical. Regarding normative beliefs, those with more egalitarian gender-role attitudes are less skeptical, whereas religiousness has the opposite effect. Differences in the perception of the negative side effects of welfare-state benefits and services are thus primarily related to normative beliefs rather than to self-interest.

Taking the policy context into account shows that country-level differences in the degree of skepticism are not systematically related to the four family-policy clusters.

The results of Chapter 4 demonstrated that the family-policy typology is only partly suited to explain country-level differences in public opinion. However, these results do not imply that the current policy setup does not matter. Instead, it was argued that processes of social and cultural change (such as the trend toward more egalitarian gender-role attitudes, increasing female labor-market aspirations and participation rates, changing family forms, and increased economic necessities to be gainfully employed) might have increased the demand for dual-earner policies in many countries - independently of the type and level of existing family-policy measures. The findings corroborate the welfare-arrangement approach introduced by Pfau-Effinger (2005a). According to this approach, public attitudes interact not only with the design of existing family-policy measures but also with cultural and social structures, e.g., in terms of labor-market characteristics and opportunities, cultural norms and values, or the degree of problem pressure (e.g., in terms of low fertility rates or child poverty). Other aspects, which go beyond the institutional design of existing family policies, are thus relevant for the understanding of public opinion.

Regarding the patterns of social polarization, the results show that both self-interest and normative beliefs are important aspects when analyzing public attitudes toward family policies. Both concepts matter with regard to the public's preference for a strong role of the state in the provision of childcare services as well as regarding the level of satisfaction with existing services. With respect to the third dimension - the perception of the unintended side effects of government intervention, normative beliefs are more salient than self-interest.

Chapter 5 asked whether the consideration of the broader social context (in terms of socio-economic and socio-demographic structures) suggests a modification of the original family-policy typology and whether the adjusted version is better able to explain country-level difference in public opinion. The first part of this chapter described the social context of the original family-policy clusters and the individual countries and provided data concerning fertility, child poverty, female labor-market participation, and gender equality. These indicators mirror important aspects of a society, such as existing social inequalities, labor-market characteristics, and the degree of problem pressure.

The analysis of these indicators suggested an adjustment of the original family-policy typology. The main adjustments were twofold. First, the low support cluster was split into two groups - a group of low support / Southern European countries on the one hand, and a group of low support / liberal countries on the other. Second, Finland was assigned to a group of dual-earner support / Nordic countries consisting of itself, Denmark, and Sweden.

The second part of this chapter asked whether public attitudes are systematically related to the adjusted family-policy clusters and presented a series of multilevel regression models in order to investigate this question. To sum up, the results show that the adjusted family-policy clusters are better equipped to explain differences in public attitudes at the country level, compared with the original typology that focused solely on family-policy indicators. The explanatory power of the adjusted clusters is strongest with regard to responsibility, slightly lower regarding the level of satisfaction, and lowest with respect to the degree of skepticism.

Comparing public attitudes among the five adjusted family-policy clusters, the following patterns emerged: The group of dual-earner support / Nordic countries demands a strong role of the state; is comparably satisfied with existing childcare services; and is not skeptical regarding the negative side effects of benefits and services. The group of low support / Southern European countries also demands a high level of government responsibility; is not skeptical either; but is not satisfied with existing childcare services. In the general family support cluster (represented by Germany), demand for a strong role of the state is strong, the level of satisfaction is low, and skepticism is moderate. The group of low support / liberal countries, in contrast, demands the lowest level of state intervention; is rather skeptical toward negative side effects; but is also not very satisfied with existing childcare services. In the pluralistic support cluster, finally, demand for government responsibility as well as the level of satisfaction is reduced, compared with the dual-earner / Nordic countries, and skepticism is high (see also Table 7.1, below).

The low level of skepticism in the dual-earner support / Nordic countries confirms the results provided by Kumlin and Rothstein, who showed that "universal welfare-state institutions tend to increase social trust, whereas experiences with need-tested social programs undermine it" (Kumlin and Rothstein 2005: 339). The low level of skepticism in the Southern European countries, in turn, might be explained by the strong tradition of familism in these countries (see Jensen and Svendsen (2009) for a similar argumentation).

Table 7.1: Public attitudes in the adjusted family-policy clusters

Adjusted family-policy cluster	Responsibility	Satisfaction	Skepticism
Dual-earner support / Nordic countries (DK, SE, FI)	Strong demand	Rather high	Low
Low support / Southern Europe (ES,GR, PT)	Strong demand	Low	Low
Low support / liberal countries (IE, UK, NL)	Low / Moderate demand	Moderate	Moderate / high
Pluralistic support cluster (BE, FR)	Moderate demand	Moderate	Moderate / high
General family support cluster (DE)	Strong demand	Low	Low / moderate

Overall, the results indicate that a similar family-policy context can coincide with opposing attitudes due to differences in the broader social context these policies operate in or differences in cultural and political traditions. In the low support / liberal countries, the public prefers a low level of state intervention suggesting approval of the status quo, whereas the public in the Southern European countries clearly favors a strong role of the state. The situation in the Southern European countries indicates a considerable gap between the status quo and public preferences, which might indicate a lack of democratic legitimacy of the current arrangements (Svallfors 2010). As Borre (1998b) pointed out, huge discrepancies between the public's policy preferences and the actual policy of the government might even reduce public support for the political system as a whole.

The preference for a low level of state intervention in the group of low support / liberal countries suggests that the status quo (i.e., a low level of government support for families) is accepted by a majority of the population. Nevertheless, satisfaction with existing childcare services is only moderate. Regarding this particular institution, the needs of the population are not met – however, the public does not agree that the government should be responsible for the provision of childcare services. These results can be explained by the fact that childcare services are very expensive in Ireland, the UK, and the Netherlands and out-of-pocket childcare costs range among the highest in comparison with other European countries (OECD 2007). The cost barriers to purchase private childcare services are thus high in these countries. In the UK and the Netherlands, the state primarily supports the use of childcare services through demand-side incentives, such as tax relief for parents or companies (Mahon 2002; Rostgaard 2002; Lewis et al. 2008b). Consequently, employers play a key role in the provision of childcare services. This fact partly explains the rejection of a strong role of the state in the provision of childcare services.

A major concern regarding tax relief, however, is that this type of benefit is more attractive and profitable to high income earners and might generate social inequality of access (Mahon 2002). As pointed out by the OECD (2007: 126), "[...] many lower-income earners may be exempted from paying taxes altogether or pay very low rates. [...] Moreover, future tax reductions offer little help to parents with limited budgets who cannot afford non-parental childcare in the current period." The UK provides a high share of means-tested benefits to low-income families, however, "once the family income surpasses a certain level, and a rather modest one at that, these benefits are no longer available and the total family package is sharply reduced" (Fagnani and Math 2008: 72).

The last part of the chapter elaborated on economic aspects of the family-policy field. The consideration of several economic indicators revealed that the proportion of GDP spent for families as well as the type of benefits these resources are spent for varies considerably among the countries. A high level of spending, however, does not univocally coincide with a high level of actual support for families in terms of work-family compatibility, the case of the UK being a good example. Consequently, a high level of spending does not automatically increase the level of public satisfaction. However, a high level of spending for childcare services coincides with a high level of satisfaction with existing services. These results are supported by several authors, who concluded that certain outcomes, such as poverty or social inequality, can only be partly attributed to the level of public spending (Castles 2009; e.g., Fagnani and Math 2008).

Within the group of countries taken into account here, the Southern European countries are not only the poorest countries in terms of GDP per capita, but these countries also spend the lowest share of available resources for families (measured as percentage of the GDP). Public support for families is clearly not a priority issue in these countries. This situation explains the very low levels of satisfaction and the strong demand for government intervention, and emphasizes the distinctiveness of this group of countries. Simultaneously, the low level of economic wealth in these countries (indicated by the GDP per capita) limits the potential scope for government intervention in the near future and the recent financial and economic crisis has even worsened this situation.

The findings of this chapter clearly corroborate that the Southern European countries form their own, distinct family-policy cluster (Flaquer 2000; Bahle 2008a). This group of countries faces not only considerable economic problems but also serious challenges due to processes of social and cultural change, indicated, e.g., by very low fertility rates, increasing female educational attainment, and growing female labor-market aspirations. This situation results in extremely low levels of satisfaction with existing childcare services combined with a strong demand for government intervention.

The specific situation of this group of countries has already been described by earlier studies. Sjöberg (2010), e.g., showed that the growth of female educational attainment has outpaced the growth in female labor-market participation in the Southern European countries. This situation results in a mismatch between women's aspirations to pursue a career and the structural possibility of realizing those aspirations (see also Karamessini 2008).

The combination of a troubling economical situation, a low level of government support for families with children, and the strong presence of familism results in a low level of work-family compatibility in this group of countries and simultaneously hampers the expansion of (public) childcare services. In addition, traditional care ideals may reduce the demand for childcare services and slow down their expansion. A qualitative study conducted by Sims-Schouten (2000), e.g., showed that Greek parents hold traditional care ideals and are very suspicious toward formal childcare options.

In many countries and especially in the Southern European countries, the lack of (public) childcare services forces mothers either to leave the labor market in order to provide care or to find alternative ways to combine work and family responsibilities, which is often only possible with the help of grandparents, other family members, or friends (Leira et al. 2005; Sims-Schouten 2000; Kreimer 2006). However, as the younger generation of women is better educated and much more involved in the labor market than their mothers, the availability of grandparents cannot be taken for granted in the future. Furthermore, informal (mostly female) caregivers often have no or limited access to the social security system with consequences for their economic well-being in times of divorce, unemployment, or old-age (Kreimer 2006; Lewis et al. 2008a). These arguments emphasize the necessity of addressing the current challenges and increasing welfare needs of the population.

Chapter 6 approached public attitudes from a micro-level perspective and investigated to what extent self-interest and cultural values explain differences in public opinion among individuals. Moreover, this chapter asked whether these concepts are equally relevant regarding both different dimensions of attitudes as well as different family-policy contexts and individual countries. The country-specific regression models allow for the investigation of whether the patterns of social polarization that were found at the aggregate level (see Chapter 4) can be confirmed for all countries included in the analysis. The Tables 7.2, 7.3, and 7.4 (below) summarize the key results.

With regard to government responsibility, women are clearly more in favor of a strong role of the state in most countries, but not in Greece, the UK, Ireland, and France. In half of the countries, egalitarian gender-role attitudes increase demand for a strong role of the state (i.e., Spain, Portugal, the Netherlands, France, Finland, and Denmark). Furthermore, in several countries, respondents with children demand stronger state responsibility for the provision of childcare services than respondents without children (not significant in Germany, Spain, Greece, Ireland, and Belgium). Other factors play a role in a minority of countries only (see Chapter 6).

The results support the idea that both self-interest (in terms of gender and the presence of children) and normative beliefs (i.e., gender-role attitudes) play a role in the formation of attitudes toward government responsibility for the provision of childcare services. However, it has also been shown that only some group differences are virtually universal (e.g., differences between men and women or respondents with and without children), whereas other polarization tendencies among social groups are country specific (see Table 7.2 below).

Regarding the level of satisfaction with existing childcare services, polarization among social groups is most striking concerning the households' income situation and religiousness. Poorer households are less satisfied in all countries, except in the UK, France, and Sweden; and more-religious respondents are more satisfied (except in France). Both self-interest (income) and normative beliefs (religiousness) play a role in the evaluation of existing services. The widespread income effect supports the argument that low-income groups are much more dependent on welfare-state institutions with regard to their life choices, behavior, and well-being (Wendt et al. 2011). Low-income groups do not have the financial resources to purchase private solutions, such as private childcare services, and consequently, a lack of affordable childcare services is most problematic for this group.

Regarding other group differences, however, the results are far from universal, and several characteristics have obverse effects in different countries, such as education and egalitarian gender-role attitudes. These findings suggest that attitudinal differences among social groups are mostly country specific and related to country-specific characteristics of the welfare program in question as well as to other contextual features. These factors might be especially relevant when examining the public's evaluation of a particular institution, such as existing childcare services. In future studies, an in-depth analysis of this specific institution might be necessary to understand the country-specific patterns.

Furthermore, personal experiences with the institution - the "personally experienced welfare-state information," (Kumlin 2002: 31) are an important aspect of public opinion and should be taken into account. Due to a lack of appropriate data, these aspects could not be captured in this study (see Table 7.3 for a summary of the results).

Analyzing the public's opinion toward the statement "Social benefits and services make people less willing to look after themselves and their family," finally, revealed the following patterns: Most of the variables indicating self-interest have no or only a marginal effect on skepticism toward social benefits and services (i.e., they have an effect in individual countries only). In contrast, normative aspects in terms of gender-role attitudes matter in almost all countries except in the Netherlands and Denmark. Persons with more egalitarian gender-role attitudes are less skeptical regarding unintended consequences. Religiousness has the opposite effect in several countries. More-religious persons are more skeptical in Germany, Greece, Ireland, as well as the three Nordic countries of Finland, Denmark, and Sweden. Additionally, younger cohorts are less skeptical in five countries, namely the UK, France, Belgium, Finland, and Denmark. As suggested by the aggregated analysis in Chapter 4, these results confirm that normative beliefs are more important compared with self-interest for the evaluation of potential side effects in most countries (see Table 7.3 for a summary of the results).

The skepticism item differs from the other two items in that it refers to social benefits and services in very general terms and does neither exclusively address family-policy benefits and services nor a specific group of beneficiaries (e.g., parents or children). This fact potentially weakens the salience of self-interest and highlights normative beliefs (Kangas 1997).

Table 7.2: Responsibility – main findings

Social groups	Pooled model	Adjusted family policy clusters: General family support (DE)	Low support / Southern	Low support / liberal	Pluralist. support cluster	Dual-earner support / Nordic	Country-specific models
Women vs. men	+	+	n.s.	+	+	+	DE, ES, PT, NL, BE, FI, DK, SE (+)
Young birth cohorts vs. older cohorts	+	+	+	+	-	-	DE, GR,UK, (IE) (+) ES, FR, BE (-)
Parents (children < age 3) vs. individuals	+	n.s.	n.s.	+	+	+	PT, UK, NL, FR,FI, (DK, SE) (+)
High vs. low education level	-	n.s.	n.s.	-	n.s.	n.s.	PT, UK, BE, FI (-)
Low vs. high income	+	n.s.	+	+	n.s.	n.s.	UK, FR (+)
Public vs. private sector	+	n.s.	n.s.	+	n.s.	+	NL, FI (+)
Working vs. not in the labor market	n.s.	n.s.	n.s.	n.s.	n.s.	n.s.	BE (+)
Egalitarian gender-role attitudes	+	n.s.	+	+	+	+	ES, PT, NL, FR, FI, DK (+)
Religious-ness	-	-	-	+	n.s.	n.s.	DE, PT (-) UK (+)

Note: + indicates a positive effect, – a negative effect comparing the first with the second group; n.s. = statistically not significant. Reading example: In the pooled model, women are significantly more in favor of a strong role of the state than men. With regard to the country-specific models (see last column), all countries are listed, in which the variable in question has a statistically significant effect (i.e., $p <= 0.05$).

Table 7.3: Satisfaction – main findings

Social groups	Pooled model	Adjusted family policy clusters: General family support (DE)	Low support / Southern	Low support /liberal	Pluralist. support	Dual-earner support/ Nordic	Country-specific models
Women vs. men	-	n.s.	-	-	-	n.s.	UK, IE, BE (-)
Young birth cohorts vs. older cohorts	-	(+)	(+)	n.s.	(-)	(+)	DE, GR, IE, DK youngest vs. oldest (+) SE (-) ES, PT, DK 1944/1958 vs. oldest (-) FR: 1974/83 vs. oldest (-)
Parents (children < age 3) vs. individuals	-	-	n.s.	n.s.	n.s.	-	DE, FI, (-)
High vs. low education level	n.s.	n.s.	-	-	-	+	ES, PT, UK, BE (-) FI, DK, SE (+)
Low vs. high income	-	-	-	-	n.s.	-	DE, ES, GR, PT, IE, NL, BE, FI, DK
Public vs. private sector	n.s.	n.s.	n.s.	n.s.	n.s.	n.s.	n.s.
Working vs. not in the labor market	n.s.	n.s.	n.s.	n.s.	n.s.	n.s.	n.s.
Egalitarian gender-role attit.	-	n.s.	-	n.s.	n.s.	n.s.	ES, GR, IE (-) FI (+)
Religious-ness	+	+	+	+	+	+	DE, ES, GR, PT, UK, IE, NL, BE, FI, DK, SE

Note: + indicates a positive effect, – a negative effect comparing the first with the second group; n.s. = statistically not significant. Reading example: In the pooled model, women are significantly less satisfied with existing childcare services than men. With regard to the country-specific models (see last column), all countries are listed, in which the variable in question has a statistically significant effect (i.e., $p<= 0.05$).

Table 7.4: Skepticism – main findings

Social groups	Pooled model	Adjusted family policy clusters: General family support (DE)	Low support/ Southern	Low support /liberal	Pluralist. support	Dual-earner support/ Nordic	Country-specific models
Women vs. men	n.s.	n.s	n.s	n.s	n.s	n.s	DK (-)
Parents (children < age 3) vs. individuals	n.s.	n.s	n.s	n.s	n.s	n.s	FI (+)
Young birth cohorts vs. older cohorts	-	n.s.	-	-	-	-	(GR), UK, FR, BE, FI, DK (-)
High vs. low education level	-	n.s.	-	(-)	-	-	GR, FR, FI, DK (-)
Low vs. high income	+	n.s.	n.s.	n.s.	n.s.	n.s.	GR, BE (+)
Public vs. private sector	n.s.	n.s.	n.s.	n.s.	-	-	UK, FR (-) IE (+)
Working vs. not in the labor market	+	n.s.	n.s.	+	n.s.	+	UK, FI, SE (+)
Egalitarian gender-role attitudes	-	-	-	-	-	-	DE, ES, GR, PT, UK, IE, FR, BE, FI, SE (-)
Religious-ness	+	+	+	+	n.s.	+	DE, GR, IE, FI, DK, SE (+)

Note: + indicates a positive effect, – a negative effect comparing the first with the second group; n.s. = statistically not significant. Reading example: In the pooled model, younger birth cohorts are significantly less skeptical toward negative side effects than older birth cohorts. With regard to the country-specific models (see last column), all countries are listed, in which the variable in question has a statistically significant effect (i.e., $p<= 0.05$).

In the German case, an additional factor was taken into account, namely the place of the interview. Differentiating between East and West Germany bred several interesting results, which are in line with the theoretical expectations. As expected, East Germans are considerably more in favor of a strong role of the state, and they are more satisfied with existing childcare services. Moreover, they are less skeptical with regard to negative side effects, though differences among East and West Germans are less pronounced here. More than 20 years after reunification, results corroborate earlier findings showing attitudinal differences among the two parts of the country (Edeltraut Roller 2002; Lewin-Epstein et al. 2000). These findings suggest that processes of socialization (e.g., in terms of female labor-market participation, gender-roles, or attitudes toward the socialization of childcare) might be more important for understanding the formation of public attitudes toward family policy than socio-demographic characteristics.

Several scholars have emphasized institutional variation within countries (e.g., Svallfors 1997). The level and quality of childcare service provision varies, e.g., across municipalities and regions as well as between rural and urban areas (Melhuish and Moss 1991; OECD 2001). Moreover, care ideals and cultural traditions may vary between different regions within the same country, East and West Germany being just one example, Flanders and Wallonia in Belgium being another (Kremer 2007). Further research is needed to highlight regional differences regarding both institutional characteristics as well as cultural traditions.

Regarding the five adjusted family-policy clusters, several patterns of social polarization emerged that were described in detail in Chapter 6 (see also Table 7.2, 7.3, and 7.4). A key result from this part of the study is that no polarization patterns emerged that were unique to any of these clusters and all its members. None of the cluster-specific social cleavages was unequivocally present in all the individual countries belonging to the cluster in question. The only exception is the group of dual-earner support / Nordic countries: In all three members of this cluster, a tertiary educational degree coincides with a higher level of satisfaction with existing childcare services compared with a lower educational degree. In contrast, tertiary education is associated with a lower level of satisfaction in several other countries (such as Spain, Portugal, the UK, and Belgium). It was argued that the dual-earner model of the family is more attractive to the more highly educated groups (due to their better labor-market prospects). In the Nordic countries, comprehensive childcare services exist and serve the needs and preferences of the more highly educated groups. In contrast, the more highly educated groups are less satisfied with that status quo in those countries, where childcare services are lacking.

Overall, the individual-level characteristics included in the regression models explained only a small proportion of the variance in public attitudes toward family policies. This is a common result of studies analyzing welfare-state attitudes (Gelissen 2002: 159-160) and could indicate that a considerable degree of consensus toward these issues exists, at least with regard to differences across socio-economic and ideological groups (compare Edeltraud Roller 1992: 173). From a more pessimistic perspective, it could also be argued that more specific analyses and survey data are needed in order to detect social inequalities and patterns of social polarization. Regarding both the responsibility dimension and the level of satisfaction, a differentiation between different age groups is necessary to conduct a more profound analysis of social disparities. Attitudinal differences among countries and social groups can be expected to be much more pronounced regarding childcare services for children under age three compared with that of services provided for older children (i.e., between age three and compulsory school age). Moreover, specific questions are needed in order to understand parents' dissatisfaction with existing childcare services. Is a lack of services the main problem, or are parents discontented with restricted opening hours, overly expensive childcare fees, and/or the quality of childcare facilities? The latter questions are obviously better suited for a study among parents rather than the whole population. Furthermore, qualitatively oriented case studies are a necessary addition to large-scale survey studies and can shed light on country-specific patterns of social polarization.

In conclusion, this study has provided a first overview of attitudinal differences among individuals in different family-policy contexts as well as within the individual countries and thus complemented earlier studies in the field of comparative welfare-state research.

A common approach in this research field is the combined analysis of data from different countries (which was also done in Chapters 4 and 5 of this study as well as in an earlier study (Wendt et al. 2011)). Attitudinal differences among social groups have mainly been analyzed by means of pooled regression models including several countries at the same time (e.g., Gelissen 2002; Blekesaune and Quadagno 2003; Jæger 2009). Only a few studies have analyzed patterns of social polarization within individual countries (e.g., Wendt et al. 2010), but most of these studies are limited to a very small number of countries (e.g., Svallfors 2006, 1997; Lewin-Epstein et al. 2000). The results provided in this study showed that hardly any of the patterns detected in the pooled models were confirmed univocally at the country level. This finding clearly illustrates that country-specific models are a valuable and necessary extension of the pooled analyses and can reveal which patterns of social polarization are indeed universal and which are instead specific to individual countries or certain groups of countries. An unavoidable disadvantage to this approach is its production of a huge amount of data and the risk one faces of getting lost in the details.

From a theoretical perspective, this study also contributes to institutional theory and confirms the importance of institutions for individuals. The design of the welfare state, here the family-policy context, generates differences in the level of public opinion. However, other contextual features need to be taken into account in order to understand these differences as well as their relatedness to the institutional context. These contextual features mirror important aspects of a society, such as existing social inequalities or labor-market characteristics as well as historical and cultural traditions.

An important result of this study is that similar institutions can generate different outcomes (e.g., in terms of attitudinal patterns), dependent on the broader social context. Moreover, the Finnish case illustrates that different policies can operate as functional equivalents, generating similar outcomes (e.g., in term of female labor-market participation and work-family compatibility) (see also Rostgaard 2002). Existing family-policy institutions thus differently impact public attitudes (and potentially social action, which was not analyzed in this study), dependent on the whole welfare arrangement these institutions are embedded in (Pfau-Effinger 2005a).

Scholars who are interested in the link between institutions and public attitudes or social behavior (such as female labor-market participation, families' organization of work and care, or family planning decisions) should take into account the interrelatedness of all elements of the welfare arrangement (i.e., the cultural system, the welfare system, welfare-state policies, social structures, political actors, and social practices of individuals). This interrelatedness is especially relevant when analyzing the field of family policy or social care, since culture, values, and ideals play a key role in these fields and impact both the development and change of the institutional design as well as families' choices and behaviors. In line with these thoughts, future studies could investigate to what extent families' work- and care arrangements are contingent upon particular institutional incentives and disincentives and to what extent are these arrangements 1) modified by individual preferences and 2) consciously made choices?

Existing studies that take into account the historical, cultural, and political context of the family-policy field are helpful for determining the relevant dimensions of contextual variation as well as for the explanation of emerging differences or similarities between countries, which cannot be explained solely by the institutional design of the current policy setup (e.g., Bahle 1995; Gauthier 1996; Pfau-Effinger 1996, 2005b; Kremer 2007; Strohmeier 2002; Anttonen et al. 2003).

Moreover, policy makers might want to incorporate these arguments into the processes of policy making or reform. Chapter 2 has argued that one of the key questions in future processes of family-policy reform and coalition building, is whether family policies should reward and promote female labor-market participation or instead women's caring and educational tasks (Häusermann 2008). Consequently, the position of political actors, political parties, and the electorate on these normative issues might increasingly become a decisive factor during election campaigns. A "blame-avoidance logic" might then be at work not regarding unpopular retrenchment (P. Pierson 1996; 2001: Chpt. 13), but regarding unpopular normative or ideological positions with respect to gender ideologies (for a discussion of different gender ideologies, see, e.g., Korpi 2000; Ferrarini 2006). As pointed out by Hilamo and Kangas (2009), a crucial factor in the process of policy making is also the political framing of discourses through which political actors try to appeal to their constituencies. As a prominent example, the authors investigated the framing of the political discourses concerning the potential introduction of a child home care allowance in Sweden and Finland. In Sweden, the home care allowance was primarily framed as "a trap for women" whereas in Finland it was framed as "the freedom to choose."

An interesting research perspective is thus the potential impact of public opinion on social-policy reform. However, these questions can only be tackled based on longitudinal data, which are scarce in a comparative framework. The major advantages of longitudinal data are at least twofold: 1) Questions concerning causality can be answered and 2) changes over time can be analyzed both at the macro level (e.g., changes in the policy setup) and at the micro-level (e.g., attitudinal or behavioral changes over the individual life course). Both aspects are important for our understanding of institutional change (or stability) and public opinion as well as the relationship between the two.

Moreover, a major challenge concerning data is the collection of internationally comparable contextual and institutional information. The availability of databases has increased immensely; however, the quality and comparability of available data are still limited, in particular with respect to specific institutions such as childcare services. Family policy is a very complex field of welfare-state intervention, and the diversity and quantity of existing family-policy measures makes a truly comprehensive comparison of existing family-policy packages a difficult undertaking – or as Fagnani and Math put it, "The devil is in the details" (Fagnani and Math 2008: 57).

Two of the three attitudinal dimensions analyzed in the previous chapters concern a specific institution, namely childcare services. The family-policy typology developed in this study, however, included different aspects of the whole family-policy package and did not solely focus on the characteristics of childcare services. Consequently, the institutional variation regarding this specific institution was hardly captured. Potentially, a typology, which focuses on the characteristics of existing childcare services is even better suited to both point out the consequences of particular institutional features for different social groups (e.g., in terms of affordability and accessibility) as well as explain differences in public opinion toward this institution. Such an in-depth analysis of national childcare facilities, however, is difficult to realize due to a lack of reliable and internationally harmonized data on existing childcare services (Plantenga et al. 2008; Eurostat 2004; Sipilä et al. 2003; Rostgaard 2002). This problem is partly related to the fact that childcare services are often organized at the regional or even local level. Consequently, levels and quality of childcare service provision vary not only between countries but also across municipalities and regions (Melhuish and Moss 1991; OECD 2001).

Moreover, a comparative analysis of childcare services should take into consideration not only the availability and accessibility of existing services (e.g., in terms of the number of childcare places in a region and the distance from a child's home) but also childcare fees (for different income groups), opening hours, and the quality of childcare services. At the organizational level, alternative ways of childcare service provision need to be taken into account, e.g., the role of employers (who play a key role in several countries, such as the Netherlands or the UK), the Church, or other non- and for-profit organizations as well as functional alternatives, such as cash benefits (Rostgaard 2002). Furthermore, Jensen (2009) pointed out that different curriculum traditions exist, namely the "readiness-for-school curriculum" and the "social-pedagogical-curriculum tradition" (Bennett 2005). According to Jensen, these traditions "constitute coherent and elaborate ideational traditions, or 'childcare philosophies', guiding the work of preschool teachers and pedagogues alike" (Jensen 2009: 10). Jensen showed that the prevailing curriculum tradition in a country has an impact on the speed and level of childcare service expansion. "Countries belonging to the readiness-for-school-curriculum tradition have expanded their provision considerably more than countries belonging to the social-pedagogical-curriculum tradition" (Jensen 2009: 7). These traditions and ideologies can thus hamper or facilitate further expansion of childcare facilities (for a discussion of the "limits to change," see also Sipilä et al. 2003). Moreover, they have an impact on the public's perception and actual usage of childcare services, e.g., in terms of the length of daily usage as well as the children's age (Kremer 2007; Fagnani 2007; Pfau-Effinger 2006). The distinction of different curriculum traditions might be a useful means to capture institutionalized normative beliefs and cultural traditions in this field of welfare-state intervention.

Access to childcare facilities has at least two important implications: First, it allows parents (and particularly mothers) to combine work and family life. Enabling and supporting mothers' labour-market participation is crucial in meeting the economic pressures of the welfare state and overcoming social exclusion, gender inequality, and (child) poverty. Second, equal access to childcare is important from the perspective of equal opportunity and child well-being, as childcare institutions can reduce disadvantages of children with special needs or in inferior socio-economic situations (OECD 2006). As expressed by the OECD: "Equitable access to quality early childhood education and care can strengthen the foundations of lifelong learning for all children and support the broad educational and social needs of families" (OECD 2001: 7).

The results of this study emphasize that it remains difficult to propose one ideal family-policy model for all European welfare states (Mahon 2002; Daly and Klammer 2006; Kremer 2007; Lewis et al. 2008a). However, the traditional male-breadwinner family model can no longer be considered the norm and is being progressively superseded by the dual-earner family model. Women increasingly want to participate in the labor market and pursue a career without giving up private-sphere life goals, such as becoming a mother (Sjöberg 2010). It is likely that the diversity of work-family arrangements will further increase in the near future due to ongoing processes of social change. Fathers might want to successively reduce their working hours when they have small children and mothers might increasingly prefer to work full-time or longer part-time hours during this family phase (Daly and Klammer 2006; Lewis et al. 2008a; Hobson et al. 2006; Knudsen and Wærness 2001a). An important step toward a welfare policy that takes the increasing diversity of families' work and care preferences and practices into account is the introduction or expansion of family and labor-market policies that would enable parents to combine labor-market participation with family life. Policies that are in line with the dimension of dual-earner support are especially suitable to absorb mothers' role conflicts as well as tensions between job and family demands. A combination of general family and dual-earner support policies, which is practiced, e.g., in Finland and France, would offer mothers and fathers more freedom of choice regarding the realization of individual work-life preferences and could increase families' well-being and quality of life.

However, policy makers have to be aware of the fact that some policies might be more attractive to certain groups of the population and generate unintended side effects. An example is the home-care allowance that is available in Finland and France. Several authors have argued that the take-up of low-paid, flat-rate leave benefits is more attractive to mothers with lower levels of education and fewer labor-market opportunities. The availability of these leaves could then consolidate the marginalization of certain groups of women from the labor-market (OECD 2001; Salmi 2006; Lewis et al. 2008b). This potential side effect, in turn, could generate increasing social inequalities in the quality of life and well-being of families, individuals, and children. Public subsidies for parents who care for their children at home can thus be seen either as capable of increasing parents' freedom to choose or as a trap for women (Hilamo and Kangas 2009).

The provision of childcare services is certainly only one way to support families. However, high quality, affordable, and flexible childcare arrangements range among the most important preconditions that enable both parents to enter the labor market and combine paid work and family life (Plantenga et al. 2008). The absence of work-family compatibility, in turn, has implications for individuals' labor-market and family planning decisions (e.g., in terms of delaying the decision to have children or deciding to have fewer or no children at all). The results provided in this study have shown that the public is not very satisfied with the status quo of existing childcare arrangements, the Nordic countries being the only exception. This finding clearly supports the call for more and better childcare services. Consequently, state involvement in the provision of childcare services might be a necessary policy response to rising (needs of) female employment as well as to changing gender roles in the family and the labor market; even despite the persistence of different care ideals.

8 Bibliography

Abrahamson, Peter (2007). Reconciliation of Work and Family Life in Europe: A Case Study of Denmark, France, Germany and the United Kingdom. *Journal of Comparative Policy Analysis, 9*(2), 193-209.

Alber, Jens (1984). Versorgungsklassen im Wohlfahrtsstaat. *Kolner Zeitschrift Fur Soziologie Und Sozialpsychologie, 36*(2), 225-251.

Albrekt Larsen, Christian (2006). *The Institutional Logic of Welfare Attitudes: How Welfare Regimes Influence Public Support*. Aldershot: Ashgate Publishing Ltd.

Albrekt Larsen, Christian (2008). The Institutional Logic of Welfare Attitudes: How Welfare Regimes Influence Public Support. *Comperative Political Studies, 41*(2), 145-168.

Alesina, Alberto & Glaeser, Edward L. (2004). *Fighting Poverty in the US and Europe. A World of Difference*. Oxford: Oxford University Press.

Andreß, Hans-Jürgen & Heien, Thorsten (2001). Four Worlds of Welfare State Attitudes? A Comparison of Germany, Norway, and the United States. *European Sociological Review, 17*(4), 337-356.

Anttonen, Anneli, Sipilä, Jorma & Baldock, John (2003). Patterns of Social Care in Five Industrial Societies: Explaining Diversity. In A. Anttonen, J. Baldock & J. Sipilä (Eds.), *The Young, the Old and the State. Social Care Systems in Five Industrial Nations* (pp. 167-197, Globalization and Welfare). Cheltenham: Edward Elgar.

Archer, Margaret S. (1996). *Culture and agency. The place of culture in social theory. Revised Edition*. Cambridge: University Press.

Arts, Wil & Gelissen, John (2001). Welfare States, Solidarity and Justice Principles: Does the Type Really Matter? *Acta Sociologica, 44*(4), 283-299.

Arts, Wil & Gelissen, John (2002). Three worlds of welfare capitalism or more? *Journal of European Social Policy, 12*(2), 137-158.

Bahle, Thomas (1995). *Familienpolitik in Westeuropa: Ursprünge und Wandel im internationalen Vergleich*. Frankfurt: Campus Verlag.

Bahle, Thomas (2003). The changing institutionalization of social services in England and Wales, France and Germany: is the welfare state on the retreat? *Journal of European Social Policy, 13*(1), 5-20.

Bahle, Thomas (2008a). Family policy patterns in the enlarged EU. In J. Alber, T. Fahey & C. Saraceno (Eds.), *Handbook of Quality of Life in the Enlarged European Union* (pp. 100-125). New York: Routledge.

Bahle, Thomas (2008b). The State and Social Services in Britain, France and Germany since the 1980s. Reform and growth in a period of welfare state crisis. *European Societies, 10*(1), 25-47.

Banaszak, Lee Ann & Plutzer, Eric (1993). Contextual Determinants of Feminist Attitudes: National and Subnational Influences in Western Europe. *The American Political Science Review, 87*(1), 145.

Bean, Clive & Papadakis, Elim (1998). A Comparison of Mass Attitudes Towards the Welfare State in Different Institutional Regimes, 1985-1990. *International Journal of Public Opinion Research, 10*(3).

Belsky, Jay (2001). Emanuel Miller Lecture. Developmental Risks (Still) Associated with Early Child Care. *Journal of Child Psychology and Psychiatry, 42*(7), 845-859.

Bennett, J (2005). Curriculum Issues in National Policymaking. *European Early Childhood Education Research Journal, 13*(2), 5-23.

Bielby, Denise Del Vento & Bielby, William T. (1984). Work Commitment, Sex-Role Attitudes, and Women's Employment. *American Sociological Review, 49*(2), 234-247.

Blekesaune, Morten & Quadagno, Jill (2003). Public Attitudes toward Welfare State Policies: A Comparative Analysis of 24 Nations. *European Sociological Review, 19*(5), 415-427.

Bolzendahl, Cathering I. & Myers, Daniel J. (2004). Feminist Attitudes and Support for Gender Equality: Opinion Change in Women and Men, 1974-1998. *Social Forces, 83*(2), 759-790.

Bonoli, Giuliano (1997). Classifying Welfare States: a Two-dimension Approach. *Journal of Social Policy, 26*(3), 351-372.

Bonoli, Giuliano (2005). The politics of the new social policies: providing coverage against new social risks in mature welfare states. *Policy & Politics, 33*(3), 431-449.

Borre, Ole (1998a). Beliefs and the Scope of Government. In O. Borre & E. Scarbrough (Eds.), *The Scope of Government* (pp. 367-387). Oxford: Oxford University.

Borre, Ole (1998b). Scope-Of-Government Beliefs and Political Support. In O. Borre & E. Scarbrough (Eds.), *The Scope of Government* (pp. 343-366). Oxford: Oxford University.

Bradshaw, Jonathan & Finch, Naomi (2002). A Comparison of Child Benefit Packages in 22 Countries. *Department for Work and Pensions Research Report, 174*, 1-15.

Brooks-Gunn, Jeanne, Han, Wen-Jui & Waldfogel, Jane (2002). Maternal Employment and Child Cognitive Outcomes in the First Three Years of Life: The NICHD Study of Early Child Care. *Child Development, 73*(4), 1052-1072.

Brooks, Clem & Manza, Jeff (2007). *Why welfare states persist: the importance of public opinion in democracies*. US: University Of Chicago Press.

Castles, Francis G. (2003). The world turned upside down: below replacement fertility, changing preferences and family-friendly public policy in 21 OECD countries. *Journal of European Social Policy, 13*(3), 209-227.

Castles, Francis G. (2009). What Welfare States Do: A Disaggregated Expenditure Approach. *Journal of Social Policy, 38*(1), 45-62.

Castles, Francis G. & Mitchell, Deborah (1993). Worlds of Welfare and Families of Nations. In F. G. Castles (Ed.), *Families of Nations. Patterns of Public Policy in Western Europe* (pp. 93-128). Dartmouth: Aldershot.

Coughlin, Richard M. (1979). Social Policy and Ideology: Public Opinion in Eight Rich Nations. *Comparative Social Research, 2*, 3-40.

Coughlin, Richard M. (1980). *Ideology, Public Opinion and Welfare Policy: Attitudes towards Taxes and Spending in Industrial Societies*. Berkeley, CA: University of California, Institute of International Studies.

Crompton, Rosemary, Brockmann, Michaela & Lyonette, Clare (2005). Attitudes, Women's Employment and the Domestic Division of Labour: A Cross-National Analysis in Two Waves. *Work, Employment and Society, 19*(2), 213-233.

d'Anjou, Leo, Steijn, Abram & Van Aarsen, Dries (1995). Social Position, Ideology, and Distributive Justice. *Social Justice Research, 8*(4).

Dahrendorf, Ralf (1988). *The modern social conflict: an essay on the politics of liberty*. London: Weidenfeld and Nicolson.

Daly, Mary (1994). Comparing Welfare States: Toward a Gender Friendly Approach. In D. Sainsbury (Ed.), *Gendering Welfare States* (pp. 101-117). London, Thousand Oaks, New Delhi: Sage Publications.

Daly, Mary & Klammer, Ute (2006). Women's Participation in European Labour Markets. In U. Gerhard, T. Knijn & A. Weckwert (Eds.), *Working Mothers. A Comparison of Policies and Practices* (pp. 122-143). Cheltenham, UK: Edward Elgar.

De Henau, Jérome, Meulders, Danièle & O'Dorchai, Síle (2006). The Childcare Triad? Indicators Assessing Three Fields of Child Policies for Working Mothers in the EU-15. *Journal of Comparative Policy Analysis, 8*(2), 129-148.

Del Boca, Daniela, Pasqua, Silvia & Pronzato, Chiara (2005). Fertility and Employment in Italy, France, and the UK. *Labour Economics, 19*(Special Issue).

DeMaris, Alfred, Mahoney, Annette & Pargament, Kenneth. I. (2011). Doing the Scut Work of Infant Care: Does Religiousness Encourage Father Involvement? *Journal of Marriage and Family, 73*(2), 354-368, doi:10.1111/j.1741-3737.2010.00811.x.

Ebbinghaus, Bernhard (2005). Whend Less is More: Selection Problems in Large-N and Small-N Cross-National Comparisons. *International Sociology, 20*(2), 133-152.

Ebbinghaus, Bernhard (2006). *Reforming Early Retirement in Europe, Japan and the USA*. Oxford: Oxford University Press.

Ebbinghaus, Bernhard (2011). The role of trade unions in European pension reforms: From 'old' to 'new' politics? *European Journal of Industrial Relations, 17*(4), 315-331, doi:DOI: 10.1177/0959680111420208.

Edlund, Jonas (1999). Trust in government and welfare regimes: Attitudes to redistribution and financial cheating in the USA and Norway. *European Journal of Political Research, 35*(3), 341-370.

Esping-Andersen, Gøsta (1990). *The Three Worlds of Welfare Capitalism*. Cambridge: Polity Press.

Esping-Andersen, Gøsta (1999). *Social Foundations of Postindustrial Economies*. Oxford: Oxford University Press.

Esping-Andersen, Gøsta, Gallie, Duncan, Hemerijck, Anton & Myles, John (2002). *Why we need a new welfare state* (1ed.). Oxford: Oxford Univ. Press.

Euraxess Luxembourg (2010). Parental Leave. http://www.euraxess.lu/eng/Daily-life/Allowances/Parental-leave. Accessed April 23rd 2010.

European Commission (2005). Reconciliation of work and private life: A comparative review of thirty European countries. Luxembourg: Office for Official Publications of the European Communities.

European Commission (2007). Joint Report on Social Protection and Social Inclusion 2007. Brussels: Directorate-General for Employment, Social Affairs and Equal Opportunities.

European Commission (2010). Indicators for monitoring the Employment Guidelines including indicators for additional employment analysis. 2010 compendium. Brussels: Directorate General for Employment, Social Affairs and Equal Opportunities.

European Social Survey (2008/09). *European Social Survey Round 4 Data. Edition 4.0 (published 02.02.2011). Norwegian Social Science Data Services*. Norway: Data Archive and distributor of ESS data.

European Social Survey (2011). *ESS-4 2008 Documentation Report. Edition 4.0*. Bergen: European Social Survey Data Archive, Norwegian Social Science Data Services.

Eurostat (2004). Development of a methodology for the collection of harmonised statistics on childcare. *Working Paper and Studies*. Luxemburg: Office for Official Publications of the European Communities.

Eurostat (2010a). Formale Kinderbetreuung nach Altersklassen und zeitlicher Nutzung (% der Population in der Altersklasse). http://nui.epp.eurostat.ec.europa.eu/nui/show.do?dataset=ilc_caindformal&lang=de. Accessed March 22nd 2010.

Eurostat (2010b). Tabellen pro Leistungen - Funktion Familie/Kinder. http://nui.epp.eurostat.ec.europa.eu/nui/show.do?dataset=spr_exp_ffa&lang=de. Accessed March 22nd 2010.

Eurostat (2011a). Population and social conditions. http://epp.eurostat.ec.europa.eu/portal/page/portal/statistics/search_database. Accessed January, 7th 2011.

Eurostat (2011b). Social conditions and welfare, social protection. http://epp.eurostat.ec.europa.eu/portal/page/portal/statistics/search_database. Accessed January, 13th 2011.

Everitt, Brian S., Landau, Sabine & Leese, Morven (2001). *Cluster Analysis* (Fourth Edition ed.). London: Arnold.

Fagnani, Jeanne (2007). Family Policies in France and Germany. Sisters or distant cousins? *Community, Work and Family, 10*(1), 39-56.

Fagnani, Jeanne & Math, Antoine (2008). Policy Packages for Families with Children in 11 European Countries: Multiple Approaches. *Comparative Social Research, 25*, 55-78.

Feldman, Stanley & Zaller, John (1992). The Political Culture of Ambivalence: Ideological Responses to the Welfare State. *American Journal of Political Science, 36*(1), 268-307.

Ferrarini, Tommy (2006). *Families, States and Labour Markets*. Cheltenham, Northampton: Edward Elgar.

Ferrera, Maurizio (1996). The 'Southern Model' of Welfare in Social Europe. *Journal of European Social Policy, 6*(1), 17-37.

Flaquer, Lluís (2000). Is there a Southern European model of family policy? In A. Pfennig & T. Bahle (Eds.), *Families and Family policies in Europe. Comparative Perspectives* (pp. 15-33). Frankfurt am Main: Europäischer Verlag der Wissenschaften.

Flora, Peter (1986). Introduction. In P. Flora (Ed.), *Growth to Limits: The Western European Welfare States Since World War II.* (Vol. I., pp. xii-xxxvi). Berlin: de Gruyter.

Flora, Peter, Alber, Jens & Kohl, Jürgen (1977). Zur Entwicklung der westeuropäischen Wohlfahrtsstaaten. *Politische Vierteljahresschrift, 18*, 707-772.

Gauthier, Anne Hélène (1996). *The State and the Family. A Comparative Analysis of Family Policies in Industrialized Countries*. Oxford: Clarendon Press.

Gelissen, John (2000). Popular support for institutionalised solidarity: a comparison between European welfare states. *International Journal of Social Welfare, 9*(4), 285-300.

Gelissen, John (2002). *Worlds of Welfare, Worlds of Consent? Public Opinion on the Welfare State*. Leiden: Brill.

Goerres, A. & Tepe, M. (2010). Age-based Self-Interest, Intergenerational Solidarity and the Welfare State: A Comparative Analysis of Older People's Attitudes Towards Public Childcare in 12 OECD countries. *European Journal of Political Research, 49*(6), 818–851.

Gornick, Janet C. & Heron, Alexandra (2006). The Regulation of Working Time as Work-Family Reconciliation Policy: Comparing Europe, Japan, and the United States. *Journal of Comparative Policy Analysis, 8*(2), 149-166.

Gornick, Janet C., Meyers, Marcia K. & Ross, Katherin E. (1997). Supporting the Employment of Mothers: Policy Variation across fourteen Welfare States. *Journal of European Social Policy, 7*(1), 45-70.

Gough, Ian (2001). Social assistance regimes: a cluster analysis. *Journal of European Social Policy, 11*(2), 165-170.

Haataja, Anita & Nyberg, Anita (2006). Diverging paths? The dual-earner/dual-carer model in Finland and Sweden in the 1990s. In A. L. Ellingsæter & A. Leira (Eds.), *Politicising Parenthood in Scandinavia. Gender relations in welfare states*. Bristol: The Policy Press.

Hakim, Catherine (2002). Lifestyle Preferences as Determinants of Women's Differentiated Labor Market Careers. *Work and Occupations, 29*(4), 428-459.

Hall, Peter (1986). *Governing the Economy: The Politics of State Intervention in Britain and France*. New York: Oxford University Press.

Hall, Peter A. & Taylor, Rosemary C. R (1996). Political Science and the Three New Institutionalisms. *Political Studies, 44*, 936-957.

Häusermann, Silja (2008). Changing coalitions in social policy reforms: the politics of new social needs and demands. *Journal of European Social Policy, 16*(1), 5-21.

Henninger, Annette, Wimbauer, Christine & Dombrowski, Rosine (2008). Demography as a Push toward Gender Equity? Current Reforms of German Family Policy. *Social Politics, 15*(3), 287-314.

Hiilamo, Heikki (2006). Women-friendliness and economic depression: Finland and Sweden in the 1990s. In A. L. Ellingsæter & A. Leira (Eds.), *Politicising Parenthood in Scandinavia. Gender relations in welfare states* (pp. 171-194). Bristol: The Policy Press.

Hilamo, Heikki & Kangas, Olli (2009). Trap for Women or Freedom to Choose? The Struggle over Cash for Child Care Schemes in Finland and Sweden. *Journal of Social Policy, 38*(3), 457-475.

Hobson, Barbara (2011). The Agency Gap in Work–Life Balance: Applying Sen's Capabilities Framework Within European Contexts. *Social Politics, 18*(2), 146-167.

Hobson, Barbara, Duvander, Ann-Zofie E. & Halldén, Karin (2006). Men and women's agency and capabilities to create a worklife balance in diverse and changing institutional contexts. In J. Lewis (Ed.), *Children, Changing Families and Welfare States* (pp. 267-290). Cheltenham, UK

Northampton, MA, USA: Elgar, Edward.

Hoel, Marit & Knutsen, Oddbjørn (1989). Social Class, Gender, and Sector Employment as Political Cleavages in Scandinavia. *Acta Sociologica, 32*(2), 181-201.

Inglehart, Ronald (1977). *The silent revolution: Changing values and political styles among western publics*. Princeton, NJ: Princeton Univ. Press.

Jæger, Mads Meier (2006a). Welfare Regimes and Attitudes Towards Redistribution: The Regime Hypothesis Revisited. *European Sociological Review, 22*(2), 157-170.

Jæger, Mads Meier (2006b). What Makes People Support Public Responsibility for Welfare Provision: Self-interest or Political Ideology? A Longitudinal Approach. *Acta Sociologia, 49*(3), 321-338.

Jæger, Mads Meier (2009). United But Divided: Welfare Regimes and the Level and Variance in Public Support for Redistribution. *European Sociological Review, 25*(6), 723-737.

Jensen, Carsten (2008). Worlds of welfare services and transfers. *Journal of European Social Policy, 18*(2), 151–162.

Jensen, Carsten (2009). Institutions and the Politics of Childcare Services. *Journal of European Social Policy, 19*(1), 7-18.

Jensen, Carsten & Svendsen, Get Tinggaard (2009). Giving money to starngers: European welfare states and social trust. *International Journal of Social Welfare*, doi:10.1111/j.1468-2397.2009.00668.x.

Jowell, Roger (1998). How comparative is comparative research? *The American Behavioral Scientist, 42*(2), 168-177.

Kamerman, Sheila B., Neuman, Michelle, Waldfogel, Jane & Brooks-Gunn, Jeanne (2003). Social Policies, Family Types and Child Outcomes in Selected OECD Countries. *OECD Social, Employment and Migration Working Papers*. Paris: Directorate for Employment, Labour and Social Affairs.

Kangas, Olli (1997). Self-interest and the common good: The Impact of Norms, Selfishness and Context in Social Policy Opinions. *Journal of Socio-Economics, 26*(5), 475-495.

Kangas, Olli & Rostgaard, Tine (2007). Preferences or institutions? Work-family life opportunities in seven European countries. *Journal of European Social Policy, 17*(3), 240-256.

Karamessini, Maria (2008). Continuity and change in the soutern European social model. *International Labour Review, 147*(1), 43-70.

Kaufmann, Franz-Xaver (2002). Politics and Policies towards the Family in Europe: A Framework and an Inquiry into their Differences and Convergences. In F.-X. Kaufmann, A. Kuijsten, H.-J. Schulze & K. P. Strohmeier (Eds.), *Family Life and Family Policies in Europe* (pp. 419-490). Oxford: Oxford University Press.

Kautto, Mikko (2002). Investing in services in West European welfare states. *Journal of Euorpean Social Policy, 12*(1), 53-65.

Knudsen, Knud & Wærness, Kari (2001a). National Context, Individual Characteristics and Attitudes on Mothers' Employment: A Comparative Analysis of Great Britain, Sweden and Norway 2001. *Acta Sociologica, 44*(1), 67-79.

Knudsen, Knud & Wærness, Kari (2001b). National Context, Individual Characteristics and Attitudes on Mothers' Employment: A Comparative Analysis of Great Britain, Sweden and Norway 2001. *Acta Sociologica, 44*.

Korpi, Walter (1980). Social Policy and Distributional Conflict in Capitalist Democracies. A Preliminary Comparative Framework. *West European Politics, 3*(3), 296-316.

Korpi, Walter (1989). Power, Politics, and State Autonomy in the Development of Social Citizenship: Social Rights During Sickness in Eighteen OECD Countries Since 1930. *American Sociological Review, 54*(3), 309-328.

Korpi, Walter (2000). Faces of Inequality: Gender, Class, and Patterns of Inequalities in Different Types of Welfare States. *Social Politics, 7*(2), 127-191.

Korpi, Walter (2003). Welfare-state regress in western Europe: Politics, institutions, globalization, and Europeanization. *Annual Review of Sociology, 29*, 589-609, doi:10.1146/annurev.soc.29.010202.095943.

Korpi, Walter & Palme, Joakim (1998). The Paradox of Redistribution and Strategies of Equality: Welfare State Institutions, Inequality, and Poverty in the Western Countries. *American Sociological Review, 63*(5), 661-687.

Kreimer, Margareta (2006). Developments in Austrian care arrangements: women between free choice and informal care. In C. Glendinning & P. A. Kemp (Eds.), *Cash and Care. Policy challenges in the welfare state* (pp. 141-153). Bristol: Policy Press.

Kremer, Monique (2007). *How Welfare States Care. Culture, Gender, and Parenting in Europe*. Amsterdam: Amsterdam University Press.

Kröger, Teppo, Anttonen, Anneli & Sipilä, Jorma (2003). Social Care in Finland: Stronger and Weaker Forms of Universalism. In A. Anttonen, J. Baldock & J. Sipilä (Eds.), *The Young, the Old and the State. Social Care Systems in Five Industrial Nations* (pp. 25-54, Globalization and Welfare). Cheltenham: Edward Elgar.

Kumlin, Staffan (2002). *The Personal and the Political. How Personal Welfare State Experiences Affect Political Trust and Ideology* (Göteborg Studies in Politics 78). Göteborg: Department of Political Studies, Göteborg University.

Kumlin, Staffan & Rothstein, Bo (2005). Making and Breaking Social Capital. The Impact of Welfare State Institutions. *Comparative Political Studies, 38*(4), 339-365.

Kumlin, Staffan & Svallfors, Stefan (2007). Social Stratification and Political Articulation: Why Attitudinal Class Differences Vary Across Countries. In S. Mau & B. Veghte (Eds.), *Social Justice, Legitimacy and the Welfare State* (Vol. 2). Aldershot: Ashgate.

Langer, Wolfgang (2010). Mehrebenenanalyse mit Querschnittsdaten. In C. Wolf & H. Best (Eds.), *Handbuch der sozialwissenschaftlichen Datenanalyse* (pp. 741-774). Wiesbaden: VS Verlag.

Leibfried, Stephan (1992). Towards a European Welfare State? In Z. Ferge & J. E. Kolberg (Eds.), *Social Policy in a Changing Europe* (pp. 245-278). Frankfurt a.M.: Campus.

Leira, Arnlaug, Tobío, Constanze & Trifiletti, Rossana (2005). Kinship and Informal Support: Care Resources for the First Generation of Working Mothers in Norway, Italy, and Spain. In U. Gerhard, T. Knijn & A. Weckert (Eds.), *Working mothers in Europe: a comparison of policies and practices* (pp. 74-96). Cheltenham: Elgar.

Lepsius, M. Rainer (1990). *Interessen, Ideen und Institutionen*. Opladen: Westdeutscher Verlag.

Lepsius, M. Rainer (1997). Vertrauen zu Institutionen. In S. Hradil (Ed.), *Differenz und Integration: die Zukunft moderner Gesellschaften* (pp. 283-293). Opladen: Westdeutscher Verlag.

Lewin-Epstein, Noah, Stier, Haya, Braun, Michael & Langfeld, Bettina (2000). Family Policy and Public Attitudes in Germany and Israel. *European Sociological Review, 16*(4), 385-401.

Lewis, Jane (2001). The Decline of the Male Breadwinner Model: Implications for Work and Care. *Social Politics, 8*(2), 152-169.

Lewis, Jane, Campbell, Mary & Huerta, Carmen (2008a). Patterns of paid and unpaid work in Western Europe: gender, commodification, preferences and the implications for policy. *Journal of European Social Policy, 18*(1), 21-37.

Lewis, Jane, Knijn, Trudie, Martin, Claude & Ostner, Ilona (2008b). Patterns of Development in Work/Family Reconciliation Policies for Parents in France, Germany, the Netherlands, and the UK in the 2000s. *Social Politics, 15*(3), 261-286, doi:10.1093/sp/jxn016.

Lewis, Jane & Ostner, Ilona (1994). Gender and the Evolution of European Social Policies. *ZeS Arbeitspapier 94*(4).

Linos, Katerina & West, Martin (2003). Self-interest, Social Beliefs, and Attitudes to Redistribution: Re-addressing the Issue of Cross-national Variation. *European Sociological Review, 19*(4), 393-409.

Lipsmeyer, Christine S. & Nordstrom, Timothy (2003). East versus West: comparing political attitudes and welfare preferences across European societies. *Journal of European Public Policy, 10*(3), 339-364.

Mahon, Rianne (2002). Child Care: Toward What Kind of "Social Europe"? *Social Politics, 9*(3), 343-379.

Marshall, T. H. (1950). *Citizenship and social class*. Cambridge: Cambridge University Press.

Mau, Steffen (2003). *The moral economy of welfare states: Britain and Germany compared* (1ed., Vol. European University Institute: Routledge EUI studies in the political economy of welfare). London [u.a.]: Routledge.

Mau, Steffen (2004). Welfare Regimes and the Norms of Social Exchange. *Current Sociology, 52*(1), 53 - 74.

Mau, Steffen & Burkhardt, Christoph (2009). Migration and welfare state solidarity in Western Europe. *Journal of European Social Policy, 19*(3), 213-229, doi:DOI: 10.1177/0958928709104737.

Melhuish, Edward C. & Moss, Peter (Eds.). (1991). *Day care for young children. International perspectives*. London Routledge.

Mettler, Suzanne & Soss, Joe (2004). The Consequences of Public Policy for Democratic Citizenship: Bridging Policy Studies and Mass Politics. *Perspectives on Politics, 2*(1).

Meulders, Danièle & O'Dorchai, Síle (2007). The position of mothers in a comparative welfare state perspective. In D. Del Boca & C. Wetzels (Eds.), *Social Policies, Labour Markets and Motherhood* (pp. 3-27). Cambridge: Cambridge University Press.

Milligan, Glenn W. & Cooper, Martha C. (1988). A Study of Standardization of Variables in Cluster Analysis. *Journal of Classification, 5*(2), 181-204.

Montanari, Ingalill (2000). From family wage to marriage subsidy and child benefits: controversy and consensus in the development of family support. *Journal of European Social Policy, 10*(4), 307-333.

Moss, Peter & Korintus, Marta (2008). International Review of Leave Policies and Related Research 2008. http://www.berr.gov.uk/files/file47247.pdf. Accessed March 22nd, 2010.

Motiejunaite, Akvile & Kravchenko, Zhanna (2008). Family policy, employment and gender-role attitudes: a comparative analysis of Russia and Sweden. *Journal of European Social Policy, 18*(1), 38-49.

Müller, Walter (1998). Klassenstruktur und Parteiensystem. Zum Wandel der Klassenspaltung im Wahlverhalten. *Kolner Zeitschrift Fur Soziologie Und Sozialpsychologie, 50*(1), 3-46.

Müller, Walter (2000). Klassenspaltung im Wahlverhalten - eine Reanalyse. *Kolner Zeitschrift Fur Soziologie Und Sozialpsychologie, 52*(4), 790-795.

Novack, Lesley Lazin & Novack, David R. (1996). Being Female in the Eighties and Nineties: Conflicts Between New Opportunities and Traditional Expectations Among White, Middle Class, Heterosexual College Women. *Sex Roles, 35*(1/2), 57-77.

O'Brian, Margaret, Brandt, Berit & Kvande, Elin (2007). Fathers, Work and Family Life. Global perspectives and new insights. *Community, Work and Family, 10*(4), 375-386.

Obinger, Herbert & Wagschal, Uwe (1998). Drei Welten des Wohlfahrtsstaates? Das Stratifizierungskonzept in der clusteranalytischen Überprüfung. In S. Lessenich & I. Ostner (Eds.), *Welten des Wohlfahrtskapitalismus. Der Sozialstaat in vergleichender Perspektive* (pp. 109-135). Frankfurt a. M./New York: Campus.

OECD (2001). *Starting Strong. Early Childhood Education and Care*. Paris: OECD Publishing.

OECD (2002). *Babies and Bosses. Reconciling Work and Family Life. Australia, Denmark and the Netherlands* (Vol. 1, Vol. Babies and bosses). Paris: OECD Publishing.

OECD (2006). *Starting Strong II. Early Childhood Education and Care*. Paris: OECD Publishing.

OECD (2007). *Benefits and Wages 2007. OECD Indicators*. Paris: OECD Publishing.

OECD (2010a). Family database. www.oecd.org/els/social/family/database. Accessed March 2010.

OECD (2010b). OECD Social Expenditure Database 2010 and ESSPROS. www.oecd.org/els/social/expenditure. Accessed 27.01. 2010.

OECD (2011). http://www.oecd.org/department/0,3355,en_2649_34819_1_1_1_1_1,00.html. Accessed 29 July 2011.

Oliver, Adam & Mossialos, Elias (2005). European Health Systems Reforms: Looking Backward to See Forward? *Journal of Health Politics, Policy and Law, 30*(1-2), 7-28.

Orloff, Ann Shola (1993). Gender and the Social Rights of Citizenship: The Comparative Analysis of Gender Relations and Welfare States. *American Sociological Review, 58*(3), 303-328.

Papadakis, E. (1992). Public Opinion, Public Policy and the Welfare State. [Article]. *Political Studies, 40*(1), 21-37.

Pettersen, Per Arnt (2001). Welfare State Legitimacy: Ranking, Rating, Paying. The Popularity and Support for Norwegian Welfare Programmes in the Mid 1990s. *Scandinavian Political Studies, 24*(1), 27-49.

Pfau-Effinger, Birgit (1996). Analyse internationaler Differenzen in der Erwerbsbeteiligung von Frauen: Theoretischer Rahmen und empirische Ergebnisse [International Differences in Female Labor Market Participation: Theoretical Frame and Empirical Results]. *Kolner Zeitschrift Fur Soziologie Und Sozialpsychologie, 48*(3), 462-492.

Pfau-Effinger, Birgit (1998). Gender Cultures and the Gender Arrangement - A Theoretical Framework for Cross-National Gender Research. *Innovation: The European Journal of Social Science, 11*(2), 147-166.

Pfau-Effinger, Birgit (2005a). Culture and Welfare State Policies: Reflections on a Complex Interrelation. *Social Policy, 34*(1), 1-18.
Pfau-Effinger, Birgit (2005b). Development paths of care arrangements in the framework of family values and welfare values. In B. Pfau-Effinger (Ed.), *Care and social integration in European societies* (pp. 21-45). Bristol: Policy Press.
Pfau-Effinger, Birgit (2006). Cultures of childhood and the relationship of care and employment in European welfare states. In J. Lewis (Ed.), *Children, Changing Families and Welfare States* (pp. 137-153). Cheltenham, UK: Elgar, Edward.
Pfeifer, Michaela (2009). Public Opinion on State Responsibility for Minimum Income Protection: A Comparison of 14 European Countries. *Acta Sociologia, 52*(2), 117-134.
Pierson, Christopher (1997). *Beyond the welfare state? The new political economy of welfare*. Cambridge: Polity Press.
Pierson, Paul (1996). The new politics of the welfare state. *World Politics, 48*(2), 143-179.
Pierson, Paul (1998). Irresistible forces, immovable objects: post-industrial welfare states confront permanent austerity. *Journal of European Public Policy, 5*(4), 539-560.
Pierson, Paul (2001). *The New Politics of the Welfare State*. Oxford: Oxford University Press.
Plantenga, Janneke, Remery, Chantal, Figueiredo, Hugo & Smith, Mark (2009). Towards a European Union Gender Equality Index. *Journal of European Social Policy, 19*(1), 19-33.
Plantenga, Janneke, Remery, Chantal, Siegel, Melissa & Sementini, Loredana (2008). Childcare Services In 25 European Union Member States: The Barcelona Targets Revisited. *Comparative Social Research, 25*, 27-53.
Plantenga, Janneke & Siegel, Melissa (2004). *Position Paper 'Childcare in a changing world'. Part I: European childcare Strategies*. Groningen: Rijksuniversiteit Groningen.
Powell, Martin & Barrientos, Armando (2004). Welfare regimes and the welfare mix. *European Journal of Political Research, 43*(1), 83-105.
Putnam, Robert D. (1993). *Making democracy work: Civic traditions in modern Italy*. Princeton, NJ: Princeton University Press.
Rabe-Hesketh, Sophia & Skrondal, Anders (2008). *Multilevel and Longitudinal Modeling Using Stata. Second Edition*. Texas: Stata Press.
Rake, Katherine (2001). Gender and New Labour's Social Policies. *Journal of Social Policy, 30*(2), 209–231.
Reibling, Nadine (2010). Healthcare systems in Europe: towards an incorporation of patient access. *Journal of European Social Policy, 20*(1), 5-18.
Robinson, Robert V. & Bell, Wendell (1978). Equality, Success, and Social Justice in England and the United States. *American Sociological Review, 43*(2), 125-143.
Roller, Edeltraud (1992). *Einstellungen der Bürger zum Wohlfahrtsstaat der Bundesrepublik Deutschland*. Opladen: Westdeutscher Verlag.
Roller, Edeltraud (1998). The Welfare State: The Equality Dimension. In O. Borre & E. Scarbrough (Eds.), *The Scope of Government* (pp. 165-197). Oxford: Oxford University.
Roller, Edeltraut (2002). Die Entwicklung der Akzeptanz des Sozialstaats und der Alterssicherung in Deutschland seit Mitte der siebziger Jahre. In V. d. Rentenversicherungsträger (Ed.), *Deutsche Renten Versicherung 57* (pp. 510-522).
Rosenfeld, Rachel A., Trappe, Heike & Gornick, Janet C. (2004). Gender and Work in Germany: Before and After Reunification. *Annual Review of Sociology, 30*, 103 - 124.
Rostgaard, Tine (2002). Caring for Children and Older People in Europe - A Comparison of European Policies and Practices. *Policy Studies, 23*(1), 51-68.
Rothstein, Bo (1996). *Political Institutions: An Overview* (A New Handbook of Political Science).
Rothstein, Bo (1998). *Just Institutions Matter. The Moral and Political Logic of the Universal Welfare State*. Cambridge: Cambridge University Press.

Rothstein, Bo (2001). The universal welfare state as a social dilemma. *Rationality and Society, 13*(2), 213-233.

Sainsburry, Diane (1999). *Gender and Welfare State Regimes.* Oxford: Oxford University Press.

Sainsbury, Diane (1994). Women's and Men's Social Rights: Gendering Dimensions of Welfare States. In D. Sainsbury (Ed.), *Gendering Welfare States* (pp. 150-169). London, Thousand Oaks, New Delhi: Sage Publications.

Sainsbury, Diane (1996). *Gender, Equality and Welfare States.* Cambridge: Cambridge University Press.

Salmi, Minna (2006). Parental choice and the passion for equality in Finland. In A. L. Ellingsæter & A. Leira (Eds.), *Politicising Parenthood in Scandinavia. Gender relations in welfare states* (pp. 145-168). Bristol: The Policy Press.

Saraceno, Chiara & Leira, Arnlaug (2008). Childhood: Changing Contexts. *Comparative Social Research, 25*, 1-24.

Schofer, Evan & Meyer, John W. (2005). The Worldwide Expansion of Higher Education in the Twentieth Century. *American Sociological Review, 70*, 898-920.

Scruggs, Lyle & Allen, James (2006). Welfare-state decommodification in 18 OECD countries: a replication and revision. *Journal of European Social Policy, 16*(1), 55-72.

Sellier, S & Mouris, R (2010). Brussels Takes Care of Mothers-To-Be. http://en.jobs.lu/MothersToBe.html. Accessed April 23rd 2010.

Sen, Amartya (1992). *Inequality Reexamined.* Oxford: Oxford University Press.

Sen, Amartya (1993). Capability and well-being. In M. Nussbaum (Ed.), *The Quality of Life* (Vol. 2). Oxford: Oxford University Press.

Sen, Amartya (1999). *Development as Freedom.* Oxford: Oxford University Press.

Shalev, Michael (2007). Limits and Alternatives to Multiple Regression in Comparative Research. *Comparative Social Research, 24*, 261-308.

Sims-Schouten, Wendy (2000). Child care services and parents' attitudes in England, Finland and Greece. In A. Pfennig & T. Bahle (Eds.), *Families and Family policies in Europe. Comparative Perspectives* (pp. 270-288). Frankfurt am Main: Europäischer Verlag der Wissenschaften.

Sipilä, Jorma, Anttonen, Anneli & Baldock, John (2003). The Importance of Social Care. In A. Anttonen, J. Baldock & J. Sipilä (Eds.), *The Young, the Old and the State. Social Care Systems in Five Industrial Nations* (pp. 1-23, Globalization and Welfare). Cheltenham: Edward Elgar.

Sjöberg, Ola (2004). The role of family policy institutions in explaining gender-role attitudes: a comparative multilevel analysis of thirteen industrialized countries. *Journal of European Social Policy, 14*(2), 107-123.

Sjöberg, Ola (2010). Ambivalent Attitudes, Contradictory Institutions. Ambivalence in Gender-Role Attitudes in Comparative Perspective. *International Journal of Comparative Sociology, 51*(1-2), 33-57, doi:10.1177/0020715209347064.

Sleebos, Joëlle E. (2003). Low Fertility Rates in OECD Countries: Facts and Policy Responses. In L. a. S. A. Directorate for Employment (Ed.), *OECD Social, Employment and Migration Working Papers.* Paris: OECD.

Smith, Nina, Dex, Shirley, Vlasblom, Jan Dirk & Callan, Tim (2003). The effects of taxation on married women's labour supply across four countries. *Oxford Economic Papers, 55*(3), 417-439.

Starke, Peter, Obinger, Herbert & Castles, Francis G. (2008). Convergence towards where: in what ways, if any, are welfare states becoming more similar? *Journal of European Public Policy, 15*(7), 975-1000.

Strohmeier, Klaus Peter (2002). Family Policy - How Does it Work? In F.-X. Kaufmann, A. Kuijsten, H.-J. Schulze & K. P. Strohmeier (Eds.), *Family Life and Family Policies in Europe* (pp. 321-362). Oxford: Oxford University Press.

Stropnik, Nada & Sambt, Jože (2007). Parental Leave and Child Allowances: Attitudes, Preferences and Possible Impact. *Revija za Socijalnu Politiku, 14*(3/4), 347-371.

Sundström, Eva (1999). Should mothers work? Age and Attitudes in Germany, Italy and Sweden. *International Journal of Social Welfare, 8*(3), 193-205.

Svallfors, Stefan (1995). The End of Class Politics? Structural Cleavages and Attitudes to Swedish Welfare Policies. *Acta Sociologica (Taylor & Francis Ltd), 38*(1), 53-74.

Svallfors, Stefan (1997). Worlds of Welfare and Attitudes to Redistribution: A Comparison of Eight Western Nations. *European Sociological Review, 13*(3), 283 - 304.

Svallfors, Stefan (2003). Welfare Regimes and Welfare Opinions: A Comparison of Eight Western Countries. *Social Indicators Research 64*, 495-520.

Svallfors, Stefan (2004). Class, Attitudes and the Welfare State: Sweden in Comparative Perspective. *Social Policy & Administration, 38*(2), 119-138.

Svallfors, Stefan (2006). *The Moral Economy of Class. Class and Attitudes in Comparative Perspective* (Studies in Social Inequality). Stanford, California: Stanford University Press.

Svallfors, Stefan (2007). Introduction. In S. Svallfors (Ed.), *The Political Sociology of the Welfare State. Institutions, Social Cleavages, and Orientations* (pp. 1-29). Stanford: Stanford University Press.

Svallfors, Stefan (2010). Public attitudes. In F. G. Castles, S. Leibfried, J. Lewis, H. Obinger & C. Pierson (Eds.), *The Oxford Handbook of the Welfare State* (pp. 241-251). Oxford and New York: Oxford University Press.

Taylor-Gooby, Peter (2004). New Risks and Social Change. In P. Taylor-Gooby (Ed.), *New Risks, New Welfare. The Transformation of the European Welfare State* (pp. 1-28). Oxford: Oxford University Press.

Taylor-Gooby, Peter (2009). *Reframing Social Citizenship*. Oxford: University Press.

Valentova, Marie (2007). Attitudes to Family Policy Arrangements in Relation to Attitudes to Family and division of Labour between Genders. *IRISS Working Paper Series* (Vol. 2007, pp. 1-21). Differdange: CEPS/INSTEAD.

van Oorschot, Wim (1998). Shared identity and shared utility: On solidarity and its motives. *Work and Organization Research Centre (WORC) WORC Paper, 98.11.008/2*.

van Oorschot, Wim (2000). Who should get what, and why? On deservingness criteria and the conditionality of solidarity among the public. *The Policy Press, 28*(1), 33-48.

van Oorschot, Wim (2002). Individual motives for contributing to welfare benefits in the Netherlands. *Policy & Politics, 30*(1), 31-46.

van Oorschot, Wim (2006). Making the difference in social Europe: deservingness perceptions among citizens of European welfare states. *Journal of European Social Policy, 16*(1), 23-42.

van Orschot, W. (2006). Making the Difference in Social Europe: Deservingness Perceptions among Citizens of European Welfare States. *Journal of European Social Policy, 16*(1), 23-42, doi:10.1177/0958928706059829.

Voicu, M., Voicu, B. & Strapcova, K. (2009). Housework and Gender Inequality in European Countries. *European Sociological Review, 25*(3), 365-377.

Wendt, Claus (2009). Mapping European Healthcare Systems. A comparative analysis of financing, service provision, and access to healthcare. *Journal of European Social Policy, 19*(5), 1-17.

Wendt, Claus, Kohl, Jürgen, Mischke, Monika & Pfeifer, Michaela (2010). How Do Europeans Perceive Their Healthcare System? Patterns of Satisfaction and Preference for State Involvement in the Field of Healthcare. *European Sociological Review, 26*(2), 177-192.

Wendt, Claus, Mischke, Monika & Pfeifer, Michaela (2011). *Welfare States And Public Opinion. Perceptions of Healthcare Systems, Family Policy and Benefits for the Unemployed and Poor in Europe*. Cheltenham, UK: Edward Elgar Publishing.

Wennemo, Irene (1994). *Sharing the Cost of Children* (Doctoral Dissertation Series No. 25). Stockholm: Swedish Institute for Social Research.

Wersig, Maria (2007). Gleichstellungspolitischer Durchbruch oder Kompromisspaket? Die Einführung des Elterngeldes. In K. Scheiwe (Ed.), *Soziale Sicherungsmodelle revisited. Existenzsicherung durch Sozial- und Familienrecht und ihre Geschlechterdimensionen* (pp. 131-142). Baden-Baden: Nomos.

Wolf, Christof (2005). Measuring Religious Affiliation and Religiosity in Europe. In J. H. P. Hoffmeyer Zlotnik & J. A. Harkness (Eds.), *Methodological Aspects in Cross-National Research (ZUMA-Nachrichten Spezial 11)* (pp. 279-294). Mannheim: ZUMA.

Made in the USA
Las Vegas, NV
11 November 2024

11555483R00134